DEEP AND WIDE

NML NEW MONASTIC LIBRARY
Resources for Radical Discipleship

For over a millennium, if Christians wanted to read theology, practice Christian spirituality, or study the Bible, they went to the monastery to do so. There, people who inhabited the tradition and prayed the prayers of the church also copied manuscripts and offered fresh reflections about living the gospel in a new era. Two thousand years after the birth of the church, a new monastic movement is stirring in North America. In keeping with ancient tradition, new monastics study the classics of Christian reflection and are beginning to offer some reflections for a new era. The New Monastic Library includes reflections from new monastics as well as classic monastic resources unavailable elsewhere.

Series Editor: C. Christopher Smith

DEEP AND WIDE

Reflections on Socio-Political Engagement,
Monasticism(s), and the Christian Life

EVAN B. HOWARD

CASCADE *Books* · Eugene, Oregon

DEEP AND WIDE

Reflections on Socio-Political Engagement, Monasticism(s), and the Christian Life

New Monastic Library: Resources for Radical Discipleship 15

Cascade Books
An Imprint of Wipf and Stock Publishers
199 W. 8th Ave., Suite 3,
Eugene, OR 97401

www.wipfandstock.com

PAPERBACK ISBN: 978-1-5326-8281-0
HARDCOVER ISBN: 978-1-5326-8282-7
EBOOK ISBN: 978-1-5326-8283-4

Cataloguing-in-Publication data:

Names: Howard, Evan B., author.

Title: Deep and wide : reflections on socio-political engagement, monasticism(s), and the Christian life / Evan B. Howard.

Description: Eugene, OR: Cascade Books, 2023 | Series: New Monastic Library | Includes bibliographical references and index.

Identifiers: ISBN 978-1-5326-8281-0 (paperback) | ISBN 978-1-5326-8282-7 (hardcover) | ISBN 978-1-5326-8283-4 (ebook)

Subjects: LCSH: Christian communities. | Christianity and politics. | Mission of the church.

Classification: BV4517.5 H70 2023 (print) | BV4517.5 (ebook)

Grateful acknowledgment is made to Brethren Press for permission to reprint excerpts from the poem "Confession" by Julia Esquivel from *Threatened with Resurrection: Prayers and Poems from an Exiled Guatemalan*, 2nd edition. Copyright © 1982, 1994 by Brethren Press.

To my daughters Claire House and Terese Howard,
who have become my models and mentors
in socio-political engagement, in community life,
and much more.

Table of Contents

Acknowledgments

I HAVE LONG APPRECIATED the contributions that friends have made to my writings. Yet for this book, my need for help was greater and consequently I feel a deeper sense of gratitude for the community that participated in every step of the process.

To Jonathan Wilson-Hartgrove, John and Deanna Hayes, David Janzen, Elaine Heath, the folks at PAPA fests, and more who planted the seeds that sprouted into this project.

To those who pointed me toward stories of or insights from monasticisms old—Joe Fockler, Jared Boyd, Michael O'Sullivan, and Bernadette Flanagan. Tom Rundel for tracking down quotes. Elizabeth Liebert offered guidance in discernment (as always). To those I interviewed or who in other ways provided me stories of monasticisms new—Rusty and Mary Lou Bonham, Aaron White, Kyle Lambelet, Kent Smith, Nancy and Joe Gatlin, and the wonderful Nurturing Communities Network Zoom Gatherings. My partners in the Church Page Project of the *Montrose Daily Press* wrote lovely stories of care that inspired my own search for stories. Sharon and Larry Clark gave me a year's subscription to *The Christian Science Monitor* in a season when attention to stories of goodness were vital. Jill Weber has been the consummate networker, connecting me with kindred spirits all along the way. The library services of Fuller Theological Seminary and the Montrose Public Library (and the internet more generally) helped provide me with resources that would have been inaccessible for one living far from a research university.

I am also grateful for so many with whom I had the opportunity to process this material along the way. I remember online posts by Randy Vigil, and online discussions with Josh Kauffman-Horner. I had helpful conversations with Joe Fockler, John Mitchell, Astro, and Doug

Kiesewetter. Coky Hartman has been a confidant throughout this journey, patiently listening to my questions and my concerns. I presented an early draft of biblical political reflections to All Saints Anglican Church and to Solid Rock Foundation Ministries in Montrose. And of course, there is my wife, Cheri, who has shared a lifetime of experimentation with political prayers, expressions of care, "simple living" (whatever that is), and much more.

Because of the nature of this book I have found it essential to offer drafts of the book for review at various stages of writing. The feedback offered by my readers has proved invaluable and the book would certainly not be what it is without their responses. David Janzen, Phil Harrold, Amy Schifrin, Joe Gatlin, Alden Bass, Zoe Mullery, Trevor Peterson, Lacy Borgo, Doug Kiesewetter, David Carrier, and Justy Engle have all read parts or all of the book. Jim Wilhoit, in addition to sharing thoughts and resources along the way, reviewed the entire manuscript at the last minute and provided helpful advice. Unfortunately, I did not have time to incorporate all of the resources recommended by my readers.

Many thanks go to Jennifer Seidel, Rodney Clapp, and Cascade Books for their generous help in editing and publishing.

Finally, I express deep gratitude for my daughters Claire and Terese. Each of them have lived in intentional communities for many years, communities I have shared life with along the way. Terese recommended resources at various points and when I needed someone to talk to about a sticky question, she was willing to listen and share her point of view. Claire and I had good talks about care and community life. She also provided a couple of important stories. They have modeled the spectrum of engagement for me: particularly living creatively, speaking boldly, caring deeply, and just taking action. I dedicate this book to them.

ONE

Deep and Wide

I REMEMBER VACATION BIBLE School as a child. We sat in rows on metal chairs and sang songs. Some of them had motions and I loved that. One of my favorites was "Deep and Wide." "Deep and wide. Deep and wide. There's a fountain flowing deep and wide. Deep and wide. Deep and wide. There's a fountain flowing deep and wide." Those were the lyrics. Oh, but the motions! On the word *deep* we would all touch the floor. On the word *wide* we would all spread our arms. At the phrase *fountain flowing* we would make some kind of flowy motion with our hands. However, our VBS was nothing like the videos of the song you see on YouTube. We slapped the ground. We waved our arms big when we were fountains. But most importantly, we spread our arms as wide and fast as we could, which meant that, when standing next to our neighbors, we could hit the neighbor on each side as we flung out our arms. Each time we sang a new verse we would silence one of the words such that, for example, during the second time through we would not say "deep," but we would still touch the ground. It got pretty wild at times. Sidney Cox, the composer of this song, writes in the (little-known) verses of the song about refreshment for the heavy laden, welcome and healing for the weary, and every need supplied, all offered without price.[1] All of this is available to us from the "Saviour's wounded side." The effects of Christ's life and death reach both the depths of our inner struggles and our ordinary "every need."

"Deep and Wide," to me, is a guiding image for this book. Some of my friends are in need of the "deep." Burned out from activisms of every

1. See the lyrics (and hear Sidney sing them!) at Cox, "Sidney Cox Sings 'Deep and Wide.'"

kind, some of us have a hard time getting in touch with the divine fountains within. Our orientation has been tied to the wide and we may not
know how to reach the deep. Indeed, at times we may feel guilty for even
desiring God's ministry to the deep, so keenly aware are we of people
who suffer. Others of us are in need of the wide. We have drunk from the
wells of spiritual formation, but we long to know where, and how, all this
formation should send us out. We are dissatisfied with simply a "Jesus
and me" faith, but our heritage has perhaps never showed us well how to
"go wide." Deep and wide. We need the benefits of Christ for the fullness
of our lives. Furthermore, the more I have explored this topic—and this
will become clear as the book progresses—the more I find that when we
mature in our socio-political faith we begin to discover that the "deep"
and the "wide" are not as easily distinguished as we thought. Deep and
wide blend together in a well-discerned life of following Christ.

This book began in March of 2017. I used my spring break to visit a
few people I considered to be leaders of different "new monastic" circles.[2]
On the last day, Jonathan Wilson-Hartgrove from Rutba House—a community that at that time lived in two houses in the Walltown neighborhood of Durham, North Carolina sharing daily worship, weekly meals,
and frequent service to others—was driving me to the airport to catch
my flight home. I had shared with him my interest in bringing some of
the wisdom of "old monasticism" to communities exploring new models
of wholehearted devotion today. At one point Jonathan turned to me and
said something like, "You know what we need from you, Evan, we need
someone to show the relationship between monasticism and action." I
think Jonathan was a little concerned about the political *inaction* of many
communities he had inspired. Some communities, perhaps fueled by
their desire to become monastic, had pulled back from socio-political
action. The following year, in his *Reconstructing the Gospel: Finding Freedom from Slave-Holder Religion,* Jonathan expressed his concern in print,
admitting that "many of us resident aliens from new monastic communities and postliberal congregations realized that, in our absence, extremism flourished in statehouses across the nation."[3]

---

2. For an introduction to the "new monastic" circles I visited on this trip see Rutba
House, eds., *12 Marks*; Bessenecker, *New Friars*; Janzen, *Intentional Christian Community Handbook*; Heath and Duggins, *Missional. Monastic. Mainline.* I will be introducing others throughout this book.

3. Wilson-Hartgrove, *Reconstructing the Gospel*, Kindle ed., loc. 1697 out of 2983.

I took Jonathan's comments to heart, particularly as other people in my visit also spoke about communities' interests in justice and compassion. Hmmm. "Justice" seems to call us to action. "Monasticism" seems to call us away from action. Was the idea of redesigning a life of prayer, community, and formation by employing wisdom of old holy people actually opening a path (perhaps unintentionally) toward political passivity? I had to figure this one out.

A few months later I was a speaker at the Ancient Evangelical Futures Conference, sponsored by the Robert E. Webber Center at Trinity School for Ministry, near Pittsburgh, Pennsylvania. Their topic for the gathering was "Medieval Wisdom 500 Years after the Reformation." The buzz at the gathering was all about one of the other speakers that followed me: Rod Dreher, introducing the release of his *The Benedict Option*. In his book Dreher suggests that "rather than wasting energy and resources fighting unwinnable political battles we should instead work on building communities, institutions, and networks of resistance that can outwit, outlast, and eventually overcome the opposition."[4] Having read Dreher's book prior to the conference I decided to introduce a slightly different idea: "The Beguine Option" (more on Beguines soon), suggesting that we might have much to gain by looking not to formal monastic institutions, but to informal semi-monastic expressions for contemporary models.[5] The question was now front and center.

It got interesting as I observed different groups. Some of my new monastic friends in the United States emphasized action while others tended to emphasize community. My friends in the UK tended to emphasize some blend of action and contemplation.[6] I found this fascinating because when I taught the history of monasticism(s) old and new in seminary settings I often used the categories of "cave" (contemplative), "refectory" (community), and "road" (mission and action) as a way of understanding poles that attracted different communities through

---

4. Dreher, *Benedict Option*, 12. For the talk, see http://webbercenter.tsm.edu/aefc-2017-media/. Dreher (along with Wilson, *Living Faithfully*, and others) was building upon the well-known conclusion of ethicist Alasdair MacIntyre's *After Virtue*, which anticipates the appearance of a "new Benedict" (see MacIntyre, *After Virtue*, 245). Since that time I have had a number of my students in monasticism express interest in Dreher's approach to monasticism and socio-political analysis.

5. For my talk see http://webbercenter.tsm.edu/aefc-2017-media/. I have developed this suggestion more fully in Howard, "Beguine Option."

6. For a survey of the UK stream see Cray et al., eds., *New Monasticism*.

history.[7] Were contemporary conversations regarding action, community, and contemplation replaying discussions that emerged from time to time throughout the history of monasticism? And how does this all relate to politics?

Actually, the more I examined the evidence, the more I began to see the *richness* of God's work through God's people. Nuns and monks had struggled for more than a millennium with the balance of action, community, and contemplation. And in the process they discovered lots of ways to engage in social and political spheres for the cause of Christ. Consider, for example:

The citizens of Antioch in AD 387 were in the wrong. The citizens themselves recognized this. Hearing that Emperor Theodosius was going to impose still another harsh tax on the city, they demonstrated. Things got out of hand and the demonstration became a riot.[8] Some of the rioters demolished statues of the imperial family and set fire to public buildings. Imperial troops were sent in to restore order, executing rioters of the lower class. But that was not enough. Theodosius saw the desecration of his own statues as an act of treason. He closed the baths, the theaters, the sports complex. He placed Antioch, an important city in that region, under military rule, sending in troops to establish order. He sent two officials to prosecute the perpetrators of the riot. On top of all that, various members of the city council were sentenced to exile or death. This was just too much for the populace. But time was short. Before these death penalties were carried out, the city needed to persuade the imperial officials to refer the matter to Emperor Theodosius himself and to allow Bishop Flavian to appeal on behalf of the city.

That is when the monks of the region arrived. John Chrysostom recounts, "After so many years' seclusion in their cells, when they saw a dark cloud hanging over the city, at nobody's request and nobody's prompting, they left their shacks and caves and came flooding down from all directions, like so many angels from heaven." These monks appeared before the officials, pleading on behalf of the accused. They argued that the desecration of the emperor's image in the statues was indeed deplorable, but to further slay the image of God in these human beings created irrecoverable damage. They appealed to the Christian faith of the emperor.

7. See Adams, "Cave, Refectory, Road."

8. On the riot of 387 see O'Donovan and O'Donovan, eds., *From Irenaeus to Grotius*, 90–91, 95–96; French, "Rhetoric and the Rebellion." See also van de Pavard, *St. John Chrysostom, The Homilies*. My thanks to Joe Fockler for reminding me of this story.

"If you refuse to exercise restraint," the monks proclaimed in a pledge of solidarity, "we shall certainly die at their side." The officials referred the case to Theodosius and Chrysostom reports that the monks pleaded with the emperor, reminding him of God's judgment. The efforts of the monks, along with those of Bishop Flavian and the Magister Officiorum Caesarius, succeeded. Emperor and citizens were reconciled and the *polis* of Antioch was restored to—a humbled—normalcy.[9]

Or consider the Beguines (pronounced Beh-geenes). Nobody quite knew how to label the women's movement in the thirteenth century, but "beguine" was a term many used.[10] Despite stories identifying the term with Lambert le Bègue as the movement's founder, the Beguines actually sprung willy-nilly from the plowed soil of late medieval Europe. Take the region of Liège (now in the Netherlands), for example. Historian Walter Simons identifies a number of centers of early Beguine life that emerged near Liège early in the thirteenth century.[11] Around 1181 Juetta, a twenty-three-year-old widow, left her home in Huy to serve a colony of lepers outside the town walls. Others joined her and an informal community developed. Elsewhere, around 1191 Marie at age fourteen convinced her new husband to live a life of continence and service. In time they moved to nearby Willambroux to serve the lepers there for many years until she retired to a nearby monastery. Again, people were inspired by the example and "flocks of Beguines" settled there. Marie became a sought-after guide, renowned for her wisdom. In the city of Liège itself women living alone in various parts of the city began to associate together, meeting for support, and working together in the local hospital or in the nearby leper colony. A house was donated for the women and some of them moved in and set up life together. Similar expressions appeared throughout Europe.

Nobody knew what to make of the Beguines because they were different. Priests who supported them often called them *religious*, the term used for nuns or monks. Yet they were not nuns. Beguines did not take formal vows, they traveled in and out of the cities, and were not formally subject to an abbess or bishop. They lived a life of voluntary poverty and

9. Chrysostom cited in O'Donovan and O'Donovan, eds., *From Irenaeus to Grotius*, 95 and 96.

10. In addition to my own work on the Beguines (see note 3), see especially Grundmann, *Religious Movements*; McDonnell, *Beguines and Beghards*; Simons, *Cities of Ladies*; McGinn, *Flowering of Mysticism*, 153–265; Swan, *Wisdom of the Beguines*; Miller, *Beguines of Medieval Paris*; Böhringer et al., eds., *Labels and Libels*; deVries, "Proper Beguine's Interaction."

11. See Simons, *Cities of Ladies*, 39–48.

yet managed their own textile businesses. They attended local churches and yet also kept their own times of prayer. Their very existence as communities of socially active devout women was a challenge to the political structure of the time—women were expected to live either with family or in the context of a cloistered order. Consequently, some Beguine communities were compelled to identify with formal religious orders. Others, however, were permitted to mature: modeling alternative lifestyles, giving birth to a new genre of spiritual writings, and making a significant mark on their world.

And then there is Thomas Merton (1915–1968). After an agnostic upbringing, Thomas Merton joined the Roman Catholic church, receiving baptism in 1938 and moving to Kentucky to enter the austere Trappist abbey of Gethsemani in 1941. His account of this transition, *The Seven Story Mountain,* brought Merton wide acclaim and, until his untimely death by accidental electrocution in 1968, he lived as a monk and became one of the most influential spiritual writers of the twentieth century. Merton occasionally expressed concerns regarding social issues in his personal journals prior to the 1960s, but after June of 1960—and particularly between 1961 and 1963—he invested himself fully in social and political concerns. But how could he do so as a Trappist monk? Thomas Merton asks this very question in his journal entry of June 5, 1960:

> 2. Is my commitment to religious vows enough or must it be clarified by a further, more concrete commitment . . . to a *social* viewpoint for myself and the other monks?

> 3. Are the commitments of the church and the Order such today that they necessarily involve one in a "reactionary" social situation? What are the church's politics exactly?

> Commitment—to the point at least of reading and studying fully these questions not speculatively but in order to form my conscience and take such practical actions as I can.[12]

By July 19, Merton felt that "I ought to use my voice to say something, in public." Yet he was concerned that "by the time it got through the censors

---

12. Merton, *Turning Toward the World,* 8, italics original. For my discussion of Merton throughout this book I am drawing primarily from the following sources: Mott, *Seven Mountains;* Merton, ed., *Breakthrough to Peace;* Merton, *Conjectures;* Merton, *Cold War Letters;* Merton, *Emblems of a Season;* Merton, *Original Child Bomb;* Merton, *Passion for Peace;* Merton, *Peace in the Post-Christian Era.*

it would have lost most of its meaning."[13] Indeed, in May of 1961 these "censors," representatives of Merton's monastic order responsible to review the communications of those within their sphere, refused to print something Merton wrote regarding the atom bomb. We hear Merton throughout his 1961 journals struggling how to respond to increasing nuclear tensions: as a well-known author, as a monk, and as an advocate for peace (though not a strict pacifist). He penned a few suggestive (and highly creative!) pieces in the last half of 1961.[14]

Merton reached a turning point in October of 1961. He was convinced that the threat of nuclear war was "the greatest moral crisis in the history of man" and that the best course was simply to strive for the end of war, period. He writes in his journal (October 23), "I am happy that I have turned a corner, perhaps the last corner in my life."[15] Two days later Thomas Merton wrote a letter to Etta Gullick, a theologian. He tells her of both his concern over "the international crisis" and of his intention to work "with such means as I have at my disposal for the abolition of war." But what means can a cloistered monk use? Merton proceeds in his letter, "Prayer of course remains my chief means, but it is also an obligation on my part to speak out in so far as I am able, and to speak as clearly, as forthrightly, and as uncompromisingly as I can."[16] This letter was the first of 111 letters written between October 1961 and October 1962. Merton's "Cold War Letters," as they have been named, were sent to artists, activists, intellectuals, and even politicians. We shall periodically be returning to Merton's Cold War Letters, along with his other writings of the early sixties, in this book, for they offer a superb example of the interaction of monasticism and socio-political engagement. And besides, there is a surprising end to the story!

The Challenge(s) of Socio-Political Engagement

As you can see, desert elders, monks, sort of nunish women, and so on (we'll get to these definitions soon) all engage in socio-political activities.

13. Merton, *Turning Toward the World*, 21.

14. See his "Chant to be Used in Processions around a Site with Furnaces," in Merton, *Emblems of a Season of Fury*, 43–47; *Original Child Bomb*; "A Letter to Pablo Antonio Cuadra Concerning Giants," in Merton, *Emblems of a Season of Fury*, 70–89; and "The Root of War is Fear," in Merton, *Passion for Peace*, 11–19.

15. Merton, *Turning Toward the World*, 172–73.

16. Merton, *Cold War Letters*, 9–10.

They confront local political leaders, they care for others even if it places them at risk socially, they speak out regarding global issues, and more. You will see the "more" in the course of this book. But it is not always easy. When is the time to leave your seclusion and take a stand? Can you live with the judgments hurled at you by your neighbors in their misunderstanding? Can you face your own finitude, compelled to do *something* and yet knowing your own offerings from your own small corner have so little impact? It was not always easy.

And it is not easy for us today. I think it is perhaps more challenging now than it was even in Merton's day. First, living in an information age, we are more aware of the range of issues that deserve attention. Many caring Christians experience a kind of overload when facing society. Policies that perpetuate racial inequities, practices that threaten forests or animal species, questions of immigration or abortion, repression of human dignities and freedoms, proliferation of human trafficking: I can go on and on. These are not mere "unfortunate trends." They touch our very encounter with right and wrong. But how can we respond to all of them? All at the same time? In the following chapter I will say something about the fact that in some sense, we can't avoid engagement at some level (especially those of us who suffer the consequences more keenly than others). But then how do we act? How do we sustain action for the long haul? How does engagement nourish faith and how does faith nourish engagement?

I also think that things are especially challenging today because we are so aware of the impossibility of neutrality. Eldridge Cleaver said it clearly: "There is no more neutrality in the world. You either have to be part of the solution, or you're going to be part of the problem."[17] Yet that very truth leaves us part of so many problems. We may be aware, for example, of "fair trade" but we don't always know which purchases are "fairer" than others. It can take a bit of work to find out and the answers are not always clear. We are informed about a few current hot issues, only vaguely aware of others, and almost entirely ignorant of some issues that are extremely significant (global land acquisition, for example). The breadth of issues and the complexity of factors involved, combined with our sense of responsibility to be part of the solution, make confident socio-political engagement particularly challenging.

17. Cleaver, "Speech to Barristers' Club." For more details on this quote see Hodson, "Becoming Part of the Solution," 68n1.

One of my online students described in a discussion post why he had abandoned socio-political activity. He had seen too many of his friends journey through the stages: get a little "edgy," stop attending church, get angry at "institutional" evangelicalism, become an activist, leave the faith entirely. My student's choice was to keep the faith by avoiding the activism, and by faithful service to God in the context of a local congregation. I have friends who have left faith through these very stages outlined by my student. I have other friends who kept the faith by making the same choices as my student. As a spiritual director and informal consultant, I sympathize with the difficulties of individuals and groups trying to navigate this journey. And yet I am convinced that other options are possible. That is why I wrote this book.

Maybe now is the time to say something about my own challenges with regards to socio-political engagement, the greatest of which is the question of why I can even think of writing a book like this. First, I am not a monk. I am married with two children. In fact I have never even lived in an "intentional Christian community," though I have visited many. Yes, Cheri (my wife) and I made commitments to voluntary simplicity and have kept them ever since our wedding (over forty years ago).[18] Nevertheless, we own a home (the mobile cost us $5,000) and have been generally employed (often part-time). I am white, raised middle class, male, American, educated, and I live in a rural environment. I do ranch work on land that was taken from Utes and other tribes. My education was made possible in part because of loans that in many schools were not available to people of color. I receive the benefits of patriarchy and racism even when I think I am unprejudiced and generous. When it comes to socio-political realities (and the perspectives of those who suffer from them) I should be the one listening rather than speaking. I know this, and I try to practice good listening in my personal life. And yet here I am writing this book. Lord, have mercy![19] I offer what I have gained from my circumstances to serve others in theirs. From the beginning nuns and monks have seen their task as a "work of repentance."[20] We shall see in

18. In the summer of 2021 Kirsten Dirksen, a YouTube journalist, visited us and produced a video about our home and our semi-monastic approach to things. You can find this video at https://www.youtube.com/watch?v=XDpZ4jED6zA.

19. Thanks to Tim Heatwole Shenk from the Camden Houses Community in New Jersey—a residential community that brings peace to a neighborhood in Camden struggling with violence—whose own statement inspired and shaped my own.

20. See for example in the first letter of Antony of Egypt (251–356), often called the father of Western monasticism (Antony, *Letters*, 2).

the course of this book (and especially in chapter 7) that our approach to socio-political engagement today also involves a work of repentance.

The Challenge(s) of Monasticism

A book on socio-political engagement presents its own challenges, as you can see. But a book on *monasticism* and socio-political engagement is still another thing, particularly for non-Catholic Westerners in the twenty-first century. For one, few of us really understand what "monasticism" is all about. I have had students declare to me that monasticism is irrelevant for today because it is simply a white, European phenomena. I tell them about my visits to some of the oldest Christian monasteries in the world (in Egypt), where I was the only white person there. Not to mention the tradition of Ethiopian monasticism. One monastery a few hours south of my home in Colorado had, last time I visited, monks from thirteen different countries. They generally conduct business in three different languages.

I have been studying and writing about Christian monasticism for over twenty years and I am still trying to figure out how best to define it.[21] You will probably get a better sense of things by reading the stories throughout this book than by any formal definition I can invent. But for the sake of giving readers something to start with, let me say this much: Monastic geeks will divide up different categories of "friars," "sisters," "canons," "nuns," and so on. There are those who take "simple" vows and those who take "solemn" vows. There those who receive approval by the pope and those who get their approval from a local bishop. The labels and the lifestyles have varied over the centuries but a few features seem especially significant.

Those who choose a religious life—"religious life" or "consecrated life" are common phrases to describe monasticism generally—often invest themselves in practices aimed at achieving maturity in Christ. Nuns and monks see themselves as participants in an alternative culture, different from the world of employment, family life, and parish membership.[22]

21. For a survey of my musings on monasticism(s) old and new, see https://spirituality shoppe.org/resources-for-christian-living/old-monastic-wisdom-for-new-monastic-people/. For a recent review of the technical distinctions regarding consecrated life in the Roman Catholic world, see Johnson et al., eds., *New Generations*, 25–40.

22. Working out just how "monasticism(s)" are similar and/or different than "church" is a complicated question, too large for me to expand on here. I hope to

They make serious commitments to common values like poverty and celibacy. They usually live according to a clearly defined form of life, often called a Rule of Life, which identifies the roles and rhythms of each community. Prayer is central to most monastic institutions and it is common for communities, when possible, to gather together frequently each day to pray. Thus, we can say that religious life is an embodiment of concrete means of spiritual formation, chosen in conscious distinction from others who do not share a similar way of life, and symbolized through a formal commitment to a particular way of life, a way of life the general principles of which are usually clearly articulated and which exhibit a rhythmic blend of prayer, work, study, and/or ministry. (Though—as we will see—the balance of interest in "cave" (prayer), "refectory" (community), and "road" (mission and activism) varies in different expressions of religious life.)[23]

This brings us to the second challenge of monasticism, for even with these features in mind we still have to identify which groups exhibit which features and to what degree. Is a community "monastic" when it has common times of prayer, lives together on one site, sees itself as an alternative form of life, yet contains both married and single people? What about those Beguines I mentioned above? My way of looking at all this currently is to see things on some sort of continuum. On one side are strict monastic expressions: solemn vows, cloistered living, clearly defined practices, written Rule of Life, established common times of prayer, and so on. On the other end is the ordinary devout individual or household: no necessary commitment to any living arrangement, employment as appropriate to "make a living" in the context of one's culture, prayer when seems best, perhaps a sincere commitment to Christian values but vaguely articulated. In between these two extremes there are a host of possibilities. In my study of the history of monasticism, and in my experience of devout communities and individuals today, I see an important place for this "in between." I celebrate families who live in the same urban neighborhood, who pray together daily, who commit to a

address this question more directly in future work. In the meantime, see Howard, "What Does God Expect?"

23. Both Wikipedia and Britannica Online provide helpful articles on the nature of monasticism and Christian monasticism more specifically. My favorite surveys of Christian monasticism are Laboa, *Historical Atlas,* and Peters, *Story of Monasticism.* For early monasticism I like Harmless, *Desert Christians,* and for medieval monasticism I recommend Melville, *World of Medieval Monasticism.*

life of simplicity, and who take concrete steps to follow ever closer in discipleship with Christ. I applaud individuals who meet weekly online to share how they have kept a common Rule of Life of prayerful rhythm, sexual fidelity, and humble service. Like the medieval Beguines, these contemporary "semi-monastic" expressions may be exploring valuable options for Christianity today.[24]

So then where does all this confusion leave us when talking about monasticism and socio-political engagement? I think it leaves us in a wonderful place; and here is why. If all I wanted to show you were the activities of "strict" monastic expressions (solemn vows, written rules, multiple common prayers daily) I could still demonstrate a wide range of engagement in socio-political affairs. This does not mean that all re-ligious orders are or should be heavily engaged in politics. The power of the monks coming off the mountain to protest comes from the au-thority they gained through years of contemplative life. There is an art to all this and we will get to those details. My point here is to show that monasticism and socio-political engagement are not necessarily op-posed. Indeed they have much to offer one another. What we find in the monastic records are stories of committed hermits influencing kings and policies through their writings, monastic pioneers who developed some of the earliest hospitals, enduring communities who sought to influence their neighborhoods for good, and more. If this kind of breadth can be documented for strict monastic life, how much more can it be seen in the semi-monastic, "in-between" expressions that have flowered in his-tory and are sprouting everywhere today. This is one reason I am writing this book, to display a few models old and new that can lead us into a life that is socio-politically deep and wide. If you want to know more about the contemporary models, or about how to start one of your own, be sure and check out the Appendix on "Exploring or Inventing New Monasticism(s)"[25]

As I mentioned above, I see a lovely blending together of "deep" and "wide" in a well-discerned life of following Christ. But just what does it mean to follow Christ? For members of traditional monasteries? For members of intentional Christian communities? For Christians like me, who have no formal ties to a community but want to live a devout life?

24. See my "Beguine Option" and Elm, "*Vita regularis*."

25. I treat the idea of history providing "perspectives and models" (and of the traps in "using" history) in my *Brazos Introduction*, 55–60. See also Buschart and Eilers, *Theology as Retrieval*.

These questions are why this book offers not merely reflections on socio-political engagement and monasticism, but also on the Christian life. We can't address monasticism and socio-political engagement without asking questions about salvation, church, Jesus, and more. While there is no space to develop some kind of theology of everything in a book of this sort, neither can I simply ignore important issues. Consequently, I will offer a few comments on various topics related to Christianity more generally when I think it will help us understand how a consecrated life and socio-political engagement interact.

My conviction is that nuns and monks and friars and so on have some valuable lessons to teach us about how to let God's fountain flow both deep and wide. This book, then, seeks to navigate an interaction between two spheres. One is "monasticism," which, as you now under-stand, I am interpreting broadly in terms of intentional Christian living found both in the past and among individuals and communities today.[26] The other sphere is the "socio-political" arena: the world of governments, policies, negotiations, public and private powers, populist actions, and the ordering of common life in general.[27] The interaction between these two spheres is what I am calling "engagement." As mentioned, one of my aims in this book is to introduce you to a range of perspectives and models of socio-political engagement. We engage with the socio-political arena when we choose to speak out (chapter 3) and when we consciously care for others (chapter 4). We engage when we choose to live differently, modeling a different value system than the dominant values of our sur-rounding culture (chapter 5). We engage socio-political forces when we take action: meeting, voting, lobbying, carrying signs (chapter 6). But we also engage the socio-political world through our prayers (chapter 7).

I don't think this is the book to inspire and motivate the masses into action. As community leader David Janzen from Reba Place Fellow-ship—a Mennonite-affiliated community of about fifty people that live in some nearby houses in Evanston, Illinois—mentioned after reading an earlier draft of this book, "People usually engage because their compas-sion (or anger) is stirred up by the suffering of others, or they experience oppression directly as a result of their place in society." My purpose here is probably less to offer inspiration and more to offer wisdom. My hope in this book is to help individuals and communities:

26. For a survey of intentional Christian living see Kauffman, *"Follow Me."*
27. I will speak more of my concept of "the socio-political" in the following chapter.

- to engage in the socio-political arena free *from* guilt or drivenness and *for* appropriate action,

- to learn the integrated repentance of our personal life within and structural life without,

- to confidently dream of our own life of deep and wide, having received an introduction to a range of appropriate (and realistically doable) action steps,

- to perceive that our engagement is not merely a choice of something meaningful to do with our "spare time," but rather flows from and feeds into a spiritual vitality of our whole life,

- to develop a sustainable, interpenetrating rhythm of socio-political engagement, community and family life, and rich personal relationship with God,

- to see how each of us fits into the larger picture of God, global society, and local community, and thus to understand our life and action not merely as a matter of exerting "political pressure," but also as a display of and a force for the life we want to see arise,

- to face the conflicts and trials—the possibilities, pitfalls, and practices—of socio-political engagement with both love and courage.

In one sense, this book is just another plea for formation or discipleship. For how can we be formed into the image of Christ, how can we become followers of Jesus, if this does not include our interaction with our own communities and with the larger social spheres that surround us?[28] The form of monasticism that follows the lead of St. Benedict of Nursia (480–547) speaks of this using the phrase *conversio morum* (or *conversatio morum*), the conversion of life, the process of our ever-increasing habituation to the person and gospel of Christ. Thomas Merton, in his 1966 essay on "Conversion of Life," declared it the "essential monastic vow." He writes, "An understanding of *conversio morum* is necessary if we are to evaluate the aspirations of some modern monks toward 'incarnational witness' in the world on one hand and toward greater solitude on the other."[29] I sense similar aspirations among a wide range of "modern monks" today.

28. Looking at it this way, the present book functions as an important footnote to my *Guide to Christian Spiritual Formation*.

29. Merton, *Monastic Journey*, 108. Thanks to Jared Boyd, founder of the Order of the Common Life, for pointing me to this statement.

If there was ever one "relic" toward which I have a special attachment, it would be the cross that Saint Francis of Assisi was looking at (around 1208) when God told him to "rebuild my church." I first learned of this cross in 1971 when Cheri (not yet my wife) and I went to see the movie *Brother Sun, Sister Moon*, a film about the life of Francis. Forty years—and a much-deepened appreciation for Francis—later,[30] Cheri and I visited Assisi and saw the very cross, an extremely moving experience. I came home with a twenty-seven-inch by twenty-inch quality print of this cross, which my daughter and son-in-law then proceeded to install on a piece of wood, complete with appropriate gold leafing. It now hangs in my office.

FIGURE 1 – SAN DAMIANO CROSS

---

30. See for example my essay, "Who Should be Poor?"

When you look at this cross, a few things stand out.[31] Jesus' eyes are wide open, observant of all that is going on around. And there is a lot going on around him. Jesus is surrounded by people in conversation of one kind or another. Some of them look like they are talking about him. Others seem to be in the midst of some kind of disagreement. Jesus is spreading his arms, not only in a symbol of crucifixion but also in a symbol of embrace. Finally, there is blood pouring from his hands, feet, and side: blood that is falling on some of the people underneath the wounds. A fountain flowing: not only from Jesus' "wounded *side*," but from all his wounds. Jesus, with eyes open, embraces the politics that surround him. He knowingly suffers wounds inflicted by the machinations of religious and political leaders who could not bear his radical life and claims. The fruits of Christ's atoning death—the fountain of his blood—flow both to those under his feet (deep) and to those at his side and just beneath his extended hands (wide).

I pray for socio-political things on Tuesdays (it's just the way I work my schedule). I stand in front of this cross and see Jesus looking at me and at all the socio-political situations surrounding us today. I see him suffering, eyes open, embracing us all even in the midst of our political disagreements (often I think of *this* or *that* issue), suffering for us all, offering the benefits of his life and death both deep and wide. This image guides me as I write, praying that you who read this book will receive from that fountain flowing deep and wide.

How to Read This Book

You will get the most out of reading this book if you understand how I wrote the book. I wrote this book for members of Christian communities, for people interested in "new" monasticism, and for people exploring socio-political engagement in "old" monasticism. This is not a theological treatise, but rather a collection of reflections. I tend to explore topics by reading widely, talking to others, and thinking about my own life. I like to talk to people from a variety of geographic locations and political viewpoints. All of these kinds of sources are reflected here.

---

31. For a good color file of this cross, see http://www.dioceseofsalford.org.uk/wp-content/uploads/St-Francis-resized.jpg. You can click on the file to enlarge it and examine the details more clearly.

What this means is that I have written this book in two layers. I have tried to make the text itself a straightforward, somewhat conversational account of my own reflections on the topics at hand. You should be able to follow the text without needing the footnotes (and many of you will get more out of the book if you ignore them!). Yet I am aware that sometimes you might want to know more about a monastic figure or movement. You might want to know a few of the sources that informed my own ideas, or a sample of different viewpoints regarding some debated issue. I have provided footnotes as guides for further exploration. My aim in the footnotes, however, is not to provide a "book within a book," critically evaluating every debate I introduce or figure I quote.

As I mentioned, I read widely, and I tend to quote people (1) where I find that they worded something well, (2) where I consider their statements to be a worthy expression of one relevant view, or (3) where I approve of their statements. I will quote these people even if I have problems with other aspects of their lives or their views. So be forewarned, I *will* quote someone you don't like. Yet I must say something here at the start of this book regarding one author I reference. John Howard Yoder is one of the most influential theologians in the twentieth century regarding matters of church and state, particularly significant for Anabaptist and "new monastic" types. Yoder also has been found guilty of grievous misdeeds against a number of women.[32] I interact with Yoder in this book because I find that scholarship requires attention given to his writings. Yet at the same time, I recognize that his deeds may make it hard for us to hear his words. My references to Yoder, or to other figures in this book, must not be mistaken for an endorsement of the whole of their lives or views.

One could address a wide range of "issues" in a book on sociopolitical engagement. My concern in this book, however, is not to solve the issues but rather to empower those who engage in solving the issues. For this reason I will highlight basic Christian values and avoid detailed discussion of political policy. My hope is that readers will walk away from this book not with "the answers" to political questions but with a confident sense of how they might take an appropriate next step forward in their own process of engagement.

As I mentioned above, we will explore in the course of this book a rich variety of ways we can appreciate the *deep* and the *wide* in our life

32. For a report written at the invitation of the Mennonite Church USA's Discernment Group of this matter see Goossen, "Defanging the Beast."

of devoted engagement with the socio-political world. But first we must recognize that fundamentally, underneath all our particular engagements, we are already there. We are political people from the start and, consequently, we cannot really avoid engagement. That is where we turn in the next chapter.

TWO

We Are Political People

SOMETIMES SOCIO-POLITICAL ENGAGEMENT IS something we *choose*. We select who to vote for and we determine how we will mark our ballot on the issues. We may decide that some matter is so important that we are going to "do something." And we choose to march. At other times, socio-political engagement is nearly *unavoidable*. We are Jewish in 1940s Germany and our very existence is outlawed. We sleep on the streets in Denver, Colorado and break the law by using a blanket. We get pulled over by police in St. Louis, Missouri because they were looking for a Black man. But there are also times when socio-political engagement is something we *fall into*. Take for example St. Columbanus (590–615).

After monastic training under good Irish guidance, Columbanus left Ireland for Gaul (France) with a group of partners. The land was hungry for the gospel and Columbanus ministered not only in word but also in the power of signs and wonders. The local king was impressed. He donated some land where Columbanus and his companions could lay their heads, eat their small meals, and share life together. In time Columbanus and his followers founded three monasteries on the grounds: Annegray, Luxeuil, and Fontaines. Columbanus also healed the son of duke Waldelen, who later donated property for another monastery.

But as things went, after the king's death his successors fought among themselves and Columbanus, now a well-known and important figure in the area, was caught in the middle. More particularly Columbanus and his support of marriage (rather than concubinage) kindled the ire of Brunhilda, the influential widow of one of the kings. Jonas of Bobbio's *Life of Columbanus* mentions that Brunhilda "feared that her

power and honor would be lessened if, after the expulsion of the con-
cubines, a queen should rule the court."[1] Brunhilda created trouble for
Columbanus and ultimately he left the area. Bobbio's story from then on
documents a series of Columbanus's (1) relationships with kings who
offer safe passage or property and (2) problems caused by the tensions
between various secular and ecclesiastical leaders. His successful ministry was constantly surrounded by the politics of his locations. He could
hardly have developed his monasteries without royal permission, yet it
was not easy navigating monastic life within their reach.

Historian Gert Melville writes,

> After Columbanus's death in 625, his conception of monastic
> life lived on. Numerous monastic communities shaped by his
> tradition appeared across Francia, whether with the support
> of both the secular and the episcopal nobility or through their
> direct initiative—thereby revealing with remarkable clarity
> what would become a long-lived, essential element of the *vita
> religiosa* [religious life] of the Middle Ages: the close relation-
> ship between monastery and political power, a relationship that
> often took on an almost symbiotic character and that was often
> expressed as domination over religious communities.[2]

Throughout the first half of the Middle Ages this "symbiotic" relationship
between monastery and political power often supported the development of both worlds and castle/monastery sites became centers of life in
early medieval Europe.

Yet when you own the land, you can also set the rules, and at times
secular rulers would often appoint abbots or alter requirements regarding the monastery's way of life (at times for the good of the faith and at
times for their own gain).[3] As the church gained power, conflicts with
secular leadership reached a critical juncture. We know of the fifty years
of drama surrounding this juncture (1076–1122) as the "Investiture
Controversy," centering around the rights of secular leaders to "invest"
bishops or abbots with the symbols of their office. As you can see, simply

1. Jonas of Bobbio, "Life of St. Columbanus." The drama was complicated, but the
point is that Brunhilda was more concerned about her own place than of the value of
marriage.

2. Melville, *World of Medieval Monasticism*, 22. For more on the interaction between Columbanian monasticism and local powers see Fox, *Power and Religion in
Merovingian Gaul*.

3. See Howe, "Nobility's Reform."

the act of maintaining a place to lay your head, eat your meals, and share life together can sink you into all kinds of socio-political engagement.

Sometimes nuns and monks fall into socio-political engagement simply as a natural consequence of caring for others, who need a place to lay their head, eat their meals, and share life together. Such was the case for my eldest daughter, Claire. In 2006 Claire graduated from college with a degree in psychology and joined InnerCHANGE: A Missionary Order Among the Poor.[4] She moved to San Francisco in order to live in community and to help people without homes in the Haight-Ashbury/ Golden Gate Park neighborhood. She loved sitting on the sidewalk with people while they played music or asked for spare change. They all shared a picnic pancake breakfast in the park every Monday.

But by 2010 things got complicated. They were told that the law would not allow them to sit on the sidewalk. It was illegal to lie and sleep in the locations that were safest. By 2013 park rangers and police were also visiting their pancake picnics in the park, informing them that they had to move, to acquire a permit, or to cook without an open flame.

Claire and her community found themselves recruiting people from the streets to speak at hearings. They relocated picnics, complied with requests, applied for permits, and finally asked for a formal ticket (civil disobedience) so they could learn exactly what the problem was. They had a lawyer draw up a document explaining their work and why having pancakes in the park was legal. They marched with other groups in an effort to prevent the "Sit-Lie" law from taking effect. This was politics, and Claire was not really excited about it. She wrote in her May 2013 "Haight Mail":

> This is tough. I hate legal issues, I just wanna make pancakes with my friends and share Jesus with them, but if this is what God has for us, we are in it. We see it as a cool way to model healthy conflict resolution for many of our friends in the park while not caving on what you believe! And we are not alone. Many cities around the USA made sharing food with homeless people illegal. I don't agree with that, and I don't believe the Bible does either. . . . Being a Christian affects the way we live as well as the way we see the world around us. Sometimes when we are Christians we will see things as wrong that the world thinks

4. InnerCHANGE was highlighted as one of the "new friars" in Bessenecker, *New Friars*. John Hayes, founder of InnerCHANGE, expresses their original vision well in his *Sub-Merge*.

is all right. Sometimes we are supposed to do something about that.

Falling into politics through the natural act of caring for others. It happens all the time.[5] Politics is just part of where we live. We look for housing and face racial covenants. We desire to improve water distribution and discover that it requires serious legal efforts. We buy products only to learn that they were produced under unfair working conditions. The fact is, we are political people. As you will soon find out, I consider that to be a blessing. I also consider it important. Indeed, I think it is important that we grasp three points about our political nature here at the start of this book because our approach to these matters will shape the nature of our engagement as communities and individuals of Christ. *We can't escape politics. Politics is more than statecraft. Christlike politics demands change within and without.* Each of these points flows from the previous.

1. WE CAN'T ESCAPE POLITICS

When I first came to faith in Christ in the early 1970s, I thought I could avoid politics. No, I thought I *should* avoid politics. People in my circles believed that in the near future Christians would be snatched up to heaven in the rapture and that the world, which was already headed downhill, would enter a cultural and political chaos known as "the Great Tribulation." Consequently, the idea of righting wrongs or investing in the social system seemed to be wrongheaded. What we needed to do was witness to as many people as possible so that they would be spared the trials of the tribulation and would then "soon be going home" with the rest of us believers. Christians in my crowd recommended against involvement in political issues. Yet a couple of years later I was on the edge of being drafted into the Vietnam war effort and I found myself inquiring of my youth group leader why he became a conscientious objector. I couldn't escape politics.

Whereas some cannot escape politics, others cannot engage in politics—or at least they are not *permitted* to engage. The famous democracies of ancient Greece were the preserve of landholding males.

5. See also the example of a pastor and congregation in Barber II and Wilson-Hartgrove, *Third Reconstruction*, 15–23.

WE ARE POLITICAL PEOPLE   23

Voting rights in the USA were once the preserve of non-enslaved males. Anabaptist fugitives, British nonconformists, detainees in Russian and Chinese prison camps, all would have loved to serve in public office but were denied that privilege. We still mark "the first woman" or "the first Black person" to hold this or that office. Yet this very denial of political opportunity is itself a form of "can't escape politics."

In one sense, we can't escape politics because that is the way God made things. We are *meant* to be political people.[6] The Bible begins with God's rule and within the first chapter God shares this rule with human beings (Gen 1:27–28).[7] From the very beginning we are called to care for the earth (Gen 2:15, see also verse 5), for the earth's creatures (Gen 2:18–20; Ps 8:3–8), and for one another (Gen 2: 21–24; of course, the answer to Cain's question in Gen 4:9 "Am I my brother's keeper?" is "Yes!"). Furthermore, we find mention of this same human creative cooperation with God's own rule at the very end of things. Rather than a scene of harp-accompanied singing, the final chapter of Revelation simply states that God's people "will reign for ever and ever" (Rev 22:5). The mandate to bring order within our spheres of influence presented in the first chapter of the Bible is affirmed in the final chapter. Public education, economic development, global communication, and wilderness preservation are what we are made for.

Yet what about sin? What about Jesus? What about the church? True, patterns of sinfulness affect the ways in which we order our spheres (a disordered ordering). The sins of self-interest and the Sin of Empire twist our political experience.[8] The rest of the book of Genesis describes

6. I have outlined the basic narrative structure of what I call "The Big Story" in Howard, *Guide*, 23–42. I have explored the theological structure of human experience in Howard, *Brazos Introduction*, 145–94, and the philosophical structure of experience in my "Metaphysics of Power." In the present book my aim is to situate specifically human *political* experience within biblical, theological, and philosophical perspectives and informed by dialogue with other political theologies.

7. Whereas some begin their political theologies from the prophets, others from Jesus, and still others from Paul's treatment of government in Romans 13, I wish to emphasize the place of politics/ordering as a constituent element of creation itself. Luke Bretherton seems to make a similar point in his *Christ and the Common Life*, 311. Wes Howard-Brook also begins from the creation account in his *"Come Out, My People!"* I affirm Stanley Hauerwas's recognition of the fundamental goodness of the world in his "Servant Community" (Hauerwas, *Hauerwas Reader*, 375). See also O'Donovan, *Desire of the Nations*.

8. I concur with Ibram X. Kendi's assessment of the dangers of self-interest when he states, "The source of racist ideas was not ignorance and hate, but self-interest."

a growing alienation from God, from ourselves, from others, and from the earth itself. One function of the nation of Israel—and ultimately of Jesus as the fulfillment of Israel's mission—is to embody in some measure the values of God as a model and influence for the world, a "light to the nations" (see Isa 42:6; 49:6).[9] Though we recognize that governments often preserve a measure of peace in the midst of self-interest, we also acknowledge that politics does not exist merely to restrain evil. Rather, the ordering of our own lives as communities and individuals, and our influence into the ordered lives of those around us, manifest (in our own stumbling ways) the heart and mind of the God who created and is recreating this world in and through the people of God. We will return to these themes throughout this book.[10]

We also can't escape politics because this is how we interact with the world. Theologically speaking, politics is how God structured the world. Social-psychologically speaking, politics is how groups of people navigate their world. We conduct deliberations as socially constructed groups. People assess circumstances or possibilities, in view of values, with an aim to action.[11] Politics is conducted by *agents*, those who ex-

How to Be an Antiracist, 229. Historian Erik van Alten notices similar dangers in his account of Calvin's assessment of early Anabaptists and rich Genevans. See van Alten, "'. . . all things in common,'" 188. I think that Arthur Brooks's treatment of "contempt" moves in a similar direction. It is interesting to consider how modern nations developed the separation and balance of powers in an effort to curb self-interest. And yet self-interest finds a way of exploiting even modern political structures. For more, see Brooks, *Love Your Enemies*. The Sin of Empire is the dominant theme of Howard-Brooke, *"Come Out, My People!"* For a treatment of the nuances of sin and Sin, see Croasmun, *Emergence of Sin*.

9. For a sense of the nation of Israel as an intended embodiment of the politics of God, see Brueggemann, *Theology of the Old Testament* and Wright, *Mission of God*. For Jesus as fulfillment of these ideals see Walter Rauschenbusch's understanding of the "kingdom of God" in his *Theology for the Social Gospel*, the works of N. T. Wright, and O'Donovan, *Resurrection and Moral Order*.

10. One sample: Luke Bretherton writes, "A christologically and eschatologically oriented order of blessing follows from an emphasis on what it means to participate in Christ's healing rule. To participate in the rule of Christ does not mean that the privileged exercise rule on behalf of Christ. This would legitimate preexisting forms of, for example, sexist, class-based, and racist structures of authority. Rather it entails being prepared to dis-identify with unjustly privileged forms of life in order to participate in Christ's cruciform rule." *Christ and the Common Life*, 77.

11. This is often the stuff of political philosophy. A couple of good examples of reflection on political deliberation (and the institutions that conduct this deliberation) are Rawls, *Justice as Fairness*; O'Donovan, *Ways of Judgment*.

ercise (or wish to exercise) some level of authority. This brings up the question "authority of *whom*?" and that, of course, is the point. Part of the world of politics is the grasp of how we decide who deliberates on behalf of whom.[12] Politics also involves *assessment*. It expects e-*value*-ation, conducted through somewhat clear procedures (proposals, debates, filibusters, referendums, and so on), according to a somewhat common set of values or social "goods" (rights, violations, justice, and so on).[13] Yes, good political judgment ("judgment" here as a verb) is sometimes forsaken because of the dominance of self-interest. Fair evaluation is sometimes forsaken because careful deliberation regarding the common good ends up being abandoned in the chaos of partisan lobbying. Nonetheless, political deliberation ideally moves toward a good end. Political deliberation ends in a *judgment* ("judgment" as a noun). Once assessment and evaluation are done, the issue moves toward implementation. But the end of politics is some kind of intended action. This is how we think. Whether primitive tribes, medieval monarchies, or modern democracies/autocracies, we can't escape politics because this is how we do things.

Finally, we can't escape politics because this is where we find ourselves. Some philosophers talk of our being "thrown" into the world such that we have no option but to have our own cultural biases and such. We are inescapably embedded in socio-political locations. I see our embeddedness not only as a reminder of our limitations and our need for the insights of others, but also as a reminder of the blessing of our own unique perspectives arising in the very embeddedness of our own particular locations. I like to think of our lives as "given" rather than "thrown" to earth. As the stories at the start of our chapter reminded us, our lives always emerge in contexts, and the contexts are always to some extent

---

12. Discussion of this issue is a major contribution of the theologies of liberation. See for example Gutiérrez, *Theology of Liberation*; Cone, *Black Theology of Liberation*. The "Christendom" of O'Donovan in *Desire of the Nations,* Wayne Grudem's nod toward "some kind of democracy" in his *Politics According to the Bible,* and the "consociation" of Bretherton in *Christ and the Common Life* also poke at this question of corporate political agency. Liberationists, however, will ask about "*whose* democracy" they are speaking. I read Bretherton as sensitive to that question. Similarly, we might add that economically speaking, politics often is the process of deciding how resources are distributed to meet needs.

13. I think Charles Taylor does a marvelous job of tracing a history of the "Good" lying behind the goods that are valued in individual and social assessments in his *Sources of the Self.*

(and differing in every case) politically tinged.[14] I live aside farmlands, outside of a small town. And yet politics surrounds me from every side. Who has the rights to our precious water, and why? What regulates the hunting practices on or off our property? Who can travel on what roads and when? (Just to let you know, the Forest Service often closes a gate across the road to our ranch during the winter and I am not allowed to drive to my own property. You can only imagine what some of the local ranchers think about this.) I could bore you forever with local politics, but I can't escape them. The "wide" world of politics invades us no matter who we are.

Monastic Practice: Political Self-Examination Part One— Observation

We see the presence of the wide in our lives by going deep. One of the core activities of monastic life is the practice of *self-examination*. Inspired by Ps 139:23–24 ("search me, O God," "see if there is any wicked way in me," "lead me in the way everlasting"), monks have reviewed their days, weeks, or lives with a view toward positive change. Isaiah the Solitary (fifth century) wrote, "Examine yourself daily in the sight of God, and discover which of the passions [vices] is in your heart." Gerard Zerbolt of Zutphen (1367–98), writer and early member of the Sisters and Brothers of the Common Life (a semi-monastic expression of the time) designed a set of "Three Examinations: and How a Man May Recover His Sense through Memory of his Sins." Ignatius of Loyola (1491–1556), founder of the Jesuits, designed a method for making an "examination of conscience."[15]

14. Augustine of Hippo (354–430) speaks of believers dwelling inevitably within the context of two "cities." He identifies one city as "the city of God" or the "heavenly city": the people who follow the leadership of the one true God. He names the second city an "earthly kingdom," "earthly city," or the "city of this world" (see for example Augustine, *City of God*, I.35; II.2; XVIII.1–2; XIX.14, 17). At one point he compares the earthly and heavenly cities to those who live by the flesh or the Spirit (XIV.4). Historians of Christian political theology often point to Augustine's *City of God* as an important political expression. Yet Augustine's political comments in the *City of God* are embedded within a long and elaborate defense for the worship of the Christian God. Augustine himself could not seem to separate his understanding of the Christian faith (and its superiority over other religions) from its place in the midst of Roman history, Roman political philosophy, Roman social practice, and more.

15. Isaiah the Solitary, "On Guarding the Intellect," in Nikodemos, *Philokalia*, 26; Zerbolt, *Spiritual Ascents*, 251–54; Ignatius of Loyola, *Spiritual Exercises* [#43]. For a sense of the place of self-examination in the context of colonial New England Puritan communities see Hambrick-Stowe, *Practice of Piety*, 168–75.

This practice, while valuable, can become overly self-critical (it's all about sin). It can also focus our attention upon the interior of the individual such that we fail to see the connections between personal life and socio-political conditions (it's all about me). What might help, particularly as we consider socio-political engagement, is an exercise in "political" self-examination.[16] Perhaps, inspired by Martin Luther King Jr.'s 1967 "Christmas Sermon on Peace," you might want to do this exercise early in the morning, perhaps as you eat breakfast.[17] And by the way, I will speak of this exercise as if it is practiced by an individual. But you can do it as a community just as you would as individuals. What is your communal experience of life together?

We begin our political self-examination with a simple prayer of openness to God's Spirit. "Holy Spirit, I open myself to your ministry. Show me what I need to see. Let me feel what I need to feel. Give me an increased awareness of the gifts, the distortions, and the hopes that politically surround me. Thank you for your presence. Amen." Then you begin with a simple awareness of your surroundings. What sounds do you hear? Do you hear a siren, or a wolf? You are listening to politics. (Most people are aware of policing politics, but recently Colorado voted to reintroduce wolves into wilderness areas—across the street from our ranch; I have heard and seen them). What do you see: buildings or trees? You are looking at politics (zoning regulations, building codes, logging permits). How do you feel this morning? (Now you could be talking about health care.) Then you turn to your meal. Eggs or bacon on your plate? You may be eating the politics of animal treatment. Are you having a drink with your meal? You might be drinking international trade (coffee, tea, cocoa, many juices). Are you watching the news or checking email while you eat? Where does your information come from? Thinking about going to work? Are you working from home or elsewhere? How will you get there? For whom is this means of transportation more or less available, and why? What do you do for work? Now you are facing questions of fair wages, employee safety, unionization, and more. Just become aware of what surrounds your morning.

16. Others writers have moved in this direction. I have been inspired in the development of this practice by the practice of writing an "ethnic autobiography" in Lau Branson and Martinez, *Churches, Cultures and Leadership*, 216–24 and by discussions around the "Pastoral Cycle" and "Social Analysis." For a summary and excellent contemporary presentation of the latter see Elizabeth Liebert, *Soul of Discernment*. I will be drawing on Liebert's work throughout this book.

17. See King, "Christmas Sermon," 254. Was this sermon an inspiration for the 1978 documentary, Hughes, dir., *Guess Who's Coming to Breakfast?*

Then you turn to the relational networks, the systems or structures, the institutions that are "present" with you in your morning. Why do you have *this* breakfast available to you and not another? How have the patterns of transportation in your area developed? Who makes the decisions at your place of work and how? Your aim here is simple awareness. You don't need to evaluate or critique or plan for change. In further monastic practices you will reflect more theologically, more strategically. Now the point is just to observe your political surroundings.

Well, almost. It might be good, at the end of the practice, to identify any feelings that come up in your political self-examination. Just as we sense things when we notice what lies within our hearts, so we also sense things when we notice the structures within which our life is embedded. And finally, since this is a "spiritual" exercise, perhaps you want to ask yourself where you notice God in all this (or where you *don't* notice God). Later we will explore the problems and the potentials in our politics. For now just observe in the presence of God, who put you on this earth just the way you are.

2. Socio-Political Engagement Is More than Statecraft

Now that we have a sense of our life surrounded by politics, we are in a place to ask the question just what politics (or socio-political engagement) *is*. Scholars struggle over definitions within the fields of political philosophy, political science, political theology, and public policy. Citizens discuss views of political theory, political deliberation, and political action. For our purposes—in a book on socio-political *engagement*—I will speak of politics as *an ordering activity of agents within given spheres of influence in the world*. Consequently, I will treat socio-political engagement as some *form of intentional participation* in politics or perhaps in society more generally. What I am trying to say by this definition is that politics—and even moreso socio-political engagement—is not to be restricted to mere governmental activity, something both Luke Bretherton and Rod Dreher call "statecraft."[18] Let me unpack this a bit.

18. Bretherton writes regarding his own view, "The understanding of democratic politics envisaged here is very different from that which equates democracy with legislation and bureaucratic administration (i.e. statecraft). Such state-centric and proceduralist approaches restrict democratic politics to pressure upon and action by state agencies rather than the negotiation of a common life between multiple actors of which the state is but one player." Bretherton, *Christ and the Common Life*, 455. See also Dreher, *Benedict Option*, 91.

First, politics is an *ordering* activity. This is the mandate of Genesis 1 and 2; human beings are to give order to the earth (till, care for), to animals (naming), and to fellow humans ("this is woman"). We are to designed to "reign" with Creator God (Rev 22:5) over every area of our lives. As theologian and monastic founder Augustine of Hippo (354–430) describes the goal of peace:

> The peace of the body, we conclude, is a tempering of the component parts in duly ordered proportion; the peace of the irrational soul is a duly ordered peace of the appetites; the peace of the rational soul is the duly ordered agreement of cognition and action, . . . peace between men is an ordered agreement of mind with mind; the peace of a home is the ordered agreement among those who live together about giving and receiving orders; the peace of the Heavenly City is a perfectly ordered and perfectly harmonious fellowship in the enjoyment of God, and a mutual fellowship in God—and order is the arrangement of things equal and unequal in a pattern which assigns to each its proper position.[19]

Similarly Bretherton speaks of politics as "the central way humans create and order their common life."[20] Socio-political engagement is our active co-participation with God in creating order in our common life on earth as human beings. Of course, in a fallen world our ordering can become problematic and thus there are times when what is most needed is a movement of divine dis-order (like drawing attention to corruption or oppression within an established empire). But even this divine dis-ordering is, to me, an act of bringing better order to our surroundings.

Politics—and socio-political engagement—is accomplished by *agents*. In the first two chapters of Genesis this meant Adam and Eve. By chapter 4 Cain is building a city. By chapter 9 we hear about sanctions imposed in response to the shedding of blood. At times the agents are leaders of tribes or kings or prophets. Yet we must realize that even kings and prophets are responsible to "the whole assembly" (see for example Num 14:1–10). The dynamics of Jesus' trials demonstrate the interplay of the one (Pilate), the few (the Sanhedrin), and the many (the crowd). All serve as agents in the political process: then and today. When I pray for political things on Tuesdays I think (as a citizen of the USA) of the

19. Augustine, *City of God*, XIX.13.
20. Bretherton, *Christ and the Common Life*, 18. See also more generally 16–50.

executive branch, cabinet members, Senate, House, Supreme Court, lobbyists, voters, and more.[21]

Socio-political engagement initiates activity within a *sphere of influence* in the world. Again, what I want to say is that politics is not just "government." The Beguines and my daughter Claire knew this. Their acts of care had political significance and brought down restrictions from authorities. They were not trying to influence legislation; they were just caring for people in need. Often legislative initiatives follow actions outside the "governmental" sphere. We reorder our relations to land, others, ourselves. We explore family and community. We initiate new forms of providing relief or protection. We experiment with new economy or new education. All this is socio-political engagement, even though it may not be directed toward formal governmental decisions. Politics is more than statecraft.

Finally, socio-political engagement expresses itself through *forms of intentional activity*. And there are a lot of forms. We hear that we must be part of the solution or we are going to be part of the problem. But what does it mean to be part of the solution? So far in this book I have been using an image of a fountain flowing deep and wide. In his monumental *There Is a River: The Black Struggle for Freedom in America*, Vincent Harding uses the image of a river to illustrate the diversity of forms of socio-political engagement all flowing together into a single force for freedom.[22] Harding speaks of prisoners escaping slave ships (13) or even suicide as rebellion (18). He describes runaways, and fugitives forming alternative communities hidden from the authorities (30, 39, 48, 111–12, 196). Some provided refuge (82, 116, 153, 170, 215). Others were able to speak out through writing (83, 86, 190, 207) or by making a simple demand for fair wages (241). Some were actively involved in governmental reforms (42, 54, 200–203), either cooperating with white organizations or forming their own schools, churches, and political organizations. Others despaired of reform and sought the establishment of a distinct Black nation (45, 67–68, 137) or attempted the overthrow of nondemocratic authorities (95, 104, 144, 196–97, 211–13). And then there was prayer. Harding writes,

---

21. See also Bretherton, *Christ and the Common Life*, 404–10.

22. Harding, *There Is a River*. In this section I will refer to page numbers of Harding's book within parentheses in the text.

> For instance, although it is hard to grasp in a secular age, large
> numbers of black people believed that their best contribution to
> the struggle was through unremitting prayer. Like some wide-
> spread, unorganized, unrecognized corps of spiritual resistants,
> these black men, women, and children were everywhere disci-
> plining their wills, turning themselves to the work of praying for
> freedom. (162, see also 114, 253, 332)

Harding summarizes, "Some prayed, some read by torchlight, some
fought and killed. Others ran, fighting cold and fears and sickness . . ."
(164). "Through their own lives the forerunners had established each
current as part of the river" (50; see also 107–8).

It has been striking for me, as I study the history of Christian monasticism, to see a similar range of forms of socio-political engagement.
Some nuns speak out. Others offer care. Monks gather groups who model
alternative expressions of life together. Some take action. And still others
devote themselves to prayer. Monasticism(s) both old and new bless the
world in many ways, one of which is to offer targeted influence in govern-
ment/statecraft. We will be hearing their stories in the chapters ahead.

3. SOCIO-POLITICAL ENGAGEMENT LEADS TO CHANGE WITHOUT AND WITHIN

Another Assisi story. Cheri and I had the opportunity while we were there
to receive ashes on Ash Wednesday directly over St. Francis's grave (the
lowest story of the basilica was being restored so we could not receive
them in front of the grave—we were in the next floor up, right above the
grave). As the priest was putting ashes on my head I heard a voice inside
me saying, "Evan, I want you to fast from oppression." I had been pondering things spiritual and socio-political during this trip—how can you
teach a weeklong workshop on Francis in Assisi and *not* think of these
matters?—but I was a bit confused. Fasting from oppression? Over time
it became clearer that God was inviting me to avoid the products, the
producers, and the principles that contribute to harming others. That was
a decade ago. Of course, it is impossible to address every single product,
producer, and principle. We would be more than overwhelmed. Yet we
can open our eyes, listen to God and the gospel and make a few responsible decisions. Since that moment in Assisi I have found myself changing
banks, eating different foods, using an open source operating system on

my computer, and learning to wait before I speak. The last one is the hardest. I have a need to be right and to lead decision-making processes, even if others are left out a little. Hmmm. Isn't this a use of privilege and power that in other settings has prevented people from being empowered? Come on, Evan, isn't this the heart of oppression itself? Lord have mercy! If I want oppression to end it must end within me.

Thomas Merton knew this. On November 2, 1962 he wrote in his journal a quote from Vinaba Bhave, "It is impossible to get rid of violence when one is oneself full of violence. On the contrary, one only adds to the number of the violent."[23] Merton interpreted the complacency of the church in the midst of nuclear sword-rattling to be a sign of the collapse of Christian faith. The move toward peace is not simply a matter of treaties, but moreso a matter of the transformation of our hearts. He writes in one of his Cold War Letters,

> My Mass on February 1, the Feast of St. Ignatius Martyr of Antioch, will be for all of the strikers everywhere in the world and for all who yearn for a true peace, all who are willing to shoulder the great burden of patiently working, praying and sacrificing themselves for peace. . . . Really we have to pray for a total and profound change in the mentality of the whole world. What we have known in the past as Christian penance is not a deep enough concept if it does not comprehend the special problems and dangers of the present age. Hairshirts will not do the trick, . . . But vastly more important is the complete change of heart and the totally new outlook on the world of man. . . . The great problem is this inner change, and we must not be so obsessed with details of policy that we block the deeper development in other people and in ourselves.[24]

This is "fasting from oppression." This is the realization and monastic repentance that the Sin without is also the sin within. It is the kind of revival we need today.

23. Merton, *Turning Toward the World*, 262.
24. Merton, *Cold War Letters*, 59.

Monastic Practice: Political Self-Examination Part Two—Sympathetic Identification

We are now ready for the second step of political self-examination, once again seeing the "wide" through exploring the "deep." In Part One we were just trying to get a sense *that* it is there, *that* we dwell in a world of politics that affects much of our lives whether we are actively involved or not. In this second part our aim is to go one step deeper, to get a felt sense of identification with some of the forces, the structures, and the institutions within which we are embedded.

"In the year that king Uzziah died," Isaiah writes (notice the political reference here?), "I saw the Lord sitting on a throne, high and lofty;" (Isa 6:1—again, notice that reference to the *throne*?). Isaiah is overwhelmed with the experience and he cries out, "Woe is me! I am lost, for I am a man of unclean lips, and I live among a people of unclean lips; yet my eyes have seen the King, the Lord of hosts!" (6:5) To me it is striking that in this extreme, almost intolerable, circumstance Isaiah spontaneously responds out of identification with his people. He is conscious not only of his own "uncleanness" but also that he shares this uncleanness with "a people." How do we become that conscious, how do we feel that solidarity with the life (created goodness, uncleanness, potential for restoration), even with the *political* life, of those who surround us?

Whereas in Part One we ranged far and wide in our reflections, perceiving how political realities were present somewhere in nearly every aspect of our early morning routine, in Part Two we will turn our focus on one or two aspects of that routine. So, after praying your prayer of openness, take a moment to select one element of your day (as an individual or as a community). You could think about a single possession you use (your automobile, for example), or a single activity (your employment), or perhaps even a relationship (your neighbor). When you have selected that element spend some time just "being with" it. What does this element look like? What sounds are associated with it? Any smells? How do you feel when you imagine this element of your day?

Now, begin to reflect on the created goodness of this element. How does this automobile, this job, this relationship, function naturally to advance something good? You may want to ask why you are connected with this element. Are there other "goods" connected with this element? Perhaps you are thinking of your breakfast itself and you think of the nutrition, or the taste, or perhaps that you know the people who harvested the syrup from their maple grove. Give yourself space to appreciate that which deserves to be appreciated in this element. Sometimes this can be difficult, but give it your best shot. And if you look carefully, I bet you can perceive

how politics—agent-directed ordering—is present in some of this goodness. I just now looked out my window and saw a herd of nineteen deer
munching a short distance from our house. Nice! But I also know that lots
of regulations influence the presence of those deer near my home. What
are the processes and powers that influence the ordering of the elements
in your own life?

Having examined the goodness of your political life, it is now time
to become aware of the dark side of things. As you think about those
influences that shape your life, those powers that have sway over what
you eat, how your neighbors are housed, how you spend your time, do
you notice your connection with "a people of unclean lips"? In what ways
is your life—*this* element—caught in a web of worldly, fleshly, or devilish
entanglements? Who or what suffers to create the life you live?[25] Again,
give this reflection some time. Can you observe the various strands of this
web within the context of this very element you are pondering? How does
this web feel to you?

Finally, turn your self-examination to the hope of redemption. Jesus Christ came to bring new life, and the Holy Spirit was sent to make
restoration real in our lives as communities and as individuals. So, what
could that look like in the midst of *this* element? What if Jesus were in the
automobile industry? What would be different about your vehicle? What
does God think about the herd of deer outside my window? Where is the
Spirit present among my neighbors? Get particular. Think of *this* aspect
of your employment. What could new life look like? Would you have any
part in this? What is this experience like?

Can you see that you are perceiving the depths and nuances of
socio-political engagement? As you develop an increasing sympathetic
identification with your "people" your political intuition will grow stronger.
We are a political people, and when we dwell sincerely and prayerfully
within this wide reality, we begin to grow deep roots that can support a
flourishing tree of socio-political engagement.

25. For an interesting exploration of this aspect of your life, try http://slaveryfoot-
print.org/.

THREE

We Speak

WE HAVE LEARNED THAT being "political" is only natural. God made us that way. We are also beginning to learn that there are many ways of engaging in socio-political matters—ways to enter the river, the fountain flowing deep and wide, ways to become a part of the solution. One of those ways is to speak. We do this all the time: After we learn of some news, we say to a friend, "Did you hear?" and then we begin to speak our mind. But sometimes we speak our mind not just to our friends, but to a wider audience, and we do so with the intention to influence matters through our speech.

TWO STORIES

This is the path Isaiah was invited to take. When we left Isaiah in the previous chapter—the day King Uzziah died—he was awestruck before God, keenly aware not only of his own personal uncleanness, but also of his solidarity with an unclean people. Then, after one of the seraphim touches Isaiah's mouth with a coal and declares that his "guilt has departed," Isaiah hears the voice of the Lord: "Whom shall I send, and who will go for us?" (Isa 6:8). Isaiah receives this invitation, saying "Here am I; send me!" And then the Lord tells Isaiah where his acceptance will lead him: "Go and say to this people," the Lord says. Isaiah's unclean lips, purified by the coal, will be the means by which God touches the uncleanness of Isaiah's people. The remainder of the chapter (Isa 6:9–13) describes the difficult message Isaiah is to deliver and the long, unfruitful journey Isaiah's life will take. Such is the prophetic vocation.

But this is a book about *monasticism* and socio-political engagement; so was Isaiah a monk? Well, that is actually a more interesting question than you might think. In the books of Samuel and Kings we learn about "schools" of the prophets.[1] These schools provided some kind of training and support for those who served as prophets to Yahweh's people, prophets who acted as advisors to (or critics of) the kings. Amos, a contemporary of Isaiah, mentions that he is not a "son of a prophet" (Amos 7:14), evidence that prophetic schools may have been in existence during Isaiah's time. Isaiah also mentions entrusting manuscripts to his "disciples" (Isa 8:16), so it may be that Isaiah, after receiving his calling, joined or formed a "school" of prophets.[2] But were these schools *monastic* in any way that we would recognize? We know that these schools formed their members in the ministry of speaking God's word to others, that their formation involved both theology and spiritual experience, and that the schools seemed to be organized into local cohorts. Other similar groupings of devout followers of God, like the Nazarites and the Rechabites, shared not only common tasks, but also common forms of life: for example, things they would avoid. While it might be a stretch to describe the prophets of the Old Testament as monks, I think we can at least acknowledge that some of the elements of monasticism listed in our first chapter (alternative culture, shared practices, spiritual experience, common focus) were present in these early prophetic communities and may have been part of Isaiah's context. The point is to recognize devout followers of God whose shared life forms an environment within which socio-political speech is nurtured.

Perhaps the environment at El Salvador's Universidad Centroamericana (UCA) in the 1980s was similar.[3] Indeed, it might be appropriate to call UCA at that time a "school of the prophets." It was founded in 1965 by the Society of Jesus (the Jesuits), a religious order founded in the sixteenth century by Ignatius of Loyola and dedicated to the progress of

---

1. The Hebrew is "sons" but the term is also translated "company" or "band." On the schools of the prophets see, for example, Schmitt, "Prophecy," 483, and Freeman, *New Manners and Customs*, regarding 2 Kings 2:3.

2. See, for example, Barton, *Isaiah 1–39*, 23.

3. I am drawing here from Lee, "Ignacio Ellacuría"; Ellacuría, *Essays*; O'Sullivan, "Open Eyes"; Sobrino et al., *Companions of Jesus*; and Whitfield, *Paying the Price*. Thanks to Michael O'Sullivan, SJ, for inspiration and guidance.

souls and the propagation of the faith. After the Second Vatican Council (1962–65), many religious orders—and particularly the Jesuits under the leadership of Pedro Arrupe—explicitly identified justice as one of their central values. This emphasis on the value of justice would require the leadership of UCA to rethink the mission of the university.

Then came El Salvador's long civil war, in which the poorest suffered the most. In 1980, a few months into the war, Oscar Romero, archbishop of San Salvador and outspoken advocate for the poor, was gunned down while celebrating mass. In response to the situation, Ignacio Ellacuría, the UCA's rector (North Americans would call him the "president"), articulated a clear vision for the university: As an institution of higher learning committed to truth and knowledge, it must dedicate itself to the acquisition and dissemination of truth in the midst of injustice. In a presentation to the University of Santa Clara in California in 1982, he declared,

> We as an intellectual community must analyze causes; use imagination and creativity together to discover remedies; communicate to our constituencies a consciousness that inspires the freedom of self-determination; educate professionals with a conscience, who will be the immediate instruments of such a transformation; and continually hone an educational institution that is academically excellent and ethically oriented.[4]

Having discerned this direction, the Jesuits were determined that UCA would become a center of research and communication concerning El Salvador's political and social crises. They established the Human Rights Institute to document abuses and the University Institute of Public Opinion to study social problems and potential solutions. Ellacuría himself developed the Forum on National Reality, which sought to bring together leaders of opposing parties in an effort to foster negotiated peace. Unfortunately, not all the political players respected the university's efforts—and some in fact deemed the Jesuits a threat. On November 16, 1989, a group of men dressed in military uniforms brutally murdered Ellacuría, five other Jesuit priests, a cook, and the cook's teenage daughter. As with Isaiah and many of those who speak, the message of God delivered by a consecrated people of God is not always well received.

4. Ellacuría, "Task of a Christian University," in Sobrino et al., *Companions of Jesus*, 149.

Like Isaiah and Ellacuría, those who sense a call to go deep are sometimes also called to go wide, to speak to broader socio-political concerns. We speak from where we are, whether Jesuit college professors, shepherds (Amos), or semi-solitary monks (such as Peter Damian in the eleventh century). Shenoute of Atripe, abbot of the White Monastery in Egypt (348–466), used his influence to advance the cause of justice. Historian David Brakke writes, "The biblical prophets provided Shenoute's voice with its agenda: exposure of hypocritical and concealed sin among the allegedly holy people of God, denunciation of worship of other gods by either the people of God or the surrounding 'Gentiles,' advocacy for the poor and oppressed, and criticism of the rich and powerful."[5] It was not only powerful men who did so: seemingly powerless women associated with religious orders (such as Catherine of Siena) also followed the call to speak God's voice to the highest levels of authority.[6]

What is the ministry of monastic socio-political engagement through speech? It is the act of seeking, as part of a group of devout followers of Christ (or as a consecrated individual), to influence the ordering of the common life and the world through communication. The image of the prophets surely stands strong when we think of the ministry of socio-political communication.[7] But socio-political communication invites more than the prophetic. Asking permission to establish a farmers market in the middle of an urban area where fresh produce is not easily available is just as much political speech as a rally chant is. For this reason, it is not enough to identify a *what* to speak about and then devise some clever *how* to speak about it. Christian socio-political communication is not simply a matter of topics and tactics. My aim in this chapter is to cover the what, who, why, when, and how, each in turn.

THE WHAT

Two "what" questions must be addressed as we explore socio-political speech: First, what are we doing when we speak? And second, what should we be speaking about? After I address the first question, I will introduce a central monastic practice (socio-political discernment) and then treat the second question.

5. Brakke, *Demons and the Making*, 103.
6. See Villegas, "Catherine of Siena's spirituality."
7. See, for example, Wallis, *God's Politics*, 32; Yoder, *Christian Witness*, 15.

The Act of Speaking

What are we doing when we are speaking? More specifically, what are we doing when we engage in socio-political communication in this information age? And even more specifically, what are we doing in this information age when we are speaking for socio-political purposes?[8] Communication at its most basic is the process of a *sender* sharing some element of meaning or experience to a *receiver*. Even at this most basic level, communication is complicated by the sender's choice of words, the receiver's cultural heritage, and much more. Senders can be not only individuals but groups, as when you receive that notice of a change in "company policy." When a sender speaks to a wide range of receivers, we call it "mass communication."

Speech in our current information age has its own unique qualities. For example, we do not "turn on" the internet the way we used to turn on the radio. We *live* in the internet. Our calendar, phone (text, social media), maps, music, news, devotional apps, and much more are all now continuously "on" and fully integrated. We are constantly surrounded (bombarded?) by both mass communication and what sociologist Manuel Castells calls mass self-communication: where individuals "speak" to an indefinite and potentially viral audience.[9] The public spaces where ideas are voiced and debated today are not just physical but also digital. Furthermore, as the advertising industry (including political advertising) is well aware, electronic communication has proven to be an effective means of shaping public mind and behavior. Consequently, control over the content, dissemination, and style of communication—each of which can require significant expense—is an important component of socio-political influence.

---

8. For my summary of philosophical discussions of communicative meaning see "What Does You (Language) Mean?," chapter 10 of Howard, *Love Wisdom*, available at https://spiritualityshoppe.org/chapter-10-what-does-you-language-mean/. I have also treated the communicative nature of corporate experience in Howard, *Brazos Introduction*, 95–100. My understanding is influenced by the thought of Charles S. Peirce (see Peirce, *Peirce on Signs*). Oliver O'Donovan's notions of "mediation" exaltation, and a vocation to engagement, in O'Donovan, *Desire of the Nations* speak to the character of socio-political communication generally. With regard to socio-political communication in an information age see especially Castells, *Communication Power*.

9. See Castells, *Communication Power*.

Socio-political speech comes in many flavors. Yes, there are the loud chants at the rallies and marches, but these represent only a small portion of socio-political speech. We also make presentations at legal hearings. We meet one on one with politicians to lobby for a cause. We offer lectures or workshops at colleges and community events. We navigate the bureaucratic details of making changes in the way things are done. Socio-political speech is often (though not always) mass communication, aimed at many hearers. Furthermore, whereas communication in general expresses a wide range of intent, socio-political speech usually aims to influence. Thus socio-political speech often communicates a message sent by a group (or an individual sharing a group concern) with the intent of influencing a segment of society. And in an information age, all of these involve both face-to-face and digital means of communication.

Power today is about more than military coercion or controlling the means of production. It is also about controlling communication. Political rallies and terrorist attacks are not performed for the sake of local influence; they are staged for their media value *and with the aim of disseminating a message widely*. Consequently, the media (social and traditional) has become a chief battleground (perhaps *the* chief battleground) for both the public mind and political power. Public and private powers make carefully considered use of media for the sake of political influence: keeping select issues in the public mind, targeting populations with carefully chosen stories, framing information within particular perspectives (spin), and so on. Political forces invest heavily to ensure that you hear what they want you to hear. Yet at the same time, digital technologies of mass self-communication create the potential for new forms of populist communication. As we have recently seen in the United States, one viral video can make quite a stir. And in the midst of this battleground, we are experiencing decreased trust in the media and in media politics—even as we spend more time immersed in this environment.

So what does it mean to "speak" into the socio-political world as a community of faith? When we speak, whether regarding particular practices, sustained policies, political parties, or a fundamental choice of governmental framework (as was the case in El Salvador in the 1980s), we are making choices to speak a message of influence in the midst of an information age.[10] We choose what to speak about: whether a hot topic or a neglected concern. We choose the medium of communication

10. For an outline of these four levels of engagement see Antoncich, "Discernment of Political Options."

(street-corner signs, livestreamed rallies, phone canvassing, YouTube videos, books, and articles), and in doing so we often choose our potential audience. We choose the tone and perspective of our speech. And we choose the life from out of which we generate our speech: speech that, as we shall see (in an age of decreased trust in words), carries more power than we might imagine.[11] What we *cannot* choose regarding our socio-political speech are the results. Ultimately, our socio-political speech— like Isaiah's, Jesus's, Ellacuría's—is a matter not of effectiveness, but of faithfulness.

This means that our act of speaking is not a minor matter, which brings us to the monastic practice of socio-political discernment, a practice that not only shapes the remainder of this chapter, but also—as we make decisions to care, to model, to act, and to pray—informs the rest of this book.

A Monastic Practice: Discerning Socio-Political Engagement

Discernment is a central theme in monastic literature. Desert elders discerned whether their choice of ascetical practice was oriented toward God or driven by spiritual pride. Medieval women mystics discerned whether their visions were from God or from other sources. Christians exploring vocation discerned whether they were called to a religious life.

Discernment is also a common interest for believers outside monastic life. Some of us live under harsh circumstances and are pressed into what I call a discernment of survival.[12] Others among us have joined a community and discern our life through serving and belonging. Still others discern using formalized interior reflection, which has been common among those joining monastic communities. Individuals discern a path of life; congregations discern whether to select this or that staff member; leaders evaluate whether a religious trend is genuine revival; intentional communities discern the elements of their common covenant. And more.[13]

11. John Howard Yoder, for example, speaks of our care for widows and orphans as a "reminder to those in power" (Yoder, *Christian Witness*, 41), and of the life of the church as a "pulpit and a paradigm" for others (Yoder, *For the Nations*, 37–50).

12. See for example, Reyes, *Nobody Cries*.

13. For a summary treatment of Christian discernment see Malatesta, ed., *Discernment of Spirits*. I have explored discernment generally and with regard to spiritual direction and revival in Howard, *Affirming*. I have elsewhere treated discernment in the context of personal and communal guidance (Howard, *Brazos*

More recently, the theme of discernment has been explored with direct reference to socio-political engagement: How do we prayerfully decide what postures or actions to take with regard to our socio-political life?[14]

By way of a brief guide, here are a few valuable elements from the monastic perspective for discerning communities or individuals to consider—and remember, every one of these five elements is bathed in prayer or is best viewed as an act of prayer:

- We prayerfully observe.

Remember your practice of political self-examination in the previous chapter? Return to that awareness of your surroundings—not merely sights and sounds, but also systems and structures. What feelings accompany your socio-political awareness? Are there a few situations that carry significance for you? Identify one in particular, and observe yourself in this situation. What brought you to this situation? What virtues might you bring into this situation? What vices or problems may get in the way of clarity?

We also observe our contexts. One helpful exercise as we begin a matter of socio-political discernment is what I call a "context autobiography" in the light of a situation. Recall your own personal or community story of race, class, gender, or other categories. How might your own experience shape how you perceive or feel about the situation at hand? Pay attention to the structures connected to this situation. Are there laws, controlling networks, economic forces, or social powers involved? In what ways might you sympathetically identify with "a people of unclean lips," as Isaiah was asked to do? Can you perceive the political good in this situation as well as the dark side—and the hope for redemption? What do you notice as you observe self, context, and structure? If a problem or a good idea comes to mind, see if you can articulate it in the form of a prayer: "God, we would appreciate your guidance with regard to *this.*"

Introduction, 371–401); formation to discernment and discerning formation (Howard, *Guide,* 211–228); and pastoral vocation (Howard, "Beneath the Plan"). Here my aim is to introduce the discernment of socio-political engagement.

14. The exploration of socio-political discernment has been a cumulative project with a number of important contributions. See, for example, Henriot, "Public Dimension"; Clarke, "Public Policy"; Holland and Henriot, *Social Analysis*; Shea, "Spiritual Direction"; McClain, "Spiritual Discernment"; and Cleary, "Societal Context." Elizabeth Liebert summarized the basic structure in "Linking Faith and Justice" and developed the practice further in a course on "Integrating Spirituality and Social Structures: Social Discernment" taught at San Francisco Theological Seminary. The fruit of her work is now published in Liebert, *Soul of Discernment,* and my own approach owes much to hers.

(As always, try to be as clear as possible: for example, "God, we would like to know if it is wise for us to speak out in our city at this time about housing for those who have none.")

- We also gather.

We gather the community, especially if a community is discerning as a body. But even a discerning individual is embedded within groups who can notice God in our socio-political situations. I like to think of the discerning process as cycles of listen-pray-gather. We gather information and then listen. We gather to pray and then separate to gather our individual expectations. And so on.

It is good to listen to those who might be affected by our discernment, especially if some are suffering in connection to the situation.[15] Invite and welcome any who are usually left out of decision making. Who attends—and who is not present at—the gathering process is important.

We also gather information as we discern our engagement. This requires a bit of homework. To get the best, most holistic understanding of things, check the details from all sides. Who has influence over this situation and how did they gain it? If there is a money trail, where does it lead? What are the various factors or conditions that make this situation what it is today? Explore some alternatives. Be creative in your search, and don't settle for stock answers. Gather fresh input and new approaches. Can you brainstorm a few brilliant possibilities for or resolutions to the situation?

As you go, don't forget to gather your feelings and expectations. Our political energies can be extinguished if we expect our political speech to reach this many people or this particular group and it doesn't happen. Furthermore, as we gather our spiritual noticings, we may discover "fingerprints of God," some small thing amid the larger thing God is doing all around us, even a clue pointing to the next steps.[16] Perhaps, after a season of prayerfully gathering people, information, expectations, and spiritual noticings—and with a clearer sense of what a discernment process best suited to this situation might look like—we find ourselves revising our initial questions.

- We evaluate.

As the discernment process develops, we find ourselves "weighing" the options (notice this theme in 1 Corinthians 14:29). A simple logistical factor may make one option unreasonable. Other times, that very logistical

---

15. See Bretherton, *Christ and the Common Life*, 445–47, 453.

16. My thanks to Kent Smith's Nurturing Communities Network Zoom Gathering in April of 2020 for this comment.

factor is a divine challenge to be overcome. We must evaluate both head and heart. As best we can, we try to achieve indifference or impartiality regarding the options. This does not mean that we lay aside our socio-political viewpoints or strategic preferences. That would be impossible! Rather, we come to the point that we can trust God in any case. Usually, as we gather and evaluate, we face a variety of different impressions or signs: particular Scripture passages that seem to stand out, the trajectory of the story pointing in a direction, experiences that "say something" to us, a certain fit of different tension points, advice that people of wisdom have provided, and so on.

- Ultimately, we decide.

After we observe, gather, and evaluate, we conclude that a certain path is the fitting response to a socio-political situation. It may be that we are blasted and the conclusion is obvious: The Holy Spirit falls on us and we know that we know that we must speak (or not). Other times, we are led, step by step, through recognizing signs of God's presence in our politics. There are also times where we wait for God, yet the group never reaches a consensus. But for one reason or another (deadlines, urgencies), we must choose, and so we trust that God loves us and we just make our best choice. We are entrusted with this responsibility. We do not need certainty. We do not need that ethereal peace. We do not need circumstances to line up perfectly. Our confidence is not in the precision of our procedure, but in the grace of God who loves us in the midst of our ordinary sincerity. We realize that our well-discerned socio-political decisions may not be successful. (Don't forget the prophets.) But they might be, so we hope, and that is a good thing.

- And then we act.

If this is a group discernment, we communicate the decision appropriately among the community and plan for careful implementation—which shouldn't be overlooked. Good discernments can fall apart at the implementation stage. You need to include the right people at the right time.

I also think an important part of discerning action is play. With a creative and joyful spirit, trusting in God, try something. Then review, revise, rebuild, and repeat. When we address systems and structures, they will respond, and we need to listen and pray so to gauge our actions by their ongoing response. We engage in this same process when we play, and I think it is a valuable part of socio-political engagement and ongoing discernment. Our situations are fluid, and we need to be playful as we adapt to them.

The monastic practice of discernment can be readily applied to matters of socio-political engagement. Socio-political discernment is a prayerful process of observing, gathering, evaluating, deciding, and acting—creatively, joyfully, playfully. The process is not always as neat and clean as I have outlined, either for individuals or for communities, but we do our best and God is faithful. You will see how this works as I highlight elements of this practice in the pages ahead.

Our decision to speak is not a minor matter. What we are doing in socio-political speech is choosing to create and express some content in the midst of an ongoing dialogue using a particular media of communication with the intent to influence our common life. For this reason, the monastic practice of socio-political discernment can be of great value.

The Content of Speech

Having decided to speak, we now choose to express *some content*. But what content, and why? What should we be speaking about? Perhaps a situation comes to mind. Your city is instituting a so-called camping ban on public property, for instance, effectively making it illegal for those people who struggle without homes to cover themselves at night. But the "homeless problem" is complicated. Should you speak? Or say a friend has invited you to a demonstration at a clinic that performs abortions. You agree with her that abortions are generally wrong. But if you go to the demonstration, other friends might label you as a fundamentalist. Should you speak?

Part of our deliberation is a matter of when or why—since it is impossible to speak about all important matters at the same time—but here I want to step back and look at a previous question: Of all the socio-political matters we could speak about, which ones should we, as Christians, speak about?

On occasion we are called to speak *out* about what matters to God. When I was an undergraduate student (back in the mid-1970s), I went through what I call my socio-political conversion. The Christianity I had known in high school was all about evangelism and anticipating the rapture. Now some of my college friends were talking about racial justice, the Vietnam War, feminism, and world hunger. In order to make some sense of things, I picked up my Bible and my *Strong's Concordance* and looked up every passage that mentioned the poor, justice, oppression, and so on—nine hundred verses, literally. My question was this: When it comes to how we order our common life, what kinds of things should I consider important? What issues or matters does *God* consider important?

This Bible study took me about two years, and when I was done I was a convert: not really a convert *from* anything, but definitely a convert *to* something. I did not know what political party to support, but more importantly, I knew the heart of God. I have frequently returned to my notes from that Bible study, most recently for a class I taught in 2020 on the Bible and politics. My interest all along has been to explore, and then to share, what matters to God—the very things we should be caring (and speaking) about. I've tried to pay special attention to the concerns that are central to the Bible's big story or theological core, the topics that are often repeated, or the themes mentioned when the passages condemn or praise people. In the end I summarized God's heart with regard to socio-political concerns with six values, what I call "God's political platform." My summary of these values here is woefully brief, but we shall return to them here and there throughout the rest of the book because I believe these are the socio-political matters that matter most to God and therefore should be *what* we speak about.

1. *Stewardship or care for creation, not wastefulness.*[17] This value is a little different from others. The issue is not frequently repeated in Scripture; leaders are seldom praised for their stewardship of creation or condemned for their failure to care for it. Yet creation care is absolutely core to the Bible. As I discussed in chapter 2, human beings are made to share in the ordering of creation: animals, children, our own bodies, and more. The opening passage of the Hebrew Bible (Gen 1–2) proclaims that humans are placed on the earth to care for it, and other passages systematically confirm this vocation (Gen 9; Ps 8; Rev 22:5). The Christian doctrine of the resurrection—perhaps the central doctrine of the Christian faith—demands we recognize the value of creation. For these reasons, I have included it here as one of the socio-political values central to God's heart.

---

17. For a biblical treatment see for example, Moo and Moo, *Creation Care*. Wirzba, *From Nature to Creation*, treats this subject from a more philosophical angle.

2. *Human dignity and freedom, not debasement.*[18] Humans are created in the image and likeness of God (Gen 1:26). As partners with God
in creation care, we exercise a kind of freedom not shared by other creatures (expressed even in God's choice to have Adam name the animals in
Gen 2). While the Bible does not frequently press for human freedoms
when speaking of political matters—indeed, I find that Scripture often
mentions limiting of individual freedoms in the context of the common
good—they are assumed when Scripture condemns repression and theft
or honors creativity, labor, and development. Discerning the proper balance of respect for human dignity and honoring the other concerns in
this list is one of the deepest challenges of Christian political life.[19]

3. *Righteousness, not corruption.*[20] Right-relatedness is the divine
standard for human conduct. The theme of righteousness is both central
and pervasive in Scripture (Gen 18:19; Matt 5:20; Rom 8:4), and it is used
with reference to socio-political situations (for example, 2 Chr 9:8; Ps
72:2; Isa 11:4). A rightly related society is shaped by the moral upright-
ness of society's members. The corruption of kings or the negligence of
the populace often contributes to the collapse of well-ordered life. For
Christians, the framework of righteousness is transformed as people facilitate the order of right-relatedness in their own life and in the world
less through the means of legal observances and more through freely following Jesus, enlivened and empowered by the Holy Spirit.

4. *Justice, not mistreatment.*[21] Like the theme of righteousness
(and often paired with it), the call for justice is everywhere present in
the Bible—prominent in core passages, important in both Testaments,
and frequently used with reference to socio-political matters (see Deut
10:17–19, 16:18–20; Amos 4:10–15; Luke 3:10–14; Matt 23:23; Jas 5:1–5).
Righteousness tends to speak to our character; *justice*, to our structures.
Leaders and nations are frequently condemned for their lack of fair treatment. When there were complaints in the early years of the Christian

18. For a communitarian view of humanity in the divine image see Grenz, *Social
God and the Relational Self.*

19. Catholic social teaching has honorably wrestled with this tension. For a
summary of Catholic social teaching, see, for example, Martin, *Healing and Creativity,*
1–38; Bretherton, *Christ and the Common Life,* 160–76.

20. See for example, Kelly, "Righteousness"; Evans, "Social Justice or Personal
Righteousness?"

21. See for example, Westfall and Dyer, eds., *Bible and Social Justice*; Gaudet,
Christian Utopia; Thurman, *Jesus and the Disinherited.*

church regarding mistreatment of Greek believers, the apostles delegated responsibility for addressing the problem to a committee—of Greeks. The fair ordering of society matters much to God.

5. *Compassion, not hard-heartedness.*[22] Regarding socio-political concerns, the heart of God goes beyond the bounds of fairness to actively express compassion for those with the least power or resources. Indeed, for God, justice *requires* compassion. The Bible repeatedly teaches that the poor, the widow, the alien (or immigrant), the orphan, and the needy are objects of God's special care and those for whom God's followers are to demonstrate a similar care. Again and again God encourages followers to build compassion for the powerless into their structures and institutions as well as to express a generosity that transcends legislative structure (Lev 19:9; Deut 27:19; Isa 1:17; 2 Cor 8:1–9:15). This concern is at the heart of true religion (Isa 58:6–9; Jer 22:15–16; Matt 25:31–46; Jas 1:27).

6. *Purity and holiness, not worldly conformity.*[23] In both Testaments, and in the midst of a variety of political contexts, God repeatedly express-es a desire that followers of the Lord would live as an alternative culture, distinct in worship and holy in life. While stewardship, righteousness, dignity, justice, and compassion summarize the values according to which humans *as humans* (whether self-identified as believers or not) are called to order their common life and world, God also calls a nation, a church, and some individuals within these groups to live a life set apart (for example, Lev 11:44; Rom 6:19–23; Eph 1:4; Heb 12:14–17).

Our response to the call of holiness has socio-political implications. When God's people value stewardship, righteousness, justice, and com-passion, we are joined to fellow humans in the cause of ordering a com-mon life. The value of holiness, however—and particularly the radical cruciform holiness advocated by Jesus and lived by monasticisms old and new—sets the people of God in tension with the world. In this sense, the politics of Jesus will never be understood by the world, and the standards of Christians can never be expected of the world. (Think, for example, of how Jesus invites some of his listeners to reimagine money, marriage,

---

22. See for example, Anderson, *Charity*; Hiers, *Justice and Compassion.*

23. See for example, Dieter et al., *Five Views*; Ryle, *Holiness*. I am uncomfortable with the individualist treatment of holiness in much literature on the topic and would recommend the development of a theology of holiness that emerges from a dialogue with the doctrines of salvation, church, s/Spirit, and eschatology. For these themes see Kärkkäinen, *Spirit and Salvation,* and Kärkkäinen, *Hope and Community.*

or power.) I will talk more about this in chapter 5, when we talk about modeling a good society.

Furthermore, for Christians, the means of embodying holiness are, as I mentioned with regard to righteousness, transformed. God encourages the nation of Israel to compel worship of YHWH through legal sanctions in order to secure his people's distinct religious identity, tempted as they were by surrounding nations. In the New Testament, however, we see God establishing the religious identity of God's people through the sending of the Spirit of Christ (John 4:24). Similarly, whereas God secured the national identity of Israel by imposing racial segregation and outlawing intermarriage, God works in the Christian era through the Holy Spirit to empower the church to become a model of racial integration, reconciling Jew and Gentile as one (Gal 3:28). As we shall see, the call of the church to be both in the world and not of the world complicates our socio-political engagement.

Care for the earth. Human dignity. Right-relatedness. Justice and fair treatment. Compassion for those without power or resources. And among God's people, holiness—an alternative life. When it comes to ordering our common life and world, these are the matters that matter most to God. These are the things that we should speak out about.

And yet, you might ask, stewardship, compassion, and such all sound like nice *values*, but what do they have to do with our socio-political *engagement*? What do these values have to do with the political speech of parties, policies, and platforms? Good question. Here is my answer.

First, we must remember what values do not do. Values do not determine policy. I believe that, in general, the Christian Scriptures outline key elements of a political philosophy, but they do not specify the particulars of political science. That is the hard work of each generation of Christians in dialogue with their cultures and settings. Values guide, but they do not prescribe. For example, I think God desires that we have compassion for children (including unborn children)[24] and people suffering in chronic poverty. Yet my commitment to compassion does not settle the question

24. While the Bible affirms the value of life and in a few places indicates God's care for unborn life (yet what do we make of Numbers 5:11-28?), the fact is though some of the nations surrounding Israel instituted laws prohibiting abortion (see for example, Pritchard, ed., *Ancient Near Eastern Texts*, 185), the Bible does not mention the issue specifically.

of whether life begins at conception or implantation, whether physi-
cians who perform abortions should face legal consequences, or whether
welfare (or workfare) is the most helpful means of addressing chronic
poverty. Christian inspiration does not assure effective legislation.

Yet, though Christian socio-political values do not resolve all our
policy questions, holding these values does influence our socio-political
engagement—and specifically our speech—in various ways. Embracing
values places certain issues in our awareness or "on our screen." Had I not
been exposed to God's heart of compassion and justice for socio-political
issues through my Bible study in college, I don't think I would have even
noticed issues like fair trade and responsible production for a long time.
And when an issue that we are slightly aware of buries itself a little deeper,
we begin to experience a reordering of our loves.[25] Values inspire our
choice of speech, as when my value for the care of creation leads me to
encourage a friend to recycle or when my value for human dignity gives
me the courage to inform a colleague how a specific comment might be
received by a person of color. Sometimes, our values inspire a fresh idea
that might in turn mandate a bit of political speech—speech that could
bear fruit. I know a congregation whose value for right relationship and
compassion encouraged its members to explore and then build a multi-
unit residential building to house both rich and poor, requiring a fair bit
of negotiating.

Most fundamentally for me, the discovery and adoption of biblical
socio-political values govern the configuration of concerns that I believe
ought to guide a community seeking to order itself in line with the heart
of God. These values provide criteria by which I assess the political speech
of others, and they channel my own political speech (and wider engagement). For example, however strategized in the particulars, my evaluation of a political party is guided by how central justice, compassion,
and stewardship are in the party's platform. Yes, I appreciate the value
of prayer in schools and the needs for national defense. Yet when I read
my Bible, I do not find these to be the central socio-political concerns of
God's heart. In this sense I am in agreement with Rev. Dr. William Barber
II, who often expresses concern over politicians and preachers who "say
so much about what God says so little—and so little about what God says

<hr>

25. On the reordering of our loves, see Augustine, *On Christian Teaching*, Book
One, XXVII–XXVIII, 20–22. My thanks again to Jared Boyd for reminding me of this
passage. For more on the ordering of our loves see Oliver O'Donovan, *Problem of
Self-Love*.

so much."²⁶ If I am going to cooperate with God in bringing order to my world (insofar as I have influence), I will choose to speak out about those matters that are dearest to the heart of God.

Christians are to speak out about those socio-political values that concern God the most. But even as we are representatives of Jesus Christ, we are also human beings and, depending on our context, members or citizens with a measure of influence in the socio-political communities within which we dwell: workplace, village, city, province, country. We share our communities' concerns: questions about public health, transition of elders, transportation routes, water distribution, intellectual property.

Consequently, we find ourselves both *speaking out* and *speaking with*. We participate in ordinary dialogue about the ordinary ordering of our life. This, too, is political speech, though of a different character. When we *speak with,* the content—the what—is whatever happens to be part of the current public conversation, whatever is of interest. And while there are times when, as Christians, we speak with the voice of a prophet, like Amos, there are also times when we speak with the voice of a wise administrator, like Daniel. (We shall come to the *when* of speaking soon.) One comment on this point: in unsettled times, like those we are living in today, the temperature of our talk depends on the volatility of the wider public discourse.²⁷

When is it best to speak *out,* and when is it best to speak *with*? In times that call for wise administration, our conversation with the public (of which we are a part) reflects a moral and prudential reasoning negotiated through relationship, insofar as our context enables us to navigate common values.²⁸ Of course, our wisdom is informed by faith, hopefully

26. See Barber, "Poor People's Campaign." In my reading, the Bible expresses mixed values regarding war, emphasizing trust in God over the development of standing armies of national defense.

27. I use the phrase *unsettled times* with reference to the work of Ann Swidler. See Swidler, "Culture in Action"; Swidler, *Talk of Love.*

28. For my thoughts on ethics in a pluralist environment more generally see "What is Right (Good, Happy)?," chapter 7 of Howard, *Love Wisdom,* available at https://spiritualityshoppe.org/chapter-7-what-is-right/. The question of a "common" or "neutral" place from which church and political systems can dialogue about ethics is a much-debated topic (see, for example, the concerns expressed in the works of John Howard Yoder and Stanley Hauerwas). For my part, I am less interested, when talking

increasingly so as we steep ourselves in the gospel. Yet the Bible does not necessarily supply ready and specific answers to questions of regulating online communication, genome research, or neighborhood security (though principles in Scripture will inform our reasoning). And more critical to the point, addressing an audience in our pluralistic culture requires references to others' frameworks of values—or a negotiated common ground. When we are speaking *with,* what do we speak about? We speak about whatever love for our neighbor invites of us.

We *speak out* about what concerns the heart of God. We *speak with* others about whatever issue our common ordering brings to the surface at any given point in time. But sometimes we just *speak truth.* We need to. Think of the University of Central America (also known as UCA El Salvador and Universidad Centroamericana). The faculty, administrators, and students alike spoke political truth—truth about people who suffered due to governmental practices. They documented human rights abuses. They invited diverse factions to the Seminar on National Reality not merely to develop solutions; rather, Ellacuría sensed that an understanding of the crisis itself demanded that people from diverse factions share viewpoints. All of this was a part of their commitment to "academic excellence," simply what an institution dedicated to the promotion of knowledge should do.

My younger daughter, Terese, spoke historical truth in public. It was the first time she was arrested. She locked arms in a demonstration against Denver's Columbus Day parade because she believed that the history we teach is skewed. Rather than teaching that Columbus *discovered* America, it would be better to say that Columbus—and the flood of European settlers who came after him—*conquered* America.[29] But her expression of historical truth had political implications. My brother-in-law, Alan, spoke scientific truth. He was a certified pulmonologist (a lung

---

about "speaking with," in the articulation of a "Christian" ethic (yet see chapter 5) and more interested in the place of Christian participation in the practice of "human ethics." With this in mind, I have written the current paragraph in dialogue with Williams, *Ethics and the Limits,* whom I take to be heading in a similar direction as I am with regard to the practice of "speaking *with.*"

29. On "conquering America" see for example, Tzvetan Todorov's classic *Conquest of America.* Does "colonizing" perhaps communicate something that neither "discovering" nor "conquest" communicates?

doctor) in Spokane, Washington, at the close of the twentieth century. As the regional lung specialist, he saw the odd cases, many from Libby, Montana. He ended up diagnosing and then documenting asbestosis, a poisoning of the lungs, among hundreds of Montanans for whom it was fatal. His job was to care for these patients. But his medical expertise had political implications, as it provided evidence that the asbestos company in Libby was aware of the harm being caused. Ultimately, Alan spent the latter part of his career as an expert witness in one lawsuit after another. He held his ground through the entire ordeal, just speaking truth again and again.[30]

Each generation struggles with truth—discovering it, articulating it, defending it—but the present moment seems especially fraught. Some joyfully abandon all hope of finding it and celebrate that society can finally admit that what we call "truth" is really an expression of a cultural perspective or a regime of power. Others busy themselves trying to fix the bugs in our approach to logic, empirical verification, intuition, or other ways of adjudicating truth. Still others wring their hands, grieving the loss of absolutes and bemoaning how our culture has decayed.

We overwhelm social media with hate speech and "fake news." We produce more legal paperwork than ever in order to document "truth." For many people this struggle with truth is neither a joy, nor a grief, but just a dilemma: a sense of not knowing who or how to trust, how to navigate one's way through the chaos of communication. On the one hand, we have a longing for—even a fundamental connection with—public "truth," and yet, on the other hand, we've become disillusioned about how to pursue that truth.

My own conviction is that this quandary stems in part from the proliferation of a fundamental misunderstanding of truth; it is a consequence of the faulty pursuits of the modern Enlightenment project. Truth is both more and less than we have been looking for.[31] As I have said to my philosophy students again and again, truth exists. Individual minds have a measure of truth, though small, fallible, and fallen. But intelligent

---

30. This story is told in Schneider and McCumber, *An Air That Kills.*

31. For my thoughts on truth and knowledge more generally see "What is (True) Knowledge," chapter 9 of *Love Wisdom* and available at https://spiritualityshoppe. org/chapter-9-what-is-true-knowledge/. In this particular section of this book I have also been in dialogue with Foucault, *Power/Knowledge*; Volf, *Exclusion and Embrace*, 233–74; and Williams, *Truth and Truthfulness*. I regret I was not able to work through Willard, *Disappearance of Moral Knowledge,* in preparation for this section.

and humble communities know even more. As we share our diverse perspectives within a shared community mind, so to speak—and especially as we refine our practice of sharing through mutual improvement of capacity and skill—truth is even more closely approximated. Only Infinite Mind—what I call "God"—holds all truth in certainty. Christians believe in a God who reveals truth: in nature and Scripture, in Son and Spirit. Yet we also believe that divine revelation is recognized within the community of the faithful. The principles of sincerity (truthfulness) and community (mutually reviewed evaluation) not only provide guidelines for the church, but also serve as perhaps our best access to truth as an intelligent, humble community of human beings. Consequently, at our best, we trust scientific knowledge that is based on repeated observation, over time, in multiple locations, employing a large sample size, and submitted to peer review. We consider historical speech more reliable when it examines a wide range of original sources and artifacts, incorporates often-ignored data from these sources, and consciously addresses interpretations from a number of viewpoints. We regard policy as worthy if it is based on documented evidence, addresses the relevant factors, and welcomes debate from all sides.

But does a culture of sincerity and community guarantee that our search will end in truth? No, not in the modern sense of certainty. And matters get even more complicated when we acknowledge that sometimes those who hold power are effective at hiding or manipulating truth.[32] Nevertheless, I think we can take a step toward truth—as a fallible humanity before Infinite Mind. The practices of sincerity, community, and open accountability serve as legitimate corrections to the errors we so often fall prey to. For example, where we might easily fall prey to ideology (mistaking our small truth for the Truth), we instead pursue wisdom and sincerely present our view as *our view*. Where we may be easily deceived by bias (mistaking spin for fact), we consciously listen to others and try to view things from a variety of viewpoints. Where we may be drawn aside by salience (interpreting a few well-publicized stories as normative descriptions), we evaluate stories by critically respected research. Thus, to both honor God and order our common life well, it behooves us to speak truth to the best of our abilities.

32. On propaganda see, e.g., Ellul, *Propaganda*; Castells, *Communication Power*, 165–89; Sassen, *Expulsions*. This is why movements that bring abuses of power to light—such as #BLM, #metoo, and #churchtoo—are important.

What do we speak about? In general, we *speak out* about God's concerns. We *speak with* about what is on the public agenda. We *speak truth* just to speak truth. We admit partiality and expect pushback. We welcome discussion, because we believe that ultimately truth is accessible even though our access to truth is partial. We strive for truth; we speak truth as best we can. We will touch more specifically on the what as we get to the why and the when.

THE WHO

As we move forward in our political discernments (remember your exercise on political discernment above?) we observe and we gather. When we observe and gather around the question of speaking we often find ourselves asking: Who is speaking here? There are a couple of ways of asking this question of who. We can ask about who we might become in order to be an embodied statement, a living and socio-politically engaging voice. I will touch on this a bit when I treat how we speak, but we will explore it further (albeit with a view more to the community than the individual) in chapter 5. Here I will consider who we actually *are* as ones who speak.

As I mentioned in our review of socio-political discernment, we bring our whole selves into our socio-political engagement. Our contexts and history, our personal strengths and weaknesses, the state of our relationship with God—all this and more accompany us as we speak. Sometimes we wish we could bring a different set of skills and traits into our speech, or we worry that because of our weaknesses we should not speak, but in the end it is a matter not of our qualifications but of our own faithfulness to the gospel and to our calling.

Thomas Merton was keenly aware of his own inadequacies even as he sought to speak about social issues:

> I suffer from my limitations, and I wish I were more of a professional, because an increased sophistication and a deeper experience of the problems and methods would help me serve the truth much better.[33]

---

33. Merton, *Cold War Letters*, 53.

> As a theologian I have always been a pure amateur and the professionals resent an amateur making so much noise.[34]

> I do indeed wish it were possible for the monks to come on a walk for peace from here to Washington.[35]

He even expresses doubts about his own writings: "The stuff I have written so far about peace does not have this tone [of infinite patience and understanding]."[36] Nevertheless, Merton knew that he had a voice and that he needed to use it for the cause of peace—in spite of his limitations as a scholar, an activist, and a person. "For my own part, I have one task left," he writes in his journal. "To pray, to meditate, to enter into truth, to sit before the abyss, to be educated in the word of Christ and thus to make my contribution to world peace."[37] And in a strongly worded 1961 letter, he says, "I just cannot in conscience, as a priest and a writer who has a hearing with a lot of people, devote myself exclusively to questions of devotion, the life of prayer, or monastic history, and act as if we were not in the middle of the most serious crisis in Christian history." Ten years after Merton's death, evangelist Billy Graham made a similar decision to speak out against nuclear proliferation in spite of his own sense of inadequacy to the topic. [38]

I think Merton and Graham voice our own hesitations here. They were aware of their limitations. Yet they were also aware of what they *could* do and of the need to speak. And that is the point for all of us: What can we, as small and imperfect communities, say that might have any effect? Actually, we all—both individually and as groups of believers—have real contributions to make in spite of our weaknesses. Remember Isaiah 6: "I am a man of unclean lips and I live among a people of unclean lips." For those of us who discern it, our place is to speak. The rest is up to God.

34. Merton, *Turning Toward the World*, 124.

35. Merton, *Cold War Letters*, 126.

36. Merton, *Cold War Letters*, 49.

37. Merton, *Turning Toward the World*, 166.

38. Merton, *Cold War Letters*, 36. For an interview with Billy Graham see *Sojourners*, "Change of Heart." See also O'Donovan, *Desire of the Nations*, 18.

THE WHY AND THE WHEN

Our struggles with adequacy and effect bring us to the question of why we speak. But since I see the when question as a helpful guide through the whys, I'll address both why and when together. In terms of our socio-political discernment framework, the stages of observing and gathering (looking wide) lead us to an awareness of action options, an initial sense of God's concerns, and a set of impressions regarding what we might have to bring to a situation by way of a response.

Note that I say action *options*. In your political self-examination and political discernment monastic practices, I had you focus attention on a particular situation, pretty much at random. Yet when we observe our contexts and concerns in real life, we encounter a number of potential areas for socio-political engagement; and part of our discernment has to do with which of these options we choose to address. The discerning stages of evaluation and decision, then, hone in on a particular option (the narrow what), they but also point us to the why and the when of our socio-political speech. This process involves deep reflection.

On the one hand, the question of why flows naturally from the what and the who: We become aware of an issue. We identify this issue as being either something of God's concern, a subject of public interest, or a matter of truth. Why do we speak? Because of our awareness, our sense that the topic is relevant, and our conviction that we have something to contribute. Yet this explanation of why is really more complicated than it appears. A number of factors influence our awareness, our assessment of an issue, and our intention to speak. Discerning evaluation helps us sort through these factors and identify an appropriate direction forward.

For example, personal context or social forces make it likely that we will be aware of some issues more than others. British political theologian Oliver O'Donovan contrasts the situations that have shaped the political theology of the Global South (especially Latin America) with those shaping the North.[39] Obviously, we are aware of the issues most visible in our own place. But sometimes we become aware of another political issue because of a monumental event or media attention. The twin towers are destroyed on 9/11, and all of a sudden we are conscious of Islamic fundamentalisms. A president's comments are banned from social media, and this is all we discuss, even though other significant global political issues

---

39. O'Donovan, *Desire of the Nations*, 18.

are unfolding at the time.[40] During the early 1960s, nuclear disarmament was front and center in the United States and Merton heard about it even though he lived in a monastery. Nevertheless, as I have mentioned above, those with influence sometimes exercise it to prevent others from being aware of issues that we would do well to speak about.[41]

Similarly, forces around us shape both our sense of concern and our awareness of issues. For example, we are more concerned about environmental politics now than we were fifty years ago. Or consider our understanding of racial issues in the early twentieth century: white people in power promoted stereotyped images of Black people that fostered less concern about racial inequities than ought to have been the case.[42] Even our theological background shapes our awareness or concern about socio-political issues. For example, some Christians emphasize the fall and others creation. Those who emphasize the fall are often concerned about the role of government in restraining evil or may identify government itself as a manifestation of the fall, whereas those who emphasize creation often see a more positive role of government in the world.[43] We must pay attention to the forces around us.

Even the sense of our own contribution does not simply rise from within. In addition to struggling with adequacy and possibility (affected by both personal and social factors), we develop our sense of success or effectiveness in socio-political speech in our own political contexts. The speech of Christians in North India, for instance, is the voice of a tiny minority within a region fraught with conflict between Hindus and Muslims. Our sense of being part of the majority in some settings gives us reason (we think) to excuse our mistreatment of those who are not in

40. Along with coauthors Paul Slovic and Amos Tversky, psychologist Daniel Kahneman treats this idea of our dependence on the salient in the preface to Kahneman et al., *Judgment Under Uncertainty*. He has covered similar ground in his more recent *Thinking Fast and Slow*.

41. Luke Bretherton speaks in a similar vein of the dangers of "technocracy," which while not entirely hiding awareness of political issues, deadens our sense of need to contribute to the issues. See Bretherton, *Christ and the Common Life*, 37.

42. See Gates Jr., *Stony the Road*. Stereotyped images—from ancient barbarians and medieval Jews to Indigenous people and enslaved Africans—are created and promoted by those with dominant power as part of a calculated effort to shape what the general public does or doesn't speak about or feel empathy toward.

43. It is obviously more complicated than this, but my point here is just to acknowledge these basic differences. See Bretherton, *Christ and the Common Life*, 25–26.

that majority.[44] Our religious loyalties may confuse our understanding of prophecy and policy. We can become so tied to moral codes that we lose sight of the ethics of a people.[45] In all of this—our awareness of issues, our sense of concern, our perceived contribution—we must learn to evaluate the social ecology of our own engagement. Our socio-political speech arises from a variety of factors. Hence the why of our speech is complicated and must be understood in the midst of all these factors.

It is for this reason that I like to emphasize the when. We can get lost in the aims and the motives of the whys—and sometimes we permit our uncertainties to turn into excuses for avoiding engagement altogether—but sooner or later we either decide to speak or let the moment pass. Imagine this in the context of parenting: when might you reprimand a child? When the time is right. The misbehavior must be severe enough to warrant a reprimand. You must also examine your motives to know that this correction is not merely an angry reaction on your part. You must be prepared for the child's response, though you may not be able to predict it. But if you wait too long, the child won't understand the connection between the misbehavior and the correction. The right time may be lost.

In the section on the monastic practice of discerning socio-political engagement, I mentioned three different times when we decide to step forward and speak. One of those times is when we are, as I put it, just blasted: that is, the Holy Spirit radicalizes us and we cannot *not* speak. With echoes of Jeremiah, Guatemalan believer Julia Esquivel writes to God:

> You seduced me, Lord
> and I was seduced.
>
> You grasped my heart firmly
> with the outstretched hand
> of the old Indian
> who has been dying for centuries
> without a roof,
> without medicines,
> without a doctor,
> asking for the bread of justice
> at the door of a Locked Church.

---

44. On majoritarianism, see Bretherton, *Christ and the Common Life*, 38, 85.

45. On code-fetishism, see Taylor, *Secular Age*, 707–9.

You seduced me, Lord,
and I let myself be seduced.
You have conquered me,
you have been stronger than I.

This is why those who were my friends
are retreating in fear
and close their doors to me.
Because each time
I hear your Word
I must cry out:
Violence and ruin
to those who manufacture
orphans, misery, and death!
How many times
I wanted to close my ears
to your voice,
to harden my heart,
to seal my lips,
to forget forever
the pain of the persecuted,
the helplessness of the outcast,
and the agony of the tortured,
but your pain
was my own
and your love
burns my heart.

Captivate me, Lord
to the end of my days,
wring out my heart
with your wise old Indian hands,
so that I will not forget
your Justice
nor cease proclaiming
the urgent need
for humankind
to live as our brothers and sisters.[46]

At other times we are led, step by step, into our decision to speak—
as when one member of my community shares an idea for a neighborhood garden and recreation area with the other members. Some have

46. Excerpts from Esquivel, "Confession."

questions, but we really like the idea. Because the plan depends on getting the city to donate a section of abandoned land, we will have to speak with the city council and answer questions about property maintenance and security issues. My community begins to investigate, and the more we explore, the better the plan looks. Yes, speaking to the council will get political because different residents of the city have different opinions about public property, but the community feels prepared to address others' concerns. Finally, we realize that we have done enough evaluation. We have looked deep into our calling as a community, and God has led us. It is now time to make appointments to speak with council members.

And then there are times when we deliberate over options but seem to get no direction. City residents are at odds over our plan, and we are facing a deadline. An election approaches, and if we do not deliver a land use study to the council's current leadership, the land will not be available for public use. We want the truth—that all would benefit from turning this lot into a garden and recreation area—to be known. We could do this, but producing the study would require all of our energies as a community, energies that are currently spent on a range of valuable activities. Should we put aside, for the time being, all our good works for the sake of this one effort? This is not an easy choice, but the time to decide is now. God, in love, entrusts us with such decisions, leaving us to choose as best we can in the midst of uncertainty.

As we move on from observation and gathering to evaluating and deciding, we pass through seasons of thinking about the whats, the whos, and the whys of our socio-political speech. Finally, at the point of decision, it becomes a matter of when. When are we done waiting? When is the time to speak? The prayerful process itself points the way.

THE HOW

Once we have decided to speak, we move to the discernment stage of implementation and the question of how (although I suspect we have already asked a few how questions along the way). Originally, I had thought this section would include a few "monastic tips" on speaking—practices that are valuable to monastic life and would likely improve the quality of our socio-political speech. But then, as I read through literature on interpersonal communication, conflict resolution, political organizing, and the like, I discovered that folks far and wide are growing increasingly sensitive to these very values.[47] When I teach about prayer, I describe communication as involving speaking, listening, and the space in between—the latter being the relational dynamics that provide the environment within which speaking and listening have their meaning.[48] It seems appropriate here to describe a few central values of monastic listening, speaking, and the space in between with illustrations to show how people writing about communication and politics are affirming these values.

But I start with a quote not from a nun or a monk, but from political activist adrienne maree brown, who, in writing about political organizing, recommends the development of "depth."

> In my longing for depth I have been re-rooting in the earth . . . honing in on work that is not only meaningful, but feels joyful, listening with less judgment to the ideas and efforts of others, having visions that are long term.
> Another part of walking this path has been the practice of humility—enough humility to learn, to be taught, to have teachers. . . .
> I am listening now with all of my senses, as if the whole universe might exist just to teach me more about love. . . .
> In all these ways, I meditate on love.[49]

Listening, humility, love. She did not mention wisdom here, though a few pages earlier she states that her book is for those who want "to tap into the most ancient systems and patterns for wisdom as we build tomorrow."[50] These themes—which are central to monastic communication—are what I wish to explore next.

---

47. Literature I have consulted in preparation for this section include Sande, *Peacemaker*; Bahnson, "Peacemaking in the Midst"; Lederach, *Moral Imagination*; Patterson et al., *Crucial Conversations*; Moe-Lobeda, *Resisting Structural Evil*; Pranis, *Little Book of Circle Processes*; Rosenberg, *Nonviolent Communication*; brown, *Emergent Strategy*; Brooks, *Love Your Enemies*. For John Howard Yoder's treatments of speaking to the state, see *Christian Witness*, 38–44, and *Discipleship as Political Responsibility*, 23–25.

48. See Howard, *Brazos Introduction*, 314–18; Wilhoit and Howard, *Discovering Lectio Divina*, 92. I use this framework when talking about prayer, but I understand human-to-human communication (and even socio-political communication) to involve these same elements.

49. brown, *Emergent Strategy*, 10.

50. brown, *Emergent Strategy*, 6.

Deep Listening

The most powerful speech comes from a context of deep listening. This has been the assumption of Christian monastic life since the earliest communities. In traditional Benedictine practice, for example,

> Silence was to be kept during three periods with varying intensity: 1) during periods of work when talking upon business and utility was allowed in the cloister; 2) during reading when silence was kept though it could be broken for a reasonable cause; 3) from late afternoon until the next day at mid-morning during which silence was rarely to be broken and then apparently only in the room set aside for such purpose.[51]

Early French religious "had to school themselves to long silences designed not only to promote dedication but to avert the impulses to gossiping and pontificating which generally irritate any social group."[52] The practice of silence was accompanied by an emphasis on listening. *The Rule of Benedict* begins with the words, "Listen carefully." Abbots were instructed to listen to their communities, disciples were to be silent and listen to their elders, members were to attend to the readings, and all were to listen to God.[53] Monastic communication in many traditions is rooted in a life of deep silence and listening. And while they are not a monastic order, the Society of Friends, also known as the Quakers, has honored this same value since its foundation.[54]

People writing about communication, including political communication, today are catching on to the value of listening, perhaps realizing that when we don't listen to one another, things don't go well—especially when the issues at hand are political in nature. I have already mentioned activist adrienne maree brown's intentions to listen with less judgment to the ideas and efforts of others. Arthur Brooks, a conservative author and public speaker, talks of the need to develop relationships and conversations outside our own political bubbles: "This is hard, not just because

51. Daly, *Benedictine Monasticism*, 206.

52. Donatus, *Rule*, 7.

53. See Benedict, *RB 1980*, 3.2 (179); 6.6 (191); 4.55 (185); Prologue 9 (159).

54. See, e.g., founder George Fox's sensitivity to the movements within in his Journal (Fox, *Journals*); the connections between listening to Spirit, self, and others, particularly regarding socio-political issues in Woolman, *Journal of John Woolman*; and in the precious treatment of listening to God and one another in Steere, *On Listening to Another*.

you have to find them, but also because you have to listen. (Our society has become pretty incompetent when it comes to listening.)" He encourages readers to "obliterate your silos by listening, reading, and watching media on the 'other side.'" He summarizes the message of his entire book with this sentence: "Go find someone with whom you disagree; listen thoughtfully; and treat him or her with respect and love. The rest will flow naturally from there."[55] Notice also how political theologian Luke Bretherton employs monastic language as he endorses the value of listening: "Attentiveness and reception—characterized by a posture of listening and contemplation—are the precursor of shared speech and action and thence the coming into being of a common life."[56] The act of listening to another is an opening of ourselves, a welcoming of the otherness of the other. Deep listening is thus a necessary path to the ordering of our common life.

Listening—to one another, to God, to our situations—is more than a vehicle of healing divisions. It is central to socio-political action. Remember the process of discernment: listen, pray, gather. Listening with discernment is not just about hearing widely or just about hearing one another, though those certainly are important. Good listening involves hearing deeply, hearing the voice of a situation, and asking yourself, what cries do I hear as I *listen* to this socio-political situation? Good listening involves hearing the voice of God, through Scripture, community, Spirit, and more.[57]

Different types of socio-political speech (legislative hearings, consciousness-raising rallies, lobbying appointments) require different kinds of hows, and careful listening will guide us to the kinds of speech necessary for a given situation. "In sum," writes Bretherton, "listening is vital to deepening our moral conversion in relation to God and others and thus our ability to reason rightly about what is the just and truthful judgment to be made with these people, at this time, in this place. To know what is true, we must first listen. In certain configurations, democratic politics

---

55. Brooks, *Love Your Enemies*, 186, 210, 213.

56. Bretherton, *Christ and the Common Life*, 186. Bretherton also emphasizes the importance of listening with regard to the relationship between representatives and their constituents (430).

57. The community of Englewood Christian Church, Indianapolis, for example, has a practice they call "communal conversation," which has helped them discern direction concerning socio-political issues.

is one such way of listening well."[58] I will discuss the strategies born of prayerful listening in the chapter on action (chapter 6).

Listening also, as Bretherton mentions, deepens "our moral conversion." Through contemplative listening we become aware of the many temptations of socio-political communication: to reduce our voice to Christian hate speech, to have ever-slicker presentations, to generate news through spectacular events, to employ expensive media because that's what everybody is doing, or to despair and withdraw from socio-political speech entirely. As you can see, attentive listening may be the cutting edge of effective socio-political communication for the next generation.

Wise Speaking

Christian monasticism developed within an environment of seeking wisdom.[59] I already mentioned the wisdom of pioneer Beguine Marie d'Oignies in chapter 1. Another characteristic example of monastic wisdom is found in the story of Abba Macarius, the brother, and the cemetery:

> A brother came to see Abba Macarius the Egyptian, and said to him, "Abba, give me a word, that I may be saved." So the old man said, "Go to the cemetery and abuse the dead." The brother went there, abused them and threw stones at them; then he returned and told the old man about it. The latter said to him, "Didn't they say anything to you?" He replied, "No." The old man said, "Go back tomorrow and praise them." So the brother went away and praised them, calling them, "Apostles, saints and righteous men." He returned to the old man and said to him, "I have complimented them." And the old man said to them, "Did they not answer you?" The brother said no. The old man said to him, "You know how you insulted them and they did not reply, and how you praised them and they did not speak; so you too if you wish to be saved must do the same and become a dead man. Like

---

58. Bretherton, *Christ and the Common Life*, 175.

59. For an account of the development of wisdom speech with regard to the writings of Evagrius Ponticus (345–399), see Driscoll, ed., *Evagrius Ponticus*, 155–214. For a treatment of early monastic wisdom speech with attention to Scripture, see Burton-Christie, *Word in the Desert*.

the dead, take no account of either the scorn of men or their praises, and you can be saved."[60]

William Harmless, in his own monumental study of early monasticism, comments on this passage:

> This story is remarkable—for its humor and its unexpected poignancy. Beneath its spare narrative is a wisdom, an intensity of insight, that leaps out and touches something deep in us. It touches on something universal: the way we all can let our lives be determined by praise and blame, by honors and curses. . . . This story gives a good first glimpse of the *Apophthegmata* [Sayings] as a whole, and why its wisdom has been compared to a "flash of a signaling lamp—brief, arresting, and intense."[61]

Harmless, acknowledging that his attraction to the wisdom of the early monastic tradition has influenced his research and writing, recounts a time during his service in the Peace Corps when he was reading Thomas Merton's *The Wisdom of the Desert* while stationed near the Sahara in 1975:

> I was impressed then, as I am now, by the desert fathers' unflinching vision of things, their knack for cutting through our intricate self-deceptions, and their willingness to help us humbly face our fragile dignity. I am convinced that their wisdom has something to say to contemporary spirituality. The translation from a fourth-century desert to a twenty-first century city is not easy, but I think that we ignore the desert fathers at our peril.[62]

I agree and would add that people writing about politics are beginning to realize that this kind of wisdom has something to say to contemporary socio-political engagement as well.

Christians debate whether we should (a) soften our Christian language when we speak in order to facilitate a natural, neutral ground of political dialogue in a pluralist society or (b) admit that there is no true common ground between Christ and the world and just be honest about

---

60. Ward, tr., *Sayings*, "Macarius the Great," 23; p. 132. Of course in this more anchoritic desert context, the emphasis is on the pursuit of God (salvation), which must not be driven by others' opinions. A community context might require other wisdom.

61. Harmless, *Desert Christians*, 171–72.

62. Harmless, *Desert Christians*, x. See also Merton, tr., *Wisdom of the Desert*.

the source of our values.[63] Perhaps we could make progress on this debate by pursuing wisdom. Wise speech—communication that provides penetrating insight into a state of affairs—is forged through a synthesis of the following: a life well lived (not a perfect life, but at least one lived *well* with regard to the matter at hand); a broad range of observation or experience; carefully considered reference to an honored set of values, which gives the wise speaker a sense of integrity in relationship to some larger tradition; and a sensitivity to the audience. And like individuals, communities can offer wise speech as their shared life, experiences, and values coalesce to give rise to a single profound voice.[64]

John Paul Lederach, a pioneer in international justice and peacebuilding, suggests that peacebuilding is more of an art than a formula, and that part of this art is learning to adapt to serendipity: "Serendipity is not just openness to the unexpected," he writes. "It requires us to hone the disciplines that build both knowledge and wisdom."[65] Rev. Dr. William J. Barber II and Jonathan Wilson-Hartgrove, leaders of the Poor People's Campaign, identify "[using] moral language to frame and critique public policy" as the second of their fourteen "steps forward together." "[Lifting] the voices of everyday people impacted by immoral policies" is the fourth step, and "[making] a serious commitment to academic and empirical analysis of policy" is the ninth.[66]

I see these suggestions—this art—as steps toward the political wisdom outlined above. Moral language points to *values*. Lifting the voices of those who suffer (which often go unheard) promotes access to a broad range of *experience*. Academic rigor likewise ensures that our access to observation and experience are *broad*. Activist adrienne maree brown's approach to political organizing is deeply informed through observation

63. This is the classic conflict between the approaches of Reinhold Niebuhr and Stanley Hauerwas.

64. I have explored the notion of wisdom with reference to philosophy in "Philosophy and the Love of Wisdom," chap. 1 of *Love Wisdom: A Global and Practical Introduction to Philosophy*, https://spiritualityshoppe.org/chapter-one-philosophy-as-the-love-of-wisdom. For a review of scientific studies on wisdom, see the Wisdom Page, http://www.wisdompage.com/wisresearch00.html, and especially Richard Trowbridge's dissertation, "Scientific Approach to Wisdom," http://www.wisdompage.com/uchicagopgm.html.

65. Lederach, *Moral Imagination*, 174.

66. Barber II and Wilson-Hartgrove, *Third Reconstruction*, 127; this list is excerpted at https://www.beaconbroadside.com/broadside/2016/01/fourteen-steps-forward-together-for-americas-third-reconstruction.html.

and reflection on the behavior of the natural world, and in this context, activists become "conduits of the wisdom of this planet."[67] I sense from many angles a developing consensus that our socio-political engagement needs to move beyond ideology and tactics to *wisdom*. I will speak about the well-lived aspect of wisdom and socio-political engagement when we get to chapter 5, on modeling.

Let me make one final comment regarding wise speech: I think a fruit of socio-political wisdom is the discovery of "appropriate language" for our speech. This is complicated, and words can wound, which is why wisdom is needed. Moral language is helpful; it points us toward values. But how do we distinguish Lederach's "moral imagination," Jerry Falwell's "moral majority," and William Barber's "moral Mondays"? Wisdom is needed to evaluate the language of values itself. Sometimes what is important is that political opponents acquire the skills of mature disagreement.[68] Thomas Merton was nervous about well-meaning activists who employ an inappropriate tone of voice. He writes in one of his Cold War Letters: "You must be very careful of a false and noisy zeal that talks loudly about plans for action and conquest. . . . These people, without meaning to, and in all good faith, will do much harm."[69] At other times the greatest need is simply an opportunity for opponents to tell their stories.[70] Still again at times it is important to ignore Merton's recommendation and just to be loud, to bring pressure on those who might wish another voice was not heard. Lord give us wisdom to know how to say what we say!

Honoring the Space in Between

Listening and speaking are embedded within our sense of each relationship itself—what I call the space in between (as I mentioned above). For example, we could compare a conversation I might have about romance with a stranger on public transportation with a conversation I might have on the same topic with my spouse. While the particular matters discussed would likely be similar, the communication itself would be radically different. Our gestures, tone of voice, and choice of words would certainly differ, but underneath all this is our own sense of how we are

67. brown, *Emergent Strategy*, 39.
68. Brooks, *Love Your Enemies*, 175–200.
69. Merton, *Cold War Letters*, 64–65.
70. On the value of storytelling, see Pranis, *Little Book of Circle Processes*.

in relationship. I might be cautious about discussing romance with a stranger, not wanting that person to draw any false conclusions about my intentions. But I might also be cautious discussing romance with my spouse if I have recently offended her and now must tenderly win back her trust. So much is present in that space in between!

The same is true of socio-political speech. Contrast, for example, a speech on regulating businesses to a rally of political allies with a speech on the same topic to a hostile audience. Our barely conscious perception of these relationships governs so much. Consequently, when learning how to speak in the midst of our socio-political engagements, it behooves us to honor the space in between by consciously fostering ways of perceiving and being in relationship that reflect the character and concerns of the Almighty and Most Merciful One. I will address this more fully in the chapters on care and modeling, but here I'll note a couple of virtues that are quite influential in our socio-political speech and central to monastic life.

Humility is one of the primary virtues of monastic life.[71] The desert elders of the fourth century highly commended it. Saint Benedict penned an entire chapter on humility in the *Rule of Life*, written as a guide for communities of his followers, which was then developed further in a twelfth-century treatise written by Bernard of Clairvaux. Monastic reform movements, appealing to the virtue of humility, often sought to level distinctions of class or caste within the cloister. Catherine of Siena, who confronted kings with her prophetic words, often writes of the value of humility toward God and others. Ignatius of Loyola, founder of the Jesuits, included a specific exercise in his *Spiritual Exercises* designed to facilitate our growth in humility. Protestants outside the monastic tradition have also praised humility: for example, Jonathan Edwards's (1703 -1758) treatment of humility and spiritual pride in the Puritan classic *Treatise Concerning Religious Affections*.[72]

I've taken part in socio-political discussions for over four decades, and I am noticing that the value of humility is affirmed in socio-political discussion now more than ever. For example, in conversations regarding race, I am hearing white folks recommend that we "put ourselves in

71. For overviews of this theme, see, e.g., Dryer, "Humility"; Chittister, *Wisdom Distilled*, 51-66.

72. See for example, Catherine of Siena, *Dialogue*, 222-26; Ignatius of Loyola, *Spiritual Exercises* [#165-68]; Edwards, *Religious Affections*, 311-340.

places [of service] with people of color."[73] This posture reflects the character of our relationships, the space in between. Just as the "humility" that white supremacy has enforced among those it seeks to marginalize has restricted the speech of people of color for centuries, so too the measure of humility we embrace will shape our socio-political speech. Counselor Ken Sande, in his biblical approach to interpersonal conflict, exhorts readers to start the journey to reconciliation by getting the log out of their own eye (Matt 7:3; Luke 6:41). In the spirit of our socio-political examen, I suspect that there is fruitful place for recognizing and removing a few socio-political "logs" as we look toward peacemaking. I think that Bretherton expresses the value for humility in socio-political engagement excellently in his treatment of "poverty of spirit as a therapy for privilege." He argues that the practice of humanitarianism would benefit from a correction stimulated by the value of humility, a value treasured by nuns and monks for centuries.[74]

Similarly, love—which has always been a value central to monastic life—is now a theme repeated by those writing about socio-political speech. To demonstrate the centrality of practicing love in Christian monasticism, I need only reference the three most influential monastic Rules of Life. Basil of Caesarea's (330–79) "Long Rules/Longer Responses" are structured to orient the reader to the love of God and neighbor. After introducing these two great commands, he writes, "This, at all events, must be recognized—that we can observe neither the command of the love of God itself nor that referring to our neighbor, nor any other commandment, if our minds keep wandering hither and yon."[75] Basil's conviction is that a monastery provides a worthy environment to foster our loves. Augustine of Hippo similarly begins his *Ordo Monasterii* with the encouragement that "before all else, dearest brothers, let God be loved and then your neighbor, because these are the chief commandments which have been given us."[76] Augustine's Rule then develops from this starting place.

---

73. Thanks to Elizabeth Dede, who offered this comment nearly word for word in a Nurturing Communities Network Roundtable Zoom Meeting on October 17, 2020.

74. Bretherton, *Christ and the Common Life*, 65–70.

75. Basil, "Long Rules" Q.5, 241.

76. Augustine, "Ordo Monasterii" 1, 106. On the authorship of the "Ordo Monasterii," see the treatment of authorship in this volume, 23–49. Augustine's mention of the two loves are replete throughout his works.

Finally, we examine Benedict of Nursia. Though he does not structure his Rule according to the two loves, the notion of love is central to it. In "The Tools for Good Works," a key chapter near the beginning, he writes, "Respect the elders and love the young. Pray for your enemies out of love for Christ. If you have a dispute with someone, make peace with him before the sun goes down." Similarly, in the penultimate chapter of the *Rule*, Benedict reminds his monks that

> This, then, is the good zeal which monks must foster with fervent love: *They should each try to be the first to show respect to the other* (Rom 12:10), supporting with the greatest patience one another's weaknesses of body or behavior. . . . To their fellow monks they show the pure love of brothers; to God, loving fear, to their abbot, unfeigned and humble love.[77]

It may be fairly said that the development of a sincere love for God and others is *what monasticism is all about*. Needless to say, the environment of love is a framework for our perceptions of relationship. It governs the space in between our speech.

Several contemporary thinkers and activists also emphasize that love is a valuable component of socio-political speech. Arthur Brooks's plea for political relationship is titled *Love Your Enemies: How Decent People Can Save America from the Culture of Contempt*. The title of Cynthia D. Moe-Lobeda's plea for social engagement is *Resisting Structural Evil: Love as Ecological-Economic Vocation*. And in the closing pages of *Emergent Strategy*, which are filled with the word *love*, adrienne maree brown writes this:

> It feels important to end this book with an admission. It is possible that this whole book is about love. My love of this planet, my love of human beings. . . . My love of Black people. . . .
>
> So practice emergent strategy, yes, but only as much as you understand that it is a way to practice love.[78]

Literature on interpersonal communication warns of the dangers of contempt, and now some are warning us of the same dangers in the arena of political speech.[79] Literature on communication emphasizes the

---

77. Benedict, *RB 1980* 72, 292–95.

78. brown, *Emergent Strategy*, 201–2.

79. See Arthur Brooks's discussion of the work of social psychologist John Gottman in his *Love Your Enemies*, 22–26.

importance of respect, and political writers today are emphasizing the same.[80]

What would happen if we exchanged our "hate speech" for "love speech"? What would happen if we exchanged "cancel culture" for "listen culture"? What would happen if we exchanged political contempt for political humility? What about "wisdom" instead of "ideology"? I know there are times to exert pressure—to hold others accountable and to magnify the voices of those who have been intentionally marginalized—and to be loud. Unacceptable situations need to change. I'm asking, what is going on in the space in between our speech and how does that influence both our communication and the consequences of our communication?

How do we enter the river of socio-political engagement? Sometimes we speak, as nuns and monks have done for centuries (and still do today). What do we speak about? We speak about those issues that matter most to God. We speak with our neighbors about whatever burdens them. We speak truth. We speak as a "who" that is present with a variety of gifts and limits. Why do we speak? Well, that gets a bit complicated because our aims, backgrounds, and motives are all mixed together. So it's better to focus on the when. We speak when it seems best to take the next step, whether blasted, led, or entrusted. Once we decide to speak we address the question of how we speak. It brings me joy to see that writers on socio-political engagement are beginning to notice (whether consciously or not) the lessons on speech taught throughout the history of Christian monasticism. We shall see, in the chapters ahead, that these lessons regarding speech also teach us much about the other ways we engage.

80. See for example, Patterson et al., *Crucial Conversations*, 79–90 and the entire June 14, 2021 issue of *The Christian Science Monitor Weekly*, devoted to "The Lost Art of Respect."

FOUR

We Care

SOME ENGAGE THROUGH SPEAKING. Others engage through caring. St. Basil of Caesarea (330–379) did both.[1] He established himself as an influential speaker, and was ordained as a deacon in 362 and a presbyter in 365. He was well known for his theological writings and his influence in ecclesiastical leadership (which at that time also involved a fair amount of politics). In 369 there was a famine in Basil's homeland (modern Turkey), "the most severe one ever recorded [in the area]."[2] Basil's response to the famine was twofold. First, he spoke, perceiving God's warning in the famine. He declared, "This is why God does not open his hand: because we have closed up our hearts towards our brothers and sisters. This is why the fields are arid: because love has dried up."[3] But he not only spoke, he cared. He sold his own possessions and gave them to those who suffered. He "attended to the bodies and souls of those who needed it, combining personal respect with the supply of their necessity, and so giving them a double relief."[4] Basil also rallied his parishioners and began to organize support.

By 372 Basil had constructed a collection of buildings within which care was provided. In a letter appealing for approval to Elias, the governor

---

1. On Basil generally see Gregory of Nazianzen, *Oration 43*; Clarke, *St. Basil the Great*; Rousseau, *Basil of Caesarea*; Holmes, *A Life Pleasing to God*; Silvas, *Ascetikon*. More specifically with reference to the Basilias, see Heyne, "Reconstructing"; Patitsas, "St. Basil's Philanthropic Program."

2. Gregory, *Oration 43*, #34.

3. Basil the Great, *On Social Justice*, "In Time of Famine and Drought," #2, pp. 75–76.

4. Gregory, *Oration 43*, #35.

of the province (notice the necessity of socio-political speech for the expression of socio-political care), he queried the governor about the project:

> But to whom do we any harm by building a place of entertainment for strangers, both for those who are on a journey and for those who require medical treatment on account of sickness, and so establishing a means of giving these men the comfort they want, physicians, doctors, means of conveyance, and escort? All these must learn such occupations as are necessary to life and have been found essential to a respectable career . . .[5]

Basil personally provided care and also established a monastery/church-supported institution to maintain this care on an ongoing basis.[6] Basil called the site "The New City." Over time, Caesarea decayed and The New City thrived. Timothy Patitsas writes, "Some two hundred years later, when Emperor Justinian ordered that the major cities of Asia Minor be walled in for their defense, walls were built around the Basileias [or "Basilead"—as others have named it] and the new economy and settlement that had continued to emerge around it—and not around the original Caesarea."[7] In founding the Basileas, Basil pioneered the first hospital, a form of care that has developed from that day till now.[8]

Our second story is about how two communities cooperated to provide care. The story is also known among the communities as the "Good Samaritan and Innkeeper" story (see Luke 10:25–37). InnerCHANGE San Francisco (you met them in chapter 2), spent time with folks who did not have homes. Some of these folks, after experiencing—as Gregory said

5. Basil of Caesarea, *Letter 94*.

6. See Silvas, *Ascetikon*, 201 (regarding LR 15.1), 356 (regarding SR 155), and 430 (regarding SR 286) with the accompanying footnotes to get a sense of the relationship between the monastic community and its various buildings and activities. C. Paul Schroeder, in his introduction to Basil's homilies on social justice describes a "regular and rotating service among the monastics" (Schroeder, "Introduction," 37).

7. Patitsas, "St. Basil's Philanthropic Program," 270.

8. See Crislip, *From Monastery to Hospital*; Watson, *On Hospitals*. For Basil's own views see Basil the Great, *On Social Justice*. Philip Rousseau summarizes Basil's contribution specifically mentioning the blend of monastic, charitable, and political elements. He writes, "Care of the sick, provision for the needy, formation in asceticism, together with 'political' elements, heralded nothing less than a major social revolution, setting in place patterns of collaboration and economic and political patronage that challenged directly the hypocrisy, corruption, and uncontrolled self-interest governing, in Basil's eyes, the society in which he had to operate." (See Rousseau, *Basil of Casarea*, 145.)

of Basil—both "personal respect" and a "supply of their necessity" from InnerCHANGE members, felt ready to take a next step. But where could they go? The temptations of the street were not helpful. Local churches invited them to a small group in a posh high rise (where they felt out of place) or offered inappropriate measures to "fix" them from being dirty and jobless. It was too much responsibility to leave people with serious problems in the hands of one generous Christian family. Social programs often treated them as "cases." The InnerCHANGE house itself was inappropriate, because it was often frequented by people in the grip of some of the same addictions the others were seeking to leave behind and the staff were often out on the streets and could not provide the kind of home-based oversight that was needed.

At some time in her San Francisco years, Claire, who worked with InnerCHANGE, also developed an affiliation with the Church of the Sojourners community.[9] "Sojo" has been around since the late 1980s, with a membership of around twenty to forty over the years, living together in three large houses in San Francisco's Mission District. They share cars, meals, and money, along with prayer, worship, and discernment. Every once in a while, Claire would talk to Sojo about a friend in need and a member of the community would invite that person for lunch. If all went well, they would move into the community for a time. Sojo was a place where drugs were not present. Someone could be nearby around the clock. The community was a calm environment, unlike the chaos Claire's street friends had often experienced in their childhood homes. A community was able to provide care that was beyond the capacity of an individual or a nuclear family. Claire served as caseworker, acting as a liaison with agencies, programs, and the like. Sojo became family, inviting people into meal preparations, birthday celebrations, and ordinary life. This was radical hospitality: many street dwellers know no housed person that they would consider a personal friend. InnerCHANGE was the good Samaritan, finding the injured person along the way and seeking to provide assistance. The Church of the Sojourners was the innkeeper, offering a place to rest and heal. Sometimes Sojo provided care for a few days, weeks, or months; once for a few years. I think the relationship between the two groups nourished them both.

Caring is an act of bringing order into the world, of shaping the *polis* where we live. We invite one who is sick to a place of healing. We sit

9. See https://churchofthesojourners.org/.

on the sidewalk sharing a sandwich with a traveler. When appropriate, we may introduce the traveler into an "inn" or a hospital, a community that can provide a new kind of welcome. Each of these acts brings a small measure of change to a state of affairs. When acts of care become habits and structures, they acquire socio-political implications.

Questions arise, even as we hear these stories: Is "charity" always good? Does it really help people? Should we be offering relief for those who suffer most or should we be changing the socio-political structures so people suffer less? Does the development of a caring institution simply create one more bureaucracy to avoid? What best should be the works of the people of God and what best the works of various government agencies?

These are the kinds of questions we address in this chapter. And we must address these questions while examining *monastic* expressions of care. I will first give a sense of how I see the character of Christian care, especially as a form of socio-political engagement. I will illustrate how care has been offered by monasteries. Then we can begin to think about how we do care today.

WHAT IS CARE?

A few introductory matters.[10] I understand "care" to be an intentional giving of oneself (a community or an individual) for the enrichment of another (individual, group, or creation itself). The term "care" ("I care for my grandmother") can communicate either attitude or action. Our life of care emerges in distinct contexts: households, faith communities, voluntary associations, one-on-one relationships. Even solitude can be a context of care (as Thomas Merton perceived). The very fact that we can talk about offering ourselves in care implies that human beings possess some level of "response-ability" with relationship to our world.[11] One aspect of care that is fascinating to me is that what we offer in care is *difference*. You are hungry. I have some food. I offer that difference to you.

---

10. I have discussed "The Life of Care" generally in Howard, *Brazos Introduction*, 337–69. Here I wish to explore more particularly how care functions as a means of socio-political engagement.

11. I have spoken about this in a video lecture. See https://www.youtube.com/watch?v=aWlTV25NoHc&list=PLiw_vQbcv1gMGh53m631rHEDqSGlgMK3M&index=7. People with different views of divine and human agency will word this idea variously.

In offering our difference, we also exercise *power*, our capacity to influence. That is the point of care. We will get into the relationship between care and power below. Care also often aims at change, the "enrichment" of another. Finally, care—like all aspects of human experience—is expressed in a mix of greatness, fallenness, and restoration. Consequently, while care seems to be a good thing, it can get a bit twisted at times. All of this must be remembered when we explore care as socio-political engagement.

The Christian God is a God who cares. The Christian Trinity we worship is a mutually self-giving unity of persons.[12] God's righteousness—as theologian James Cone asserts at the beginning of his *A Black Theology of Liberation*—is not merely a static ideal of perfection, but "God's active involvement in history, making right what human beings have made wrong. The consistent theme in Israelite prophecy is Yahweh's concern for the lack of social, economic, and political justice for those who are poor and unwanted in society."[13] God's acts of creation (Job 38–39), providence (Ps 104), and deliverance (Lev 26:12) are consistently described as acts of care.[14] God is the One who declares, "When Israel was a child, I loved him, and out of Egypt I called my son. . . . I led them with cords of human kindness, with ties of love; I lifted the yoke from their neck and bent down to feed them" (Hos 11:1,4).

The universe God created works through a process of mutual self-giving. Take, for example, the biblical portrait of creation itself as compared with other ancient Near Eastern creation myths. "What we find in the Genesis account," write Douglas Moo and Jonathan Moo, "is a startlingly distinct understanding of deity and a radically different assessment of the significance of creation and human life than what is depicted in these other stories." Creation is fundamentally an expression of God's creative purposeful grace.[15] Land itself is a space of mutual self-giving, as

12. See for example, Kärkkäinen, *Trinity and Revelation,* 250–82.

13. Cone, *Black Theology of Liberation,* 14. See pp. 39–42 as well as Kelly, "Righteousness," 193, and Evans, "Social Justice or Personal Righteousness," 98.

14. For creation and providence see Moo and Moo, *Creation Care,* 53–60. For God's caring deliverance as the foundation of Israelite law see Hiers, *Justice and Compassion,* loc. 2066 of 3625. That God's care is a care for both individuals and communities, see locs. 1611, 2106, 2111. On God's character as actively present in love, see Howard, *Brazos Introduction,* 127–28.

15. Moo and Moo, *Creation Care,* 47. See further on pp. 47–53. I consider a perspective of the universe as purposeful, creative gift to lie—at least inchoately— behind Paul's inquiry regarding the Corinthians' charismatic gifts, "What do you have

soil (including decomposed organic matter) produces food, which facilitates plant and animal life, which when ended contribute to the health of the soil.[16] God fashions human beings as participants in creation, giving them the fruits of creation and giving them *to* this same creation (Gen 1:28–30).[17] God's gifting of humans to creation is also an assignment of intentional human self-giving for the enrichment of both human and nonhuman creation itself.[18] Needless to say, God's sending of Jesus to creation as a human child and raising Christ bodily from the grave is itself a supreme affirmation of this mutually supporting relationship between God, human beings, and creation.

Finally, God's covenant relationship with Israel and the church initiates communities of care. The righteous God who acts on behalf of the least instructs the nation of Israel to act in solidarity with the least, reminding them that "you were aliens in the land of Egypt" (Exod 23:9).[19] The value of justice or fair treatment of others is understood as an expression of the care-full ordering of things. God's people are exhorted to structure their common life not according to the self-serving and stratified principles of

---

that you did not receive?" (1 Cor 4:7).

16. Norman Wirzba speaks of the "processes of life and death" as "sacred" (Wirzba, *From Nature to Creation*, 100). On the one hand I can totally appreciate the beauty of this mutually self-giving (though unintentional) circle of life. At the same time, it is dependent upon the perpetuation of death, not to mention the importance of symbiotic organisms for the preservation of life as we know it. Is the beautiful cycle of life we currently experience part of divine providence post-fall?

17. Wirzba speaks of our participation as living a "creaturely" life (Wirzba, *From Nature to Creation*, 95–129). Moo and Moo speak of being "members" of the community of creation (Moo and Moo, *Creation Care*, 69–72). I speak of our distinct, dependent, participation in creation in Howard, *Brazos Introduction*, 147–48.

18. Humans value earth and care for it (Moo and Moo, *Creation Care*, 76–87). Oliver O'Donovan writes, "The order of things that God made is *there*. It is objective, and mankind has a place within it. Christian ethics, therefore, has an objective reference because it is concerned with man's life in accordance with this order" (O'Donovan, *Resurrection and Moral Order*, 17). Humans also value other human beings as created in the image of God. This value of human life and our obligation to care-fully honor it is reflected, for example in biblical law (see for example Hiers, *Justice and Compassion*, loc. 2116 of 3625).

19. On these "motive clauses" see Evans, "Imagining Justice," 7. The term "righteousness" as applied to both God and humans is a slippery and much-debated term (see Kelly, "Righteousness," esp. p. 193; Evans, "Social Justice or Personal Righteousness?"). Note also how the Hebrew term for righteousness (*tsedaqa*) eventually became employed as a moniker for the giving of alms (see Anderson, *Charity*, 19, and throughout his book).

surrounding nations, but rather to act "neighborly," exercising their "duty to care," to "dissolve the boundaries" characteristic of other groups.[20] In addition to the structures of justice, the Christian faith invites God's people into a generous charity: a free-willed self-giving for the benefit of others.[21] God's Spirit empowers us to move from self-centered living into communities of care, from economies of extraction to economies of fellowship, from socially stratified identities to universal acceptance. All of this is rooted in the foundational Christ-gift of God's own self-offering.

All of this biblical/theological account of care, of course, begs further socio-political questions: Who are the intended recipients of Christian care? Is this alternative, generous, egalitarian vision meant for the community of Christ or for the whole world? Where does vision end and realistic strategy begin? Who should be the performers of care? Are these instructions exclusively for the community of Christ or do they have relevance for "secular" government? I will touch on these questions below and address them more fully in the forthcoming chapters. Nonetheless, this much can be said as a way of summarizing the basics of my approach to care in this chapter. First, I do not see the Scriptures demanding a *proscription* of care or socio-political engagement outside the community of faith. Indeed, rather than denouncing care for unbelievers, I suspect that Christian Scripture points toward expressions of care that transcend parochial interests.[22] At the same time I find no *prescription* of programs or institutions for care outside the church family within Scripture. No

20. Acting "neighborly" is a key theme in Brueggemann, *Money and Possessions*. The "duty to care" is a prominent theme in Hiers, *Justice and Compassion*. For Paul's understanding of the church's need to dissolve boundaries and form a "counter-institution" to Roman society, see Porter, "Reframing," 141–42. See also Evans, "Imagining Justice," 26–27; Westfall, "Continue to Remember," 156; and Hasselhoff, "James 2:2–7."

21. See Brueggemann, *Money and Possessions*, 49; Boda and Baines, "Wisdom's Cry," 59; and especially Anderson, *Charity*. I think that Evans, "Imagining Justice," 27–29, on Jesus's hermeneutic of suspicion, expresses an idea worthy of consideration. I also think that Buell, "Be Not One," along with (diverse!) studies of the Pauline ecclesial economy (Gaudet, *Christian Utopia*; Brueggemann, *Money and Possessions*, 219–38; Porter, "Reframing Social Justice") all point us beyond a shallow "capitalist" or "communist" interpretation of the New Testament church. As I will address in the following chapters, I suspect the employment of such concepts as "gift economy" can serve us in our attempts to understand both early and contemporary models of communities of care.

22. For a selection of views see for example, Westfall, "Continue to Remember," 170; Longenecker, *Remember the Poor*; Porter, "Reframing Social Justice."

specific political strategies or institutions are normatively established. What the Bible does provide is positive *permission*: a vision and an encouragement that gives perspective and a trajectory whereby various forms of compassionate socio-political engagement for all people may be seen as appropriate in the right context. This is precisely what we find in the history of Christian monasticism.

MONASTICISM AND THE HISTORY OF CHRISTIAN CARE

Now that we know something about what care is, and how it is woven into the fabric of Christian life and teaching, we can explore the ways monasticism has lived out this vision of care and has done so as a form of *socio-political engagement*. In doing so, we must remember that the basic ordering structures of common life have changed significantly from late antiquity until today. Byzantine Turkey is different than medieval France, is different than nineteenth-century United States of America. My point, as you will see, is that monastic communities pioneered and developed institutions of health, education, welfare, and more, which in their settings became dominant providers of care for that place and time. Particularly in medieval Europe, the monastery—in the midst of their vows, prayers, and community life—*was* the "Department" of (no, let's use the British term, the "Ministry" of) health care, welfare, and education.

Medieval monasteries built upon the experiments and expressions of the Christian church prior to Roman emperor Constantine (reigning from 306–337) and the collapse of the Roman Empire in the fifth century. The Christian church was caring for widows, educating (catechizing) seekers, and welcoming abandoned children long before the formal institution of monasticism was known.[23] Gary Anderson in his treatment of charity cites the well-known comment of emperor Julian ("the Apostate" reigned 361–63), regarding Christians: "The impious Galileans support not only their own poor, but ours as well."[24] During the fourth century when monasticism(s) were being formed, care for others was regarded as an acceptable expression of the monastic life. Thus we learn in the *History of the Monks in Egypt* about Serapion, who

> successfully administered a considerable rural economy, for at
> harvest time all of them came as a body and brought him their

23. See for example Sittser, *Resilient Faith*, 135–54; Kreider, *Patient Ferment*.
24. Anderson, *Charity*, 17.

own produce, which each had obtained as his harvest wage, filling each year twelve *arbatas,* or about forty *modii* [ten bushels, 350 litres], as we would say. Through Serapion they provided this grain for the relief of the poor, so that there was nobody in that district who was destitute any longer. Indeed, grain was even sent to the poor of Alexandria.[25]

With the fall of the Roman Empire, and the collapse of Roman systems of poverty relief and education, monastic communities frequently filled in—and creatively addressed—the gaps which the Roman government left behind.[26]

Medieval monasteries functioned as the primary Ministry of Welfare for centuries. As Michel Mollat states at the start of his *Poverty in the Middle Ages,* "Poverty moved from the declining cities into the countryside, and charitable services tended to move with it from the episcopal cities to the rural abbeys. In the monasteries, hostels were open to all comers, especially pilgrims, and these hostels assumed responsibility for the distributions of goods formerly associated with the [Roman] poor lists."[27] The value of charity was written into monastic foundation documents. Chapter 53 of the *Rule of Benedict* for example, reflects on the themes of Matt 25:31–46 when it instructs that "Great care and concern are to be shown in receiving poor people and pilgrims, because in them more particularly Christ is received."[28] The "almoner," who oversaw the distribution of charitable gifts, became a significant position in medieval monastic communities.

Perspectives regarding the order of things were shared by medieval peoples. One was a perspective regarding the divisions of society. There were those who prayed (clergy and religious); there were those who ruled and fought (kings and knights); and there were those who

25. Russell, tr., *Lives of the Desert Fathers,* XVIII.1, "On Serapion," p. 102. See also the story of Paesius and Isaias in Palladius, *Lausiac History,* 49–51; and the comments on Evagrius of Pontus in Brakke, "Care for the Poor." I have already mentioned Basil's hospital, to which we will return.

26. Monastic charity developed differently in the Byzantine East and the medieval West, due in part to different government structures. I will here focus my attention on the development in medieval Europe. For Byzantine charity, see for example, Caner, "Wealth," and Hatlie, *Monks and Monasteries,* 143–47, on the Monophysite monasteries.

27. Mollat, *Poor in the Middle Ages,* 41.

28. See also Mollat's treatment of the Benedictine porter in Mollat, *Poor in the Middle Ages,* 47–48.

worked (peasants). Another perspective regarding the order of the times was what historian of charity Carter Lindberg calls the "poverty-alms-salvation complex": there were those who gave alms to aid their salvation and there were those who suffer in poverty (or live in voluntary poverty in monasteries), receive alms, and pray for those who give as part of their own salvation.[29] Thus, monastic structure and medieval perspective blended in the "customary role" of care that monastic communities exercised within the order of medieval society for over six hundred years.[30]

After the twelfth century things began to change. Migration to the cities, devastating plagues, lay interest in charity, the birth of money economy, and other factors stimulated shifts in the way poverty relief was arranged. Yet even within this transition, communities of consecrated Christians (canons, mendicants, Hospitallars, Beguines) often led the way in pioneering new forms of compassionate care.[31] Mollat states of the traumatic transition from late medieval to early modern that, "traditional forms of charity, though less methodical and more frequent than direct or posthumous alms, nevertheless fell short of meeting society's new needs."[32] By the sixteenth century, as Lindberg summarizes, "The major responsibility for welfare shifted from the church to governmental and economic institutions," a shift that Marvin Olasky suggests—due to unique circumstances in the early modern New World—did not materialize in the United States until the late nineteenth century.[33]

During the Middle Ages monasteries also served as medical centers, a "Ministry of Health." Lindberg summarizes: "Monasteries were the refuge of the poor. This role extended to concern for the sick poor and

29. Lindberg, *Beyond Charity*, loc. 838 of 3712. See also locs. 318, 356.

30. Mollat, *Poor in the Middle Ages*, 47. For examples, see the tenth-century *Monastic Agreement of the Monks and Nuns of the English Nation* (Symons, tr., *Regularis Concordis*, xxxvi); and the comments on the monastery at Cluny in Constable, *Abbey of Cluny*, 67–70; 299–300.

31. On canons see Mollat, *Poor in the Middle Ages*, 89–92. On lay initiatives see pp. 93–95, along with Vauchez, *Laity in the Middle Ages*, 95–117, and Thompson, *Cities of God*, 70–77. I have already mentioned the Beguines in chapter 1 and will address the Hospitallars soon.

32. Mollat, *Poor in the Middle Ages*, 266.

33. Lindberg, *Beyond Charity*, loc. 73 of 3712. See also locs. 122, 436, 532, 622–700. See also Olasky, *Tragedy of American Compassion*.

included the development of simple and inexpensive remedies."[34] As with poverty relief, churches paved the way prior to the fourth century. Historian Andrew Crislip, making reference to a wide range of early Christian charitable services and places of care, states that "it is no surprise that Basil's hospital was understood as the continuation, if not the zenith, of the Christian charitable tradition."[35] The monastic institution itself was a community and a place where the securities of family were left behind. The monastic experience of common care and the Christian heritage of compassion served as the soil out of which the institution of the hospital emerged during Basil's famine of 369. The Basilias was only the start. Crislip recounts: "By the turn of the fifth century, the establishment of hospitals had become a common vocation of ecclesiastical and ascetic leaders, . . . by the fifth century the hospital was an accepted feature of the landscape of Late Antiquity."[36]

The structure of care for the sick was written into the monastic *Rules*. The *Rule of Benedict*, citing Matthew 25:36, gives explicit instructions regarding the procedures of sick care, assigning a "separate room" for their care.[37] It was only natural that this structure would be expanded to offer care to "externs" as well as members of the monastic community. Monastic hospitals were founded throughout medieval Europe. Distinct religious orders were established during the Crusades to care for sick. Women's houses dedicated themselves to care for the sick in a somewhat invisible hospital movement.[38] Mendicant orders, Beguines, and lay groups pioneered expressions during the late Middle Ages. As with poverty relief, a major transition from late medieval to early modern systems of health care occurred when "urban authorities began to bring under their jurisdiction those hospitals that were under the oversight of the bishop and cloisters."[39] Yet even in the modern period, religious orders

34. Lindberg, *Beyond Charity*, loc. 718 of 3712.

35. Crislip, *From Monastery to Hospital*, 108. See this book further for an account of the early development of medical care from monastic settings to what we know as hospitals.

36. Crislip, *From Monastery to Hospital*, 103.

37. Benedict, *RB 1980*, 36 (p. 235). See Kardong, *Benedict's Rule*, locs. 6556–6751 of 13811 for a commentary on chapter 36 and comparison with other early monastic Rules.

38. See Melville, *World of Medieval Monasticism*, 173–76; Berman, *Cistercian Evolution*, 232–33;

39. Lindberg, *Beyond Charity*, loc. 767 of 3712. See locs. 738–48. See also Watson, *On Hospitals*.

(and particularly women's apostolic orders) continued to found hospitals, which is why so many hospitals in our day have "Catholic" names.[40] To summarize in the words of historian Lowrie Daley, "the monasteries provided for many centuries almost the only organized type of medical care."[41] Out of the deep, prayerful environment of the monastery arises the wide-reaching care of hospitals.

It is only possible here to present a few portraits of the influence of monasticism in the world of education. The importance of education as a form of care is well known ("teach a person to fish and you feed them for life"). We have seen how the Basilias not only provided medical care, but also training in the trades. Basil also welcomed children into his monasteries, stressing the importance of education for these children.[42] In time monasteries, cathedrals, and parishes were all establishing schools. Higher education, however, was a special preserve of the monasteries, again filling in a gap after the collapse of Roman systems. Monastic education was unlike "secular" education however, in that it was oriented toward growth in Christian maturity. As medieval historian Jean Leclercq describes regarding the monastic approach to Scripture, "This application of grammar to Scripture has been practiced in monasticism in a way which is entirely its own because it is linked with the fundamental observances of monastic life. . . . In the monastery, the *lectio divina*, which begins with grammar, terminates with compunction, in desire of heaven."[43] Schools for conversion.

This monastic approach to learning passed from monastery to monastery and found a special home in the British Isles. Thus Thomas Cahill proclaims with perhaps a bit of an overstatement, "Without the Mission of the Irish Monks, who single-handedly refounded European civilization throughout the continent in the bays and valleys of their exile, the world that came after them would have been an entirely different one—a

40. See McNamara, *Sisters in Arms*, 622–25. For an interesting exploration of the interplay between state and religious orders, particularly in the modern period, see Wittberg, *Rise and Decline*, 97–100.

41. Daly, *Benedictine Monasticism*, 265.

42. See Silvas, *Ascetikon*, 199–204. For the welcome of children in the Benedictine Rule see, Benedict, *RB 1980*, 39 with the commentary in Kardong, *Benedict's Rule*, locs. 10530–10584 of 13811.

43. Leclercq, *Love of Learning*, 72.

world without books. And our own world would never have come to be."[44] Monasteries served as soil from which the university emerged. In the late medieval and early modern periods, the mendicant orders (Franciscans and Dominicans) and then the Jesuits pioneered forms of higher education. Still later an army of women joined "teaching congregations." Patricia Wittberg declares that "over 600 new religious communities were founded in Catholicism worldwide during the nineteenth century." and that "the vast majority—as high as 90 percent in some dioceses—were involved in teaching."[45] While monasteries were not the only venue for education in medieval culture, they offered a significant contribution to the ordering of the common life: a Ministry of Education.

Ministries of Health, Education, and Welfare: Care, when it reaches a certain scale, can become socio-politically significant, depending on the context within which the acts of care are exercised. Washing wounds, teaching Scripture, offering meals. These all seem like such mundane tasks. But as means of enriching others they can become vehicles of ordering common life. And that can get political. Negatively, communities of faith turn caring ministries into private fiefdoms: institutions that end up undermining God's own concerns for compassion, justice, and the like. History shows examples of "caring" institutions that have perhaps less consciously served to maintain an oppressive status quo or more consciously to advance self-serving ends at the expense of others. But, as we have seen, Christians can also pioneer the improvement of life for some who may not have opportunity. Space prohibits us talking about the role of monasticism in the arts, in agriculture, in the rise of womens' voices, and much more. What is clear is that monastic communities have expressed care in a variety of ways, from a variety of faith perspectives, and with a variety of church-government relationships. Some ancient monks were slaughtered by the government. Some medieval monasteries were political powerhouses. Modern religious communities have found ways to operate alongside national and local governments.

Monastic expressions of care can contribute much to the ordering of society. It did long ago and it still does today. I see today the same variety of care offered by new monastic groups and intentional Christian

44. Cahill, *How the Irish Saved*, 4. See also Hill, *What Has Christianity*, 87–88.
45. Wittberg, *Rise and Decline*, 39.

communities that I read about in medieval monastic history. Jubilee Partners, a rural community in Georgia, USA, welcomes refugees from all over the world. The L'Arche communities, which started in France in 1964 and then spread throughout the world, often care for people with intellectual disabilities. Rutba House (I mentioned this North Carolina, USA community in chapter 1) along with other kindred groups have sponsored "Schools for Conversion," and Jesuits still manage universities. I know many households that welcome neighbors for an open dinner on a regular basis.[46] Some expressions of care are small (buying groceries for an elderly neighbor who may not want to be exposed to COVID-19).[47] Others are much larger (would the Mennonite Central Committee qualify here?). Some offerings of care appear to have little socio-political impact. Others (remember the Beguines, or InnerCHANGE pancakes?) "fall into" more direct socio-political engagement. Still others, such as the Sisters of St. Joseph of Peace, see direct action *as* their expression of care. And of course, our opportunities for care and the socio-political engagement required will depend on our context. A ministry of welfare will look very different in France, in the United States, or in Chad.[48]

OFFERING CARING CARE

We have thus far gained a biblical/theological perspective of care, and have witnessed the historical/contemporary precedents of Christian care by communities or consecrated individuals. We have seen these expressions of care as means of ordering common life in different contexts, and therefore as appropriate forms of socio-political engagement, though periodically requiring more direct "governmental" activities (for example requiring permits to build hospitals). We are now in a place where we

46. To learn about Jubilee Partners, check out https://jubileepartners.org/. For John Howard Yoder on the value of founding institutions of care, see Yoder, *Discipleship as Political Responsibility*, 44.

47. By the way, on "neighboring" see Bretherton, *Christ and the Common Life*, 41–45.

48. For perspective see, for example, Weiss, "Origins of the French Welfare State"; Wuthnow, *Saving America?*; "The Future of Non-Governmental Organisations in the Humanitarian Sector—Global Transformations and Their Consequences," available at https://reliefweb.int/report/world/future-non-governmental-organisations-humanitarian-sector-global-transformations-and.

can explore the questions of how to do care well, or how our care can be really *caring*.

A few reminders might help us along the way. First—I keep saying this—politics is more than governmental action, more than merely "speaking out." I say this again here because we need to learn to think of "care" as a creative self-giving act of ordering our common life. We are the caretakers of the earth. We must see our response-ability as a freedom to creatively experiment with our socio-political realities. Again, think of Basil. Basil had resources, influence, and a crisis on his hands. But he also took the risk of exploring something new. I think we must do the same today. Global financial needs, difficulties getting resources to the right people, cooperative organization to help the people at the bottom take a first step. Bingo! Microloans; and microloan organizations.[49] How could we rethink the prison system today? Instead of thinking in terms of "punitive" justice, what about "restorative" justice, or even "transformative" justice?[50] Care as creative, socio-politically engaging, experimentation.

Second, community care emerges from community discernment. Remember the monastic practice in discernment last chapter? Consider, for example, the wonderful 2010 French movie *Of Gods and Men*.[51] A Cistercian monastic community in 1990s Algiers must decide whether to stay and care for their local friends or leave in the face of civil unrest. The film reflects the monastic rhythm of work, worship, and community life in the midst of increasing socio-political tensions. Key conversations around a table present the community's developing discernment process. Our journey of discernment into care often develops organically through prayerful observation, growing interest, personal service, formation of structure, and navigating tension.[52] Be willing to let the journey take its course.

This kind of discerning, creative use of resources—what I earlier called *difference*—reflects my positive view of "power." Power, in my view,

---

49. For a fascinating reflection connecting Basil with microlending, see Patitsas, "St. Basil's Philanthropic Program."

50. See for example, Zehr, *Little Book of Restorative Justice*; Dixon and Piepzna-Samarisinha, eds., *Beyond Survival*; Gilliard, *Rethinking Incarceration*.

51. Beauvois, dir., *Des Hommes et des Dieux*. This award-winning movie was inspired by a true story.

52. On this process see Howard, *Brazos Introduction*, 357–61. I think that Norman Wirzba suggests a similar process toward learning to care for creation. See Wirzba, *From Nature to Creation*.

is not just power *over*, but power *to*. I (or *we*) have the ability to influence some segment of a state of affairs for the enrichment of a group of people (or other beings). Yes, power corrupts, and our inattentive or self-interested relationships with structures of power can prove to be devastating. Nevertheless, when we pay attention to our ability to influence in the context of a humble Christlike love, we learn to offer ourselves (our own power) for the sake of the betterment of others. This is what I mean by "power *to*." By the way, do you see that this idea also reinforces the notion that politics is not just talking *against* things?

Monastic practice—Hospitality

Biblical hospitality is a rare and wonderful virtue, and a practice that characterizes authentic monastic life. We might think of monasteries as "private," but their value for hospitality made them havens for strangers. Recently there has been renewed interest in the practice of hospitality, an interest I support wholeheartedly.[53] Indeed, I think it might be nice to think of hospitality as a spiritual practice of care, a deeper way of reaching wide.[54] Whereas today we think of hospitality as the art of "entertaining" peers, biblical (and monastic) hospitality is a practice of welcoming strangers, those most in need of care. While some spiritual practices are performed alone (such as taking retreats) and others are performed together (such as worship singing), hospitality is performed partly alone and partly together. Let's explore hospitality in four parts symbolized by four steps of sharing a meal:[55]

1. Setting the Table

53. Resources for this section include Kärkkäinen, *Trinity and Revelation*, 310–39; Pohl, *Making Room*; Chittister, *Wisdom Distilled*, 121–32; Oden, ed., *And You Welcomed Me*; Pratt, *Radical Hospitality*; Bretherton, *Christ and the Common Life*, 258–88; Volf, *Exclusion and Embrace*. See also Butterfield, *Gospel Comes with a Housekey*. I have touched on hospitality in Howard, *Guide*, 159–61.

54. See Calhoun, *Spiritual Disciplines Handbook*, 138–40.

55. These steps are my own improvisation informed by Oden, ed., *And You Welcomed Me*, 145–214; Volf, *Exclusion and Embrace*, 140–47. Of course, the practice of hospitality is exercised in all kinds of settings: the hospitality of simple listening, the hospitality of offering a ride, the hospitality of giving someone a room for the night. There is also the—important—practice of what is called "reverse hospitality," when we welcome another by receiving what they have to offer. I offer what follows as a mere "taste" of the practice. Of course, connections between this illustration and the Christian practice of Eucharist are obvious.

We set the table. Our guest is not physically present yet, but is present in our minds as we place the plates and utensils that will be appropriate for the meal. We prepare our soul and our space to receive a guest. What are we serving and why? What do we have to offer and who are we who offers it? In what ways are we also strangers, aliens on this earth? When we set the table we try to think of the world from our guest's perspective. Would a white tablecloth communicate our appreciation, or would it alienate them, accentuating our differences and making them afraid to get anything dirty? Setting the table is a time to review our motives and to anticipate the meeting. Perhaps we will be "entertaining angels unaware" (see Heb 13:1–2). The transition between preparation and celebration is the moment we open the door. What might it mean for you to open the door, to wait while a stranger enters?

2. Serving the Food

The stranger-guest enters in to our space. Now host and guest are together. And we serve: restoring the guest by meeting an immediate need, the need for food. Other acts of hospitality used to include foot washing, clothing, offering prayer. What does another need and what do we have to offer now that they are here?

3. Sharing the Meal

Serving the food is the first part of sharing a meal. In sitting together, *sharing* the meal, we mutually offer our lives to each other. The simple offering of the time sitting together is itself an act of care. As we offer food, we receive from our guest, appreciating their stories, loving them just as they present themselves. This moment is a profound reframing of social relations. Decisions regarding passing the salt, clearing a plate, or moving to another room for tea and desert become fruits of the relationship, not expectations of status. It is a deep spiritual practice. It is OK if it feels awkward. Strangers feel awkward all the time. Serving the food is a moment of charity. Sharing the meal is a moment of solidarity.

4. Letting Go

It is rare when hospitality becomes a permanent arrangement. Most often the meal ends, the tea is finished, and it is time to return to something else. Hospitality avoids creating systems of dependence, but rather empowers another to move on, even if this empowerment is only a single meal and some friendly conversation. Once again we open the door, and opening a door to let someone go is just as meaningful as opening it to let someone in. Perhaps we send them off with a gift or a prayer or the name of someone to contact further on. Both the "host" and the "guest" are changed through the encounter. Notice what has transpired. As the first step moved from alone to together in anticipation, this last step moves from together to alone in gratitude. Make space for that moment of private gratitude. Let the presence of Christ given through the guest fill you who are the guest of Christ who meets your needs.

Now a few suggestions.

First, start with yourself. Michael Jackson's "Man in the Mirror" spoke to me at a time when I had made some big mistakes. It still speaks to me today. Remember Merton's quotation from Vinoba Bhave, "It is impossible to get rid of violence when one is oneself full of violence."[56] I have already mentioned the importance of humility and love in the previous chapter. In a more practical vein, Douglas and Jonathan Moo suggest that our steps into creation care may require us to reexamine our own standard of living.[57] As we shall see in the following chapter, the changes we make in ourselves *are* changes in society.

Second, match your care to the complexity of the human condition. Face it, there is no single "cause" of suffering. You are not going to end homelessness simply by starting drug treatment programs. Notice that Ignatio Ellacuría, in his presentation of the work of the University of Central America I described in the previous chapter, specifically mentions the need to "analyze causes." Scripture itself describes human suffering as influenced by a variety of factors.[58] We must acknowledge the interplay of personal, circumstantial, structural forces, and more. Then—in the context of this knowledge—we discern where and how we can offer care best.[59] Remember the question at the beginning of the chapter: "Should we be offering relief for those who suffer most or should we be changing the socio-political structures so people suffer less?" A

56. Merton, *Turning Toward the World*, 262. The theme of the need to address the problems of society within is pervasive in Merton's 1960–63 writings.

57. Moo and Moo, *Creation Care*, 177–79.

58. See for example, Boda and Baines, "Wisdom's Cry," and Friesen, "Injustice or God's Will." Friesen's work is based on a previous study. See Friesen, "Poverty in Pauline Studies," and the critique by John Barclay (Barclay, "Poverty: A Response").

59. For reflections on the definition(s) of "poverty" and the consequential implications of these definitions, see Bretherton, *Christ and the Common Life*, 60–65. For an overview of the various factors involved in offering care see Howard, *Brazos Introduction*, 364.

well-known "ambulance story" addresses this question, telling of a town near a mountainside. Periodically people driving on the mountain road fall over the edge. One family in the town decides to care by offering first aid. Another decides to pioneer an ambulance service. Another decides to build a guardrail. Still another petitions the town to redesign the road. Who offers care? All of them, each in their own way.

Another question we asked was "Is 'charity' always good? Does it really help people?" My third suggestion addresses this question: Think Christian solidarity, offer Christian charity.[60] As we have seen above, the Christian tradition encourages charity. Charity is best done, however, from a perspective of solidarity ("remember you were once aliens"). I will stereotype some differences for the sake of making a point:

- "Charity" tends to assume you are helping someone because they are incapable of helping themselves and need you to save them. "Solidarity" assumes you are helping someone because we all need to help each other as we are all interdependent.

- Charity is focused on one-sided giving, from the well-off to the helpless. Solidarity is focused on networks of mutual aid that support each other.

- Charity says, "Poor them, I'm so glad I will never be like that." Solidarity says, "It could be me." Or perhaps in the frequent care from one in need to another in need, "It *is* me!"

- Charity sees no responsibility to undo oppression in a context of privilege. Solidarity recognizes responsibility with privilege to rectify oppression often caused by the existence of that privilege.

People of privilege can offer care for the sake of those without and still express solidarity. We just approach this care as an act of solidarity, knowing (1) that with privilege comes responsibility, and (2) that the person we are helping deserves our help in part (personal, circumstantial, *structural* factors) due to histories of oppression which lead them to need help. In solidarity we offer care knowing that the goal is for other people to have access to the means necessary to care for themselves, but that often systems of government, economy, or the like operate such that some people have little or no access to means that are readily available to others.

60 Thanks to a conversation with Terese Howard for both ideas and wording here.

The steps from patronizing charity to charity-with-solidarity involve paying attention to ourselves, to others, to the time we have together, and to God. Charity can be *wide*. Solidarity requires *deep*. It is a practice of simple, monastic mindfulness. With attention we learn to recognize our sins of self-doubtful shrinking back from action, of overconfident complacency, of prejudice, of impatience.[61] It is a practice of noticing and appreciating the presence of God. Terrance Kardong comments on St. Benedict's instructions for the monastery "infirmarian": "The one who cares for the sick must be acutely aware of the presence of God."[62] When we truly appreciate the presence of Christ in those for whom we care (Matt 25:40), and we desire to come to know Christ in the other, we learn to shed expressions of care that communicate self-importance and we begin to see care—and even the exercise of power—as a divinely gifted system of mutuality. And when that happens, others notice. This is so important today, for today people do not care what we know until they know that we care.

Movement toward charity-with-solidarity also requires some education. At times, people have relocated to areas of need in order to offer care, an expression of what was called "incarnational ministry." Good intentions. Sacrificial giving. Others move into the same neighborhood. When does compassionate incarnation become harmful gentrification? When does generosity become bureaucracy? Offering care that is truly caring often depends on our concrete knowledge of the history, the conditions, and the heart of a neighborhood and a people.[63] Through prayerful, humble, discerning attention the Spirit of God can begin to transform our socio-political care from the development of structures of "beneficence" to structures of "blessing."[64]

Those who go deep in love for God also find themselves going wide in love for neighbor. Care is important both theologically and practically in our society today. Monasteries have pioneered important expressions

---

61. For a further development of these "sins" and more see O'Donovan, *Finding and Seeking*.

62. Kardong, *Benedict's Rule*, loc. 6636 of 13811.

63. Compare Lupton, *Toxic Charity*; Bryan Stevenson's presentation on "The Power of Proximity" at https://www.youtube.com/watch?v=1RyAwZIH04Y; Corbett and Finkkert, *When Helping Hurts*; and Wuthnow, *Saving America?* Also of interest is Patitsas, "St. Basil's Philanthropic Program." For reflections on caring care within the helping professions, see Phillips and Benner, eds., *Crisis of Care*.

64. On orders of beneficence and blessing see Bretherton, *Christ and the Common Life*, 70–79.

of care in the past, expressions that became woven into the socio-political fabric of their time (for better and for worse). I think that new monastic groups and intentional Christian communities have a unique opportunity to pioneer fresh expressions of care today. They may or may not become politically significant. What matters is offering caring care. I remember visiting Coptic monasteries in Egypt a few years ago. Something I noticed was how the monasteries employed nearby (Muslim) peasants, and how well they were treated. Was this politically significant? Not yet, but if tensions escalated . . .

Yet—you have probably observed—we have been dancing around one question throughout this chapter and are still left with it. How do we divide care? What are the works of the people of God and what are the works of various government agencies? What is the relationship between the two? This is the question of "Christ and culture" or "the church and the world" and we will be exploring that question further in the chapters to follow.

FIVE

We Model a Good Society

SOMETIMES WE CHOOSE TO speak. Sometimes we choose to care. Sometimes we choose to live a different life and others notice. I call the latter *modeling a good society*. Some people are less comfortable with this word "model" and might prefer "witness," "exhibit," "embody," or something else. I will stick with the term "model" because I want to emphasize how we—for example, in the engineering and organization fields—create "models" that attract attention and are then developed into more sustainable realities. Our practice as individuals and communities "model" life possibilities: they express creative designs that attract attention and draw others into developing these designs such that over time they became viable options for many. Remember Vincent Harding's account of those who "entered the river" of the struggle for Black freedom? He specifically includes secessionist movements and fugitives who formed alternative communities hidden from the authorities.[1] Some of the secessionist dreams were consciously designed with hope that a wider society would take notice and realize that Black freedom could be life giving for all. Some alternative communities were hidden from the authorities but known to other freedom strugglers. Folks knew that "outlyer communities" were an option. Still others just chose to live differently. It was what they had to do. That's the way it is with "modeling." Sometimes our impulse to model a new way of life is intentional: we want the world to see and perhaps try it out. Often we just live and others notice. The fact that people notice or might want to imitate our life ends up more as a

1. For fugitive movements, see Harding, *There Is a River,* 30, 39, 48, 111–12, 196. For secessionist movements see 45, 67–68, 137.

94

by-product. But from the perspective of the people looking at our life and "trying it on," it is modeling either way.

In one sense we are always modeling, whether we intend to or not (for better and for worse). We live the gospel in the sight of a watching world. And the fact of the matter is, what we model *does* have socio-political implications. When we are at our worst, our way of life may demonstrate a contented complicity in oppressive socio-political arrangements, or an anxious trust in political tactics for change, or perhaps a hopeless abandonment of society as a whole. Monasteries have, at times, been guilty of all of these. When we are at our best, however, the forms of life through which we respond to God in our midst display that another way is possible.

In our previous chapter on care, my first practical suggestion was to start with yourself. Believe me, the changes we make in ourselves *are* changes in society. When I teach pastors in seminary I plead with them: Who you are is the most important thing you can give to your congregations. When I address churches and communities I say: Who you are is the most important thing you can give the world. The deep is our gift to the wide.

JESUS'S FOLLOWERS AS AN ALTERNATIVE CULTURE

Consider Jesus and his followers. What were they about? How do we make sense of those three years of Jesus's ministry on earth? Scholars have struggled to summarize Jesus's earthly ministry through their "quests" for the historical Jesus. More recently, proposals have been offered that emphasize similarities between the Jesus movement and one or another of the socio-political-religious factions of his day: rabbis, zealots, Essenes, peasants, and so on.[2] When I speak of "socio-political-religious factions"

2. For surveys of historical Jesus studies see, for example, Beilby and Eddy, eds., *Historical Jesus*; or for a more comprehensive treatment see Holmén and Porter, eds., *Handbook*. I explored the socio-political backgrounds of the Gospels in two unpublished papers I wrote in the early 1980s ("An Economic, Literary, and Theological Look at the Rich Young Ruler," and "New Testament Studies in the Sociologist's Den: A Review of Recent Hermeneutical Trends") and will not rehearse the bibliography that informed those explorations. For my treatment here I have consulted works by a few of the key contributors to the most recent quest (John Dominic Crossan, John P. Meier, N. T. Wright, James Dunn, Luke Timothy Johnson). In addition to these Yoder, *Politics of Jesus*; Horsley, *Bandits*; Horsley, "Jesus-in-Context"; and Brueggemann, *Money and Possessions*, 185–204, have been helpful for considering Jesus in his

I refer to what many scholars identify as "Jewish sects." In their time, they were more than schools of religious belief. Just as "Moral Majority" or "Christian anarchist" identify socio-political-religious self-identities, so also groups of "Jews" at the time of Jesus (under Roman rule) understood themselves through a blending of theological, social, and political categories. I aim to suggest in what follows that Jesus and his followers also lived and expressed a blended identity and hoped that others would follow them in this self-identity.[3]

Jesus was a Jew. What I mean by this is that Jesus perceived himself (and promoted a movement that saw itself) in continuity with the big story of the Mosaic people, a story where at least one function of their life and mission as a people was to embody the values of God as an influence for the world, a "light to the nations" (see Isa 42:6; 49:6).[4] Gerhard Lohfink calls this the "social dimension" of God's work: a work not just for the individual, the invisible, or "the world" in general, but the salvific creation of a new people who embody the heart and life of God.[5] By the time of Jesus, different factions interpreted their fulfillment of this mission in different ways vis-à-vis their context under the Roman Empire. Some saw Roman rule as providing security and permission to serve God in their land. They thought perhaps a righteous people could live (or would have to live) within the empire framework. Others perceived the compromises as unacceptable. Some established semi-isolated alternative communities. Still others fomented rebellions. All of them interpreted God's activity within the trajectory of their own religious-socio-political movements.[6]

---

socio-political-religious environment.

3. I will not try to sort through sources (whether oral, pre-canonical, or extra-canonical) to retrieve some "real" or "historical" Jesus." I only share my own perception of the Jesus movement as presented in the canonical texts. I have tried to stay true to broadly recognized features of Jesus's life and ministry.

4. For a sense of the nation of Israel as an intended embodiment of the politics of God, see Brueggemann, *Theology of the Old Testament*; and Wright, *Mission of God*. For Jesus as fulfillment of these ideals see Walter Rauschenbusch's understanding of the "kingdom of God" in his *Theology for the Social Gospel*; the works of N. T. Wright; and O'Donovan, *Resurrection and Moral Order*.

5. See for example Lohfink, *Jesus and Community*, 165 and elsewhere in this work, and Lohfink, *Does God Need the Church?*

6. On the relationship between "Jewish apocalyptic" and "Jewish sects" see for example Richard Horsley's treatment of popular movements in *Bandits* and Meier, *Marginal Jew: Mentor*; Meier, *Marginal Jew: Companions and Competitors*.

. Jesus entered this scene proclaiming that "the kingdom of God is at hand" (or "has come near," Mark 1:15—notice the socio-political language: *kingdom*). What is this "kingdom" and in what ways is it "at hand"? I think insight can be found if we examine not only Jesus's teachings, but also the life he and his followers led. The Gospels portray Jesus as consciously re-establishing the people of God through his followers. Twelve tribes of Israel, twelve disciples. This fact—that Jesus founded a movement—itself had socio-political implications. Both those who applauded him and those who crucified him interpreted his movement as politically significant. Were they all mistaken, only to discover later that Jesus really promoted a "spiritual" kingdom, having no interest in politics (see John 18:36)? Let's examine a few elements of the life of Jesus and his followers.

Consider, for example, Jesus's approach to money and possessions. He often calls those he invites to "leave all and follow." His band of disciples confirms that they have done just that (Luke 18:28). They appear to have shared their meager livelihood in common (John 13:29). Jesus repeatedly warns of the dangers of "mammon." John Dominic Crossan calls the economy Jesus lived and encouraged a "*communal* program," a "*share* community from the bottom up as a positive alternative to Antipas's Roman *greed* community established from the top down."[7] Walter Brueggemann speaks of this aspect of the Jesus movement as the "performance of an alternative economy."[8] This sounds like a visible exhibition of the value of holiness (distinction from the world) that I mentioned in chapter 3.

Or consider Jesus's attention to outcasts. N. T. Wright proclaims wryly, "There is a more or less universal consensus among scholars— something as rare as snow in midsummer . . .—that Jesus offered welcome to, and shared meals with 'sinners.'"[9] Darrell Bock states further, "His association with people regarded as the fringe of society, as unclean or as likely reprobates was something that created both reaction against him and interest in him."[10] Bock mentions tax collectors, lepers, and the poor, but one could also speak about his treatment of women, Samaritans, Roman centurions, "zealots," and the demon-possessed. Jesus offered welcome to the least and he encouraged his followers to do the

7. Crossan, "Jesus and the Challenge," loc. 1797 out of 6531.

8. Brueggemann, *Money and Possessions*, 185. See also Wright, *Jesus and the Victory*, 403–5.

9. Wright, *Jesus and the Victory*, 264.

10. Bock, "Historical Jesus," loc. 3745 out of 6531.

same (Luke 14:13–14; Matt 25:31–46). Here we find a visible expression of the value of compassion mentioned earlier.

Finally, consider Jesus's approach to power. On the one hand, Jesus had lots of power: healing leprosy, raising the dead, calming storms. He also had social power. He could gather a crowd and he knew it. He could have been the political savior his admirers wanted and his opponents feared. But he chose—and advocated—another way. Mind you, he was tempted to place himself on the pinnacle of the temple and "take power" as the world takes power.[11] But he chose the way of collaborative power, using his own abilities to care for those who suffered and to equip and release others into ministry (Luke 10:1–12). Jesus castigates the use of authority by those who surrounded him and encouraged his disciples to follow his example in living another way (Matt 20:20–28). I perceive here (see also Luke 11:42) a visible step toward modeling a society of justice.

Though he could have, Jesus did not organize an armed rebellion. Nor did he form an isolated community like the Essenes. Through his earthly career, Jesus uniquely reframed some of the basic elements of personal and socio-political identity: family, finances, authority, membership, virtue, and more. John Howard Yoder summarizes this aspect of Jesus's ministry well:

> Jesus was not just a moralist whose teaching had some political implications; he was not primarily a teacher of spirituality whose public ministry unfortunately was seen in a political light; he was not just a sacrificial lamb preparing for his immolation, . . . Jesus was, in his divinely mandated (i.e. promised, anointed, messianic) prophethood, priesthood, and kingship, the bearer of a new possibility of human, social, and therefore political relationships.[12]

Jesus modeled a new way: by his own life, and the life he encouraged others to live. Furthermore, the vision of an ordered common life that Jesus taught and exhibited (shall we say the "politics" of Jesus?) was understood

---

11. Yoder provides interesting reflections on Jesus's temptations in Yoder, *Discipleship as Political Responsibility*, 54–56 and Yoder, *Politics of Jesus*, 30–34. See also Douglass, *Resistance and Contemplation*, 71–77.

12. Yoder, *Politics of Jesus*, 62–63. Pay careful attention to the word "just." We are here exploring a single aspect of Jesus's life and ministry. I have summarized the broader range of Jesus's work in Howard, *Brazos Introduction*, 181–89.

in his own time as an alternative to the familiar socio-political options of his surroundings—so much so that in the end he was put to death for it.[13]

THE CHURCH AS A MODEL OF GOOD SOCIETY

The book of Acts begins with an account of a unique ordering of society. The Holy Spirit descends and those affected find themselves living a transformed life: "All who believed were together and had all things in common; they would sell their possessions and goods and distribute the proceeds to all, as any had need" (Acts 2:44). This account not only describes a fulfillment of the Jubilee laws in Leviticus 25, but more. J. Schattenmann, after describing utopian descriptions of "fellowship" (*koinonia*) in ancient classical and Jewish literature, writes of this passage authored by Luke likely to a Gentile of rank, that "the educated reader would have got the impression that here the Greek ideal of society had been realized."[14]

I see the account in Acts as the record of an ideal achieved through the work of the Spirit. The renunciation that the rich young ruler was unable to complete (Luke 18:18–30) and stepping toward which Zacchaeus was declared "saved" (Luke 19:1–10), the renunciation into which Jesus urges his "disciples" (Luke 12:33–34), this Luke describes twice in Acts in language that unmistakably declares the inauguration of a new society through the ministry of the Spirit of Christ. Though we do not find evidence of a consistent mandate or practice of this comprehensive sharing of possessions, we do find in Acts 2 a model of the kind of generosity encouraged throughout Acts and the Epistles.

It is striking to see in Acts and the Epistles—reflecting the spread of Christianity over a wide range of populaces and geography—the degree of consistency that the church of Christ kept to the life Jesus modeled. Jesus challenged the common understanding of family (Mark 3:31–35). The early church referred to one another as sister and brother.[15] Jesus chose the way of collaborative power, a pattern the church followed even

13. I recognize the multiple concerns shaping the opposition to Jesus: blasphemy, treason, sectarian revolt, and more. Nevertheless, the sign over Jesus's cross remains, "This is Jesus, king of the Jews."

14. Schattenmann, "*Koinonia,*" 642. For more on the book of Acts, see Jennings, *Acts.*

15. On Jesus see Wright, *Jesus and the Victory,* 398–403. On the church and family see Clapp, *Families at the Crossroads;* Lohfink, *Jesus and Community,* 106–8.

in difficult decisions (see Acts 15:1–29).[16] Jesus encouraged his followers to welcome the stranger. The church opened doors to both Jew and
Gentile, and we find in James the affirmation that "religion that is pure
and undefiled before God, the Father, is this: to care for orphans and widows in their distress" (Jas 1:27).[17] Following the lead of Jesus, the church
became the salt of the earth, the light of the world, a royal priesthood, a
fragrance of something more. Following the model of Jesus, the church
itself became a model of good society, a contrast-society, a "sacramental
community," that "should signify in its own internal structure the salvation whose fulfillment it announces."[18] It is perhaps in this sense that the
church's first mission is to *be* the church.[19]

The church developed as a counterculture in a context of minority
status. It was misunderstood and mistreated by Jews and Romans alike.
Though the life of the church itself confronted the socio-political realities
of its surrounding cultures, it had no realistic opportunity to influence
governmental policies or social practices. What it could do was to care
for widows and orphans and "to keep itself unstained from the world,"
an ideal it struggled to realize from the start.[20] Yet in time the Christian
church gained increasing recognition and voice in the socio-political
arena. Perhaps it is fair to speak of some kind of "Constantinian shift,"
both within the church and with regard to church-state relations, if by
this we mean a transition especially during the fourth and fifth centuries
in which (1) Christianity moved from minority to majority status, and
(2) the elements of church life itself (doctrines, texts, buildings, authorities, community structures) acquired a greater measure of formalized

16. Wayne Grudem draws attention to this passage as an example of the value of
"separation of powers" (Grudem, *Politics According to the Bible*, 102). More generally,
see Lohfink, *Jesus and Community*, 115–122. Both Gerhard Lohfink (*Jesus and
Community*, 121) and John Howard Yoder (*Christian Witness*, 17) speak of the distinct
practice of the church with regard to legal proceedings.

17. See Barclay, *Paul and the Gift*, 510–11.

18. Gutiérrez, *Theology of Liberation*, 147. On the church as a contrast-society see
Lohfink, *Jesus and Community*, 122–32. In his later work Lohfink uses the language of
"new society" (see Lohfink, *Does God Need the Church?*, 150–53).

19. Stanley Hauerwas communicates this notion often (*Vision and Virtue*, 211,
240; *Hauerwas Reader*, 149, 374; *Community of Character*, 85). See also Hauerwas and
Willimon, *Resident Aliens*, 38; Yoder, *Politics of Jesus*, 153; Dreher, *Benedict Option*,
101. Note the word "first," not "only." See also Alexander, *Being Church*.

20. I do not believe in some kind of "primitive purity" of the early church (see Acts
5–6 for starters).

synthesis.[21] Greater freedom and structure enabled the church to pioneer new ways of modeling good society (like founding hospitals) and thus to explore the fulfillment of its missional vocation.[22] In addition it made "keeping oneself unstained from the world" challenging in new ways. It was also during this transition between ancient and medieval that monastic forms of life began to be more clearly identified.

ON FORMS OF LIFE

"Forms of life." I have used this phrase occasionally since the first chapter. There, when defining monasticism, I mentioned that nuns and monks usually "live according to a clearly defined form of life." Just what is a "form of life" and what significance does it have for monasticism(s) and socio-political engagement?[23]

Seventy or eighty years ago most white, middle-class folk in the United States of America lived in the context of two-parent families, a single full-time occupation, dwelling in the same general vicinity for a length of time. Whether you lived in the city or the country, this was the dominant shape or *form* of "modern" life—securing a family, a job, and a location.

But it wasn't the only form of life people lived. Some joined the military, whose patterns of sleeping, eating, and more were all subject to their own form of life as soldiers. Some people were migrant farm workers,

21. On the "Constantinian shift" see Yoder, *Priestly Kingdom*, 135–47; Leithart, *Defending Constantine*; and Roth, ed., *Constantine Revisited*.

22. On the missional vocation of the church see Kärkkäinen, *Hope and Community*, 366–476.

23. Some have mentioned that the word "form" is difficult to grasp. Others have suggested "manner" or "rhythm." I retain the term "form" because of its close connections with monastic history and with philosophy. My thoughts on forms of life have been developing in dialogue with a variety of sources. Historically, Charles Taylor's treatment of the models of warrior, philosopher, and such in his *Sources of the Self* suggests not merely intellectual but embodied goods. The Roman orator Cicero speaks of the best "form of life" involving a combination of contemplation and action. Philosopher Ludwig Wittgenstein has spoken of "forms of life" as establishing grounds from which patterns of language emerge. Sociologically, Pierre Bourdieu's notion of *habitus* and Michel de Certeau's discussion of the "practice" of everyday life also point in this direction. Kees Waaijmann discusses "forms of spirituality": family, schools, and countermovements. For forms of life and monasticism more specifically, see for example Lawrence, *Medieval Monasticism*; Melville, *World of Medieval Monasticism*; and Agamben, *Highest Poverty*.

living in towns or cities part of the year and traveling the harvests through the rest of the year, sleeping in labor camps and sharing life together as a community of workers. There were also some who chose what they considered to be a *religious* form of life: Amish families, sharing cooperatively as rural farming communities; celibate nuns taking vows of poverty and praying in convents; or missionaries who left the country to share Christ in the context of unfamiliar cultures. And every once in a while you could find others who pushed the boundaries of the normal forms of life: they were called "beatniks" back then. But they were rare.

So what is a form of life? In every culture and in every period of history, society is set up with a finite collection of ways of living that most everybody understands. Human beings live within generally expected *ensembles* of practices, sentiments, relationships, values that are held somewhat in common and provide a sense of identity for those who share them. I was a migrant farm worker myself for two summers and I learned something of how to store your possessions under a bunk bed in barracks with a group of strangers. I learned about the kinds of relationships that will help you get promoted to a desired position, or who might protect you when you needed it. Housing arrangements, relationship structures, patterns of employment, even the feeling all share at the end of the day's work: when all this is put together in a single whole then we can begin to understand a "form of life." The term "life" speaks of something fluid and vibrant: ever changing, becoming something. The term "form" speaks of something rigid and structured. That is the ironic tension about forms of life. Form can provide a safe haven or an experimental region within which we thrive and grow and develop influence. But forms can also squash life into shallow con-*form*-ity.

What I am trying to get at here with this notion of "forms of life" is: (1) that we seem to order the basic elements of our lives in somewhat recognizable patterns or shapes, (2) that we do so in dialogue with the various possibilities and limitations that surround us, (3) such that novel ways of living are called "alternative" communities or "countercultures," (4) that our own ordering exhibits ("models," consciously or unconsciously) forms of life for others, and (5) that depending on the situation, the way that one or another group orders a form of life may have political significance.

Monastic Forms of Life as Socio-Political Models

Biblical scholar and communitarian Gerhard Lohfink suggested that
the "Constantinian shift" (he calls it the "Constantinian Turn") could be
dated more precisely: specifically with the publishing of Augustine's *City
of God* (written 410–426). In Lohfink's reading of *City of God*, "It is hard
to see how this church could become a contrast-society in the world; the
church is hardly recognizable in its already experienced salvation."[24] Lohfink sees, in Augustine's portrait of the church as a mixture of sin and
salvation, a diminishment of the Christian ideal of the body of Christ as
a model society. I currently, following the lead of other scholars, would
interpret Augustine differently on this point. Augustine was significantly
inspired to become a Christian after hearing of the model virtues of
Egyptian monks. In his "The Ways of the Catholic Church" he affirms
this role of monks as examples. Indeed, historian Robert Markus states of
Augustine's perspective, noting how Augustine writes of the monastery
in the same terms as he speaks of the City of God:

> The monastic life displays, in a special way, the Church's calling
> to be the perfect community which can be realized only in the
> City of God *qualis tunc erit*, beyond history. It is a privileged an-
> ticipation of the Church's eschatological realisation. The Church
> could be no alternative society in which men could take refuge
> from the dislocated and tension-torn society in which it was,
> always and inevitably, placed; but the monastery was called to
> be a visible anticipation, a showing forth here and now, of the
> shape of the society that would be embodied in the Church in its
> final state, no longer the "mixed body" (*corpus permixtum*) but
> purified on God's threshing floor.[25]

Augustine actually *did* understand the City of God as potentially realiz-
able: at least to a greater measure by those who had the freedom. And this
brings us to an account of monasticism and monastic modeling.

What I have not yet said, in my treatment of Jesus and the early
church, is that we find in the record of Scripture multiple forms of life
represented and encouraged. Jesus invited the rich man to sell all and
follow, whereas he encouraged the Gerasene demoniac to go home (Mark

24. Lohfink, *Jesus and Community*, 184. See also Alan Kreider's treatment of
changes in the Patristic views of conversion in Kreider, *Change of Conversion*.

25. Markus, *End of Ancient Christianity*, 79–80. For Augustine on monasticism
more generally see Zumkeller, *Augustine's Ideal*.

10:21; 5:19). To those he sends on mission, Jesus gives specific instructions regarding message and life habits, instructions which we know are not meant for all of those who would follow Jesus (Matt 10:1–15). While Jesus assumes that most people will remain married, Jesus recognizes that some will desire the life of a eunuch (Matt 19:12). Similarly within the record of the New Testament church we find counsel—not command—toward celibacy (1 Cor 7:25–26) and encouragement—not compulsion—of sacrificial giving to meet others' needs (2 Cor 9:7). These were patterns of living that were not expected of the entire church. It appears that the Spirit invites people to embody the heart of Christianity through different forms of life. Some will glorify God in the commonly recognized form of employment, marriage, and service to congregation and culture. Others will (like Jesus himself) abandon family, employment and possessions, freeing themselves up to serve the glory of God through a consecrated life. Still others, I contend, find a vocation somewhere in between.[26] The point here is that the monastic or "religious" life (or to some extent, a semireligious life) offers unique, undistracted opportunities to experiment with models of Christian life and service. Let's examine a few.

First, we turn again to Benedict of Nurcia, and what the Benedictines accomplished by their model of stability. Though not entirely novel, a distinctive element of the Benedictine form of life was their commitment to remain in a given monastery for life.[27] Members did not leave to get married. They did not follow the most attractive employment option. They carved out a life together for a long time. A grounding in stability of community and place enabled Benedictine monasteries to become centers that locals turned to in need, in friendship, or in appreciation. Their commitment encouraged them to learn righteousness and justice among themselves, how to work through conflict and remain in a healthy community. Needless to say, the Benedictine form of life spread throughout Europe and inspired many other monastic expressions. At its best, the Benedictine form of life models a communal continuity that fosters a depth that frees members up for width. It is interesting to note that both

26. I have addressed the question of "secular" and "religious" vocations (along with the question of the possibility of "perfection" by some) at greater length in Howard, "What Does God Expect?" In future work I hope to further explore these questions of conversion, forms of life, and the nature of specifically "religious" life.

27. See Benedict, *RB 1980*, 58.9. Commentary on "stability" can be found in Benedict, *RB 1980*, 463–65; Kardong, *Benedict's Rule*, locs. 10121, 10188 out of 13811.

Jonathan Wilson-Hartgrove and Rod Dreher lift up Benedictine stability as a virtue for new monastics today.[28]

To give another sense of how the vision of holy order can spread through modeling, I recount the development of one of the "children" of the Benedictine Order, the Cistercians. One of the features of this twelfth-century monastic renewal movement was a wave of adult conversions, the most notable of which was the conversion of Bernard of la Fontaine (known as St. Bernard of Clairvaux). These adult converts gave themselves to an austere life of work, prayer, and reflection on Scripture. To use a contemporary phrase, the Cistercian model "went viral." Historian Constance Berman writes:

> Some of these adult converts would retire with their entire families to newly created religious centers whose cores were syneisactic (literally communities of men and women living together under the same roof). These family monasteries often eventually gave birth to twin reform communities, one for men and one for women. Sometimes both were eventually affiliated with the Cistercians.[29]

The socio-political impact of this kind of experiment is simply the demonstration that another way, another form of life, is possible. Though precise historical connections are impossible to draw, it seems reasonable that these kinds of experiments in the twelfth century helped make room for Third Order communities in the thirteenth century, which then became precursors for Protestant and Anabaptist experiments in more recent centuries.[30] Models give birth to further models. A cloud of witnesses.

Finally, I want to point once again to Francis of Assisi. It is likely that in developing the form of life of his community, Francis was intentionally exploring an alternative economic model. Francis did not take over his father's business. Neither did he join one of the monasteries in Assisi. Nor did Francis choose to invest himself in the local religious societies. Rather, in the midst of the major economic transition to a profit economy in the thirteenth century, Francis chose to follow Jesus's own example. Inspired by the very Gospel passages Jesus used to instruct those he sent

28. Wilson-Hartgrove, *Reconstructing the Gospel*, locs. 2082–2113 out of 2983; Dreher, *Benedict Option*, 65–67. See also Chittister, *Wisdom Distilled*, 147–59; and Stock, "Stability."

29. Berman, *Cistercian Evolution*, 101–02.

30. See for example, Arnold, "Early Anabaptists Part I."

(Matt 10:9–10; Mark 6:9; Luke 9:3 and 10:4), Francis established a community of traveling ministers. He discouraged his brothers from financial or supervisory offices, desiring them to be "lesser" and "subject to all." Francis encouraged his brothers to work at a trade, receiving what they needed "excepting money." When necessary "they may seek alms," yet they must "always strive to exert themselves in doing good works."[31] Franciscan historian David Flood writes,

> With *subditi* [the term "subject" to all] the brothers imagined a new way of working. They excluded serfdom and management, seeing as neither accorded with their larger purposes. They looked like wage earners, in a way, or as day laborers, but that was a surface resemblance. They refused the social implications of wages because they defined their work differently. . . . In sum, Francis and his friends gave work a new definition, and unless we take that into account, we are not going to get very far into their history. . . . They were seeing to their sustenance in a way that held promise for others and for a transformed society as well.[32]

The early Franciscans modeled an alternative form of economy. They saw that another way—perhaps a more just or compassionate way—was possible and they wanted to demonstrate this to others. Needless to say, the Franciscans have been one of the most influential religious communities in history.

Stable Benedictines. Renegade Cistercians. Courageous Franciscans. I could go on to recount the lives of the early Amish, the Daughters of Charity, and many more. Yes, stable Benedictines can become oppressive landlords. Yes, wandering Franciscans can become deadbeats. Yet at their best communities and individuals follow divine initiative by choosing distinct forms of life in conscious dialogue with their settings with an aim to embody the values of Christ. Each expresses part of the fullness of Christ (often called a "charism") and each has its own unique impact on the socio-political world. Such is the way of monastic modeling.

---

31. "Earlier Rule." In *Francis and Clare: Early Documents,* FA:ED, 1.68–69.

32. Flood, "Franciscans at Work," 32–33. See also Flood, *Daily Labor,* and Howard, "Who Should be Poor?"

MODELING AS SOCIO-POLITICAL ENGAGEMENT: HOW IT WORKS

Actually, that is our question: just what is the "way" of monastic modeling? Just how does this modeling thing work, especially as some form of *socio-political engagement*?

Many activists these days would simply say, "Oh, what you're talking about is *prefigurative politics*." By this phrase activists indicate some kind of behavior that looks like or anticipates the social structure ultimately desired.[33] This might mean that our protest against racial oppression would be organized with leading contributions by people of color. It might mean that we hold our conference on environmental sustainability in a "green" building. It may mean that we utilize nonhierarchical means of decision-making. It may also mean that the people in our economy-rethinking collective choose (when possible) to work in cooperatively owned businesses. While the phrase has received attention recently within Western "radical" political circles, similar practices have been employed by feminist movements and liberation activists from India. Prefigurative political concepts have also been employed by Christian dissidents for centuries.

The notion of "prefigurative" points to a continuity between goal and practice, ends and means, future and present. Some activists argue that a focus on prefigurative strategies (how we live, decide . . .) creates an insular politics, more concerned about the activists than the cause. Raekstad and Gradin reply that prefiguration is simply "part of a strategic ecosystem that includes a whole host of other tools for achieving the kind of social change a group is after."[34] They contrast "vanguardist" approaches with "prefigurative" approaches. While vanguardist approaches tend to focus on nuanced laws or elite activists, prefigurative approaches extend to everyday behaviors for they insist (similar to the understanding of politics as "ordering" that I have been advocating throughout this book) "that we need to pay attention to our own social relations and behaviours."[35] My conviction is that this is precisely what we are

33. The term was coined in 1977 by Carl Boggs (Boggs, "Marxism, prefigurative communism"; Boggs, "Revolutionary Process"); and developed further by Breines, *Community and Organization*. For more recent discussion see Gordon, "Prefigurative politics"; Raekstad and Gradin, *Prefigurative Politics*.

34. Raekstad and Gradin, *Prefigurative Politics*, 143.

35. Raekstad and Gradin, *Prefigurative Politics*, 143.

doing through monastic socio-political modeling. We are living and demonstrating the eschatological community of the King (I am aware of the irony here) in the present for the sake of the future.

The power of a model depends to some degree on its visibility. Antony of the desert was only a model during his own lifetime insofar as people heard of him by word of mouth. But after Athanasius published a biography of Antony, readers could "see" the form of life in writing and Antony—along with the form of monasticism that he influenced—became a model throughout Christendom. John Howard Yoder, an Anabaptist historian keenly aware of the political implications of obedience to religious beliefs (many early Anabaptists were martyred by political authorities for their practice of adult baptism) writes regarding the Christian church that its emphasis on transcendence "can become concretely effective within the civil community only if represented by a discrete empirical community, . . . a visible body of people who are able to escape conformity to the world while continuing to function in the midst of the world."[36] The visibility of models varies: figures or movements from history provide models at a distance, while our own informal relationships provide models close at hand. Each have their own contributions and challenges.[37]

An effective model is also relevant. People need to understand how a form of life "fits" and why it is worth living. Luke Bretherton, for example, speaks of "alternative political imaginaries," mental constructions of socio-political life that may, in certain situations, be able to make sense of different ways of doing politics.[38] Yoder describes Christian practices (such as binding and loosing, breaking bread, and baptism) as "paradigms." For example, "binding and loosing [involving community accountability and co-discernment] can provide models for conflict resolution, alternatives to litigation, and alternative perspectives on 'corrections.'"[39] Sociologist of culture Ann Swidler speaks of how people

36. Yoder, *Priestly Kingdom*, 188. See also his notion of the church "casting light" beyond the borders of the church in Yoder, *Christian Witness*, 18.

37. I have discussed the modeling functions of informal relationships and history in Howard, *Brazos Introduction*, 51–60.

38. Bretherton, *Christ and the Common Life*, 361–62 and throughout that chapter.

39. Yoder, *Body Politics*, 77. This entire book presents a set of practices which Yoder feels are political models. Yoder also in *Christian Witness*, 17–20 speaks of the value of the church's witness (with regard to things like egalitarianism, use of power, compassionate service, or the refusal to cooperate with the state on certain matters) as "stimuli to the conscience of society."

"depend on explicit cultural models to learn ways of organizing selves, relationships, patterns of cooperation and authority, and other capacities for individual and group life."[40]

Consider, for example, three of the great political struggles of every age. Societies struggle with wealth and poverty. Societies struggle with marriage, family, and sexuality. Societies also struggle with issues of power. I think, for example, of our contemporary discussions concerning class, patriarchy, and race. Monastic traditions have sought to address these by means of fundamental commitments (called "vows"). Many nuns, friars, and such, upon entering, make commitments to live lives of "poverty," "chastity," and "obedience." Wow. Money, sex, power—poverty, chastity, obedience. Some new semi-monastic communities today make similar commitments to simplicity, fidelity, and humility. This is relevant alternative living.

Finally, a model is possible. If it cannot be realistically realized, people simply won't try it. The possibility of a better way was precisely what Booker T. Washington's well-known notion of "racial uplift" tried to communicate. Some models will make more sense for some people in some situations than others. We can wish that our own model of Christian social change would be considered not only possible but attractive by many, but often it seems to be a matter of certain models at certain times, under certain conditions.[41] I will go further. One of the functions of a good model is not only that it is possible but that it provides *hope*. I will speak more of this below.

Models work by being visible, relevant, and possible. How they ultimately trigger the life of an individual or group, however, is a mystery. Yoder speaks of a "moral osmosis" through which Christian witness makes its impact.[42] I think individuals or groups often "try on" a model of life and sometimes it just sticks. One may even make a commitment to live out a few, or even one aspect of the Christian faith. And then that one aspect seems to develop into something we never expected.

40. Swidler, *Talk of Love*, 99. See 99–102.

41. For a fascinating exploration of this question, see Wuthnow, *Communities of Discourse*.

42. Yoder, *Christian Witness*, 40.

Taizé: A Model of Reconciliation

Such was the story of Taizé. On August 20 of 1940, Roger Louis Schutz-Marsauche, then twenty-five years old, rode his bike to visit Taizé, a near-by little village in the Burgundy region of southern France. Roger was having difficulties continuing his education. France and Germany were at war, and much of France was already under German control. A student Christian group he led expressed a daydream about someday forming a house of reconciliation. Perhaps in Taizé? Years later Roger wrote, "The defeat of France awoke a powerful sympathy. If a house could be built there, of the kind we had dreamed of, it would offer a possible way of assisting some of the most discouraged, those deprived of a livelihood; and it could become a place of silence and work."[43]

"Brother Roger," as he is known, moved to Taizé and began to welcome war refugees. From the beginning Brother Roger prayed three times a day, at first alone, and then together with those who joined. During the war, they ministered to Jewish refugees, but after the war they also began offering care to nearby German prisoners of war, to the concern of some of the local French. Nevertheless, their commitment was to love their neighbor and offer reconciliation: even between the Germans and the French.[44]

In 1949 this group made vows together: celibacy, a life of common ownership of goods, and a life under the authority of a prior. In so doing the community of Taizé became a pioneering expression of modern Protestant monastic life. But at the same time, as a community longing for reconciliation between God's people, it began to develop relationships with Roman Catholics, ultimately in 1958 receiving official recognition by the Pope. Later, after the Berlin wall fell in 1989, Taizé welcomed Orthodox Christians from nearby Eastern Europe into their fold, thus becoming one of the first organizations to celebrate worship services incorporating this diverse a group of Christians.

During the 1960s the community of Taizé experienced another development. Youth began visiting. In large numbers. And from different countries. Community members felt they could no longer expect their guests to sing the traditional French or Latin chants. Indeed, they began to feel that their ministry was, in part, to welcome these youth. So after

43. Santos, *Community Called Taizé*, 57.

44. The commitment to reconciliation is explicitly mentioned in their Rule, chapter 7. See Brother Roger, *Parable of Community*, 27.

some collaborative experimentation, the brothers developed a form of song that could be used with many languages, and which still might be employed as means of contemplative meditation. Visitors to the community at Taizé live a rhythm of prayer (three times a day), Bible studies, and manual labor. Everybody works.

Jason Brian Santos, a youth pastor from the USA, first visited Taizé in 1995. As with any good youth pastor, he wanted to know their secret. How did they attract so many youth? Santos writes,

> When I first decided to research the community, I too was under the anticipation that I could crack the code. Once in Taizé, however, I realized there is no secret code and thus nothing really to crack, per se. What I did find was a real community of brothers who are an authentic and living example of Christ's reconciliation in the world.[45]

The ministry of Taizé and its charism of reconciliation continues to grow. As of 2008, when Santos's book was published, over 100,000 youth were visiting Taizé every year. People celebrate prayer services using the chants of Taizé in thousands of towns and cities around the world. Some of the brothers live in troubled parts of the world and offer reconciliation there. The brothers of Taizé hope that people who hear of them or who sing their chants might catch a vision to live as communities of reconciliation. Monastic modeling as socio-political engagement. I think it makes a difference.

How Christian Communities Can Model Good Society Here and Now

If we are going to offer faith, love, and hope to the world, we will need to receive and embody them ourselves.[46] First, faith. When I teach on the Bible and politics, I often say: "The first rule of politics is this: God rules (see Gen 1:1)." I say this not to encourage some passive escape from political engagement (my second rule is that "we are invited to rule"—see Gen 1:28; 2:15). Rather, my aim is to give people perspective. Tribes, cities, nations have all fought and conquered, given and received, for a long, long time. Christians and atheists alike have watched their movements

---

45. Santos, *Community Called Taizé*, 126.

46. Oliver O'Donovan's three volumes on *Ethics and Theology* are an excellent reflection on faith, love, and hope.

go awry even within recent centuries. We have seen good things as well (*The Christian Science Monitor Weekly* is especially attentive to publishing good things that happen). The point is that God is bigger than all this. God is bigger than nation, than democracy, than our understandings of "freedom." Our fears about the state of things (the "wide")—the fear that media proliferates simply to draw our attention—are reordered through a deepening faith in God. When we drink deeply of the truth, our contributions toward socio-political ordering is itself ordered within a spirit of faith-full-ness.

Faith is fundamentally a response to divine initiative, a trust in the One who first acts. Faith in the First Actor is the root of any Christian socio-political action. Socio-political engagement is a response to the prior work and the call of God, whether this call be perceived in the values of Scripture or in the cries of those who suffer. Consequently, Christian faith eschews any kind of self-trust; the object of faith and the source of our fundamental socio-political identity is the Almighty God. We discover our agency—and find its empowerment—through faith.

This is important, for if we are to help society order itself well, we will need to learn to order our own lives well as communities and individuals. The careful ordering of life is a characteristic feature of monastic forms of life. That is why monastic communities have regular times where wise outsiders visit and advise the community. Our ordering process does not go well when it is driven by guilt ("I don't have time for devotions/family/ community, I need to be in the streets"—or vice versa), by surrounding agendas ("if we were *really* living as the church we would . . .") or by shallow self-interest ("I can't make sense of all this and I need some self-care, so I'll just . . ."). When, however, we do our best to root our own life order in faith, faith in the One who transcends our feeble attempts to alter the state of things, then we are more likely to discover a free, sincere, and faith-full discernment that opens us to the wisest, most appropriate, order for *our* life in *our* context in light of *God's* values. A well-discerned order emerging from a faith-full, free, conversation with others models the kind of individual-in-community relationships we strive to see realized in society.

Next, love. "Love is kind. . . . It does not insist on it's own way. . . . It does not rejoice in wrongdoing, but rejoices in the truth" (1 Cor 13: 4–6). Oppression is the denial of just these virtues. Though we can strive for laws or structures that ensure greater measures of fairness in society, we will never be able to legislate love. But we can inspire love. We can model

love. One of my joys in visiting intentional communities is to watch nonviolent communication in action.[47] One of my joys in relating to communities of communities is to witness how diverse groups offer sacrificial
care for one another.[48] I, along with Luke Bretherton, find these kinds of
relationships significant for politics. Bretherton writes in his theology of
democracy,

> Without some kind of meaningful relationships between peo-
> ple, there are just individuals, and an atomized and disaggre-
> gated crowd. . . . If one begins with relationships, then one has
> to take seriously the arenas or forms of social life through which
> individuals develop and sustain relationships over time and in
> which they learn the art of ruling and being ruled.[49]

We train love and model love through our ordinary community relationships. If we are going to engage the divisions in our socio-political
world—race, class, ideology, and so on—we will need to face them (in
love) in our own midst.

Finally, hope. I like that phrase "prefigurative politics." As noted
some activists are recommending that the phrase be replaced with something more modest. The classless society has not come. In light of the
scope of converging planetary crises facing us, some wonder what we activists are "prefiguring."[50] As a Christian, I think it is important to retain
the phrase. We know what we are prefiguring: a concrete utopia where
"there is no longer Jew or Greek, there is no longer slave or free, there
is no longer male and female," where God makes "all things new," and
where "the Lord God will be their light, and they will reign forever and
ever" (Gal 3:28; Rev 21:5; 22:5). We Christians place our hope not in
effective tactics or the political process or shifts of power, but rather in
God whose heart we share and whose mission is sure, even when we see
little progress. The sense of hopefully embodying the future has been an
important theme throughout monastic history. And believe me, people
notice this kind of hope.

---

47. Alden Bass, in a Nurturing Communities Network Roundtable (November 7,
2020) spoke of "practices of communication for our sake and for the world."

48. For a delightful story of the relationship between the Mennonite-oriented
Shalom Mission Communities in the USA and the Roman Catholic Valle Nuevo in El
Salvador see Gatlin et al., *Compañeros*.

49. Bretherton, "Power to the People," 63–64.

50. See for example, Gordon, "Prefigurative politics."

I mentioned at the beginning of this chapter that modeling is accomplished both intentionally and unintentionally. Sometimes we choose a form of life with the conscious aim of demonstrating one or another aspect of the heart of Christ. Other times we just live a life and others notice. But in either case we face the question of how to order our lives. In many monasteries, this ordering is accomplished through the development of a Rule of Life. I think we have things to learn from this practice today.

Monastic Practice: A Rule of Life

Political self-examination (chapter 2) helps us to see who we are in the midst of our socio-political contexts and to see our politics in their goodness, their dark side, and their redemption. Socio-political discernment (chapter 3) enables us to prayerfully choose (through observing, gathering, evaluating, deciding, and acting) postures or actions with regard to our socio-political options in light of the active presence of God. A Rule of Life helps us to take the further step of integrating the postures and actions we have chosen into the ongoing realities of our common and personal lives.[51] The fact of the matter is, we are being shaped, regulated, ruled all the time: by trends, by peers, or by powers. A Rule of Life is one way of standing consciously in relationship to these forces as best we can and naming how we will be regulated.[52] As with discernment, Rules of Life are lived differently among different people. Some simply live a Rule of survival. God's Spirit is somehow present as we put together what we need to do, what is in front of our face. Others belong, and in their belonging they discover how to live. It's interesting to think that although the creation of a Rule of Life is central to the formation of a monastery, once someone joins the monastery they now *belong* and their need for developing Rules or discerning choices is minimized. Here I simply outline a reflective way of developing one's own personal or community Rule of Life.

I like to think of a Rule of Life as *a concrete expression of the life intentions of a Christian community or individual made in order to help*

51. I have developed a number of resources regarding Rules of Life. If you go to https://spiritualityshoppe.org/resources-for-christian-living/ and scroll halfway down, you will come to "Rules of Life Resources."

52. Thanks to Elizabeth Turman-Bryant at the Nurturing Communities Network Roundtable Zoom meeting, March 1, 2022, on Rule of Life, who reminded us all of this insight.

maintain or develop relationship with God and the gospel. With a view to socio-political engagement, then, a Rule of Life expresses those intentions we may have with regard to things social and political in order to help us implement those postures and actions we have discerned, in the context of the realities of our life. It is a link between the ideal and the real.

First, we start with the real. We cannot develop a budget without knowing how we spend our money. Similarly, we cannot apportion the time, relationships, and energies of our lives without knowing how we currently spend them. It might help to take a few months and examine how you spend your life. Then you can reflect and see where you may be able to adjust things.

Then the ideal. Monastic Rules often begin with some statement of vision. What are we about? (Or "What am *I* about," if this is a personal rule.) Where are we going? The 1727 "Brotherly Union and Agreement" of the Moravian Brethren, after proclaiming that their existence owes to God's grace, states that "Herrnhut, and its original old inhabitants must remain in a constant bond of love with all children of God belonging to the different religious persuasions—they must judge none, . . . but rather seek to maintain among themselves the pure evangelical doctrine, simplicity, and grace."[53] A clear statement of a commonly held ideal. What is your ideal for life? Can you state in a few words what your community hopes to model by way of the values of the gospel?

Then, back to the real. Monastic Rules specify how we intend to live out the values stated in the vision. How, for example, given the demands of family, community, and employment, will we engage in socio-political affairs? Are there aspects which require little time (and may save money —like limiting our consumption of violent movies)? Are there aspects that may require no time at all, but are matters of "attitude" to monitor (pay attention—do I allow others to speak first in a discussion)? Are there practices that might require some scheduling? How will we fit them in? (For example, instead of violent movies, let's watch stuff about the environment.) Diet, sleep, work, relationships, anything can be included.

Finally, a couple of suggestions. First, start small. Better to succeed at something small and develop from there than to try something big and give up because you couldn't live up to your unrealistic standards. Second, develop your Rule in dialogue with key friends and mentors. This is obvious for communities, but even if it is a personal Rule, believe me, others who love you will be able to spare you from much trouble if you let them speak into your life. Finally, learn to trust God through experimenting and

53. Zinzendorf, "Brotherly Union," 325.

revising your Rule. Like I said about discernment, become like a child, and play!

A Rule of Life (especially when regularly revised) can prove quite helpful in enabling us to model good society for ourselves and others, to link the real and ideal in our socio-political engagement. Through our little community and personal Rules of life, we learn to follow the bigger Rules of the Scripture and Spirit, which leads us—as best we can—to embody the supreme Rule of Christ and the gospel.

SIX

We Act

BY NOW I SUSPECT some of you are wondering, "Are we ever going to talk about *real* politics?" You might be saying, "OK, I get it, politics is more than statecraft. We care and we live good lives and it makes a difference (hopefully). Some of the 'speaking out' stuff reminded me of politics, and I can see the idea of teachers and lawyers using their influence for good. But when are we going to talk about *government*? I understand that you think Christianity is more than saving souls, but some of us are interested specifically in Christianizing the social order."[1] Well, you can breathe easy, because this is the chapter where I discuss civil disobedience, legislation, marches, voting, referendums, lobbying, "direct" action, and all that sort of thing.

But even as I propose to talk about government I am aware that I have now given others concern. There are some Christians who feel that involvement in "secular" government affairs is useless, or even worse. Some point to 1 Sam 8:1–21 and argue that God never intended human government, and that for this reason it is meaningless to try to improve an institution God never wanted in the first place. What we need is not *engagement in*, but *resistance to* government.[2] Others point to the Sermon on the Mount and urge that Christians should avoid getting involved in politics, because when they do, they are often compromised in their

---

1. See Rauschenbusch, *Christianizing*.

2. This way of expressing it is sometimes used by those who self-identify as "Christian anarchists." For various expressions of Christian anarchism, see Ellul, *Anarchy and Christianity*; Eller, *Christian Anarchy*; Steenwyk, *Unkingdom of God*.

obedience to the gospel of Jesus.[3] Still others (in the USA) contend that at least in current history, government and other cultural institutions have degenerated such that it is wiser to withdraw from politics and form monastic communities where Christians can explore and exhibit the values of faith.[4]

My response to those who express concern is simply to say that I believe Christians have both an opportunity and to some extent even a mandate to invest at some level in human government.[5] As I have already stated, I think human beings were put on this planet to cooperate with God by exercising our influence to help the earth flourish. This is a project of governing. Perhaps we can employ a few of the biblical images of Christian influence in the world to say that Christians bring forth an increase of God-oriented order in the world when they communicate the heart and concerns of God (*speak*, light), when they reach out to the broader world with the transforming love of Christ (*care*, leaven), when they live a transformed life (*model*, fragrance), and when they exercise appropriate influence within the structures of government that reflect the concerns of the heart of God (*act*, salt). Theologian Wayne Grudem, in his reply to those who suggest that we ought to "do evangelism, not politics," argues that the suggestion itself reflects an inadequate understanding of the breadth of the gospel. The work of Christ involves more than forgiveness of sins. He states, "The good news of the Gospel will result in changed lives, but Jesus wants that to result in *changed families* as well. And when the Gospel changes lives, it should also result in *changed neighborhoods*. And *changed schools*. And *changed businesses*. And *changed societies*. So shouldn't 'the Gospel' also result in *changed governments* as well? Of course it should!"[6] I am in complete agreement with

3. This is a common (though stereotyped) way of expressing it among Anabaptists. I think that one of the aims of John Howard Yoder's life work was to reconsider and clarify Anabaptist political reticence. See for example Yoder, *Christian Witness*, 16–22.

4. This is how I understand the basic message of Rod Dreher's *Benedict Option*. It must be noted, however, that Dreher makes place for socio-political engagement (see 78–99) and speaks specifically of political advocacy regarding religious freedom issues (86).

5. On Christian influence in government generally see, e.g., Hill, *What Has Christianity Ever Done?*; Stark, *For the Glory*; Colson, *God and Government*; Schmidt, *How Christianity Changed the World*; O'Donovan and O'Donovan, eds., *From Irenaeus to Grotius*.

6. Grudem, *Politics According to the Bible*, 47. Grudem presents at 45–53 a series of eight replies to the "do evangelism, not politics" suggestion.

Grudem on this point and I would add that while the New Testament may not provide a specific set of instructions for reaching those aims, it does offer reasons why, given the appropriate circumstances, Christians do well to cooperate with—or to critique—governmental institutions. We will get to this soon.

But *monasticism*? Is there a place for nuns or monks to be involved in statecraft? Didn't they join the convent to get away from all that "worldly" activity? This, perhaps, is the heart of the question Jonathan Wilson-Hartgrove put to me. How can we keep "committed monasticism" and "engaged statecraft" together in the same life?

I have saved this question until chapter 6 because I felt we first needed to appreciate the breadth of politics before we could properly—to my mind—grasp statecraft as one valuable component of a full-orbed intentional participation with God in bringing order within common life. We also needed to hear a few stories of monasticism(s) to get a better sense of what religious life is like. Now in chapter 6 we are prepared to explore statecraft—and the relationship between monasticism and statecraft—more explicitly. We begin by exploring the idea of "political action" itself.

STRATEGIES OF STATECRAFT AND TACTICS OF RESPONSE

First, let's think of human action more generally. I see human action as the exercise of agency within a framework of limits and possibilities. For example, I am five foot, one inch tall. What this means is that in many ways I am not well suited to the world the United States has constructed for me. Americans tend to sit on chairs and when I do, my feet do not touch the floor and my legs fall asleep. So, long ago I learned to sit cross-legged, even on wooden chairs. But I am great in crawl spaces. I have learned to live in light of both my own realities and those of the environment presented me. Had I lived three-thousand years ago, or been born in rural Japan, things would be different. I discovered young that I was neither "tall," "dark," nor "handsome." In my context, that meant something. The point is that human actions are performed through a navigation of both self and space.

And, of course, the same is true with regard to our political actions. Some tribal cultures negotiate the ordering of their lives through circle meetings of elders. As a tribal participant, I would learn through the course of my life how (or whether) I could exercise my agency and contribute to the life of the community. Though the tribal governmental structure may change somewhat over the course of years or generations (just as the structure of chairs have changed), I would learn to dwell, to act, through navigating myself within the space given me. Yes, even within tribal culture there are times when an individual or group decides to withdraw, to reform, or to resist. Yet these actions are performed in the context of a political "grammar" that—for the most part—makes sense of the whole, even the aberrations.

Just who is permitted to influence and the sense of how influence is to be performed are somewhat structured (given to us) through history, location, balance of power, and current circumstances.[7] The statecrafts of ancient Athens (government officials chosen by lot), early medieval France (vassals vowing fealty to regional feudal lords), and contemporary Germany (a government composed of executive, legislative, and judiciary branches) are worlds apart. Indeed, one needs training even to navigate the nuances between Canadian and USA legislative procedures. Furthermore, an unforeseen circumstance may alter familiar means of involvement in statecraft, as Britain now faces after parliamentarian Sir David Amess was brutally stabbed to death while conducting an open in-person meeting with constituents.[8] Usually "how things are done" is well enough known. With a little work most of us can navigate the accepted procedures for introducing specific governmental practices (federal funding of faith-based service agencies), for approving governmental policies (an immigration policy), or for selecting ruling governmental parties (election of representatives) because they are part of the political water we swim in.[9]

When we view political givens from the "balance of power" angle—and especially when the scale of government structure is sufficiently large or when people suffer—then we often speak of *dominant* political powers, or even *empires*. We distinguish between the politically powerful, who for

7. At least. My sense of the emergence of socio-political structures here is informed by works like Arendt, *Human Condition*; Bourdieu, *Theory of Practice*; de Certeau, *Practice of Everyday Life*; Taylor, *Social Imaginaries*.

8. See Musaddiquue, "MP's killing."

9. As in chapter 3, I am making reference to the categories described in Antoncich, "Discernment of Political Options." Antoncich also mentions a fourth category, the fundamental choice of governmental framework (for example, whether a country will choose a basically monarchical, democratic, communist, or other basic form of government). This fourth category, while not common in more stable governments, has been and continues to be a serious affair among locations around the globe.

one reason or another have more opportunity to influence governmental process, and the powerless, who do not have such opportunity, perhaps even to have voice with regard to their own situation.

It is with all these kinds of factors in mind that I distinguish in this chapter between official political "strategies" and unofficial political "tactics."[10] Official political *strategies* in most contemporary democratic countries include things like running for office, initiating legislation through a process of collecting signatures, voting, volunteering for a political party, and so on. Unofficial *tactics* include things like public demonstrations (like marches), symbolic actions (like boycotts), acts of civil disobedience (like sitting on a bus where you supposedly don't belong), social disruptions (attempting to take over a public building), or guerilla activities verging on war. I make this distinction because I am convinced we cannot begin to understand monastic political action—or even biblical political action—until we have a grasp within any given time or place of (1) the contexts (historical, location, balance of power, circumstances) that shaped the framework of socio-political engagement, and (2) the range of strategies and tactics that were available within the contexts. Let us begin by surveying a few samples of monastic political action.

Monasticism(s) and Socio-Political Action

Did Christian monasticism avoid or engage in socio-political activity? By now you should see that an answer to this question is not as simple as it may seem. We have already heard a variety of stories of monastic socio-political engagement. But what about governmental action? On the one hand, the monastic reputation for withdrawal, for avoidance of political life, is well-known. Wasn't this the heritage that Antony of Egypt passed on to the generations of monasticism that followed him: intentional solitude? Well, yes. Antony did abandon his secular occupation and withdraw to private places in order to seek God.[11] Yet through the course of his life, he returned periodically to public ministry. At one point during

10. De Certeau identifies these categories in his *Practice of Everyday Life*. He distinguishes them in terms of how people inhabit ordinary activities and places (walking streets, making conversation, cooking, and so on). My aim here is to employ his categories somewhat loosely with reference to governmentally related activities.

11. Some scholars and popular writers speak of the early ascetic removal into the desert as an "escape," or a tranquil "retreat." I believe this view misunderstands the aims of monastic withdrawal. See Howard, "Getting Away to It All."

the persecution of Maximin (perhaps around 311) Antony left his cell to support the confessing Christians in Alexandria. Athanasius writes of Antony's ministry there,

> In the law court, he showed great enthusiasm, stirring to readiness those who were called forth as contestants, . . . When the judge saw the fearlessness of Antony and those with him, he issued the order that none of the monks were to appear in the law court, nor were they to stay in the city at all.[12]

Antony refuses to obey the judge's order and appears the next day in the front of the assembly wearing freshly cleaned clothes, drawing attention to his presence. Antony first employs the legitimate *strategy* of accompanying those accused of religious crimes. Then, when the (powerful) judge sought to remove the monks' influence from the political process—and you see, by the way, that it is now not just a matter of Antony, but of a retinue of monks—Antony employs the *tactic* of civil disobedience.

As we discovered in chapter 1, early monks felt free to leave their cells in order to address political authorities as a gathered mass. I have already mentioned in chapter 3 how Shenoute of Atripe, abbot of the White Monastery in Egypt, used his spiritual/political influence to advance the cause of justice in his region. Nuns and monks employed political strategies or tactics as the need required. Peter Hatlie writes in his account of monasticism in Constantinople, "The record of local monastic political activities from 489 through 518 is long and full of intrigue. It ranges from alleged secret plots to unseat patriarchs, to public complaints voiced against the visits of a suspicious icon painter and even more a suspicious theologian to the city."[13]

True, most religious communities in most of what we know as Europe in the ancient and early medieval centuries arranged their lives around a rhythm of prayer, study, and manual labor. Nevertheless, nuns and monks would adjust this rhythm—and the regulations of the community—to suit the situation of a community or individual. Gert Melville writes of Frankish queen and founder of a monastery, Radegundis (520–587),

12. Athanasius, *Life of Antony*, #46 (pp. 65–66).

13. Hatlie, *Monks and Monasteries*, 118. If one might think that this quote merely refers to "religious" squabbles, I encourage the reading of the entire book, which, covering Constantinople from 350–850, repeatedly documents a wide range of religious/political enmeshment. The "separation of church and state" was unknown in this context.

Admittedly, the founder herself did not entirely adhere to its regulations. She never thought to renounce her noble customs but instead lived in keeping with her status in a few rooms in the monastery, receiving guests in majestic style. She also involved herself continually in the business of high politics. In that way she was a forerunner of a pattern of relationships that, despite all of the rules to the contrary, became common over the coming centuries, especially in women's religious houses.[14]

Another fascinating example of consecrated religious embodying their vows through strategic governmental activities is the case of many late medieval friars. Giacomo Todeschini writes of merchants who were representatives of the mercantile and entrepreneurial civic classes and were also Third Order Franciscans (a group who consecrated themselves to a Franciscan life, but could still be married and maintain ordinary employment). These Franciscan merchants pioneered creative economic and political measures. They "could represent the civic community as a community able to calculate its own welfare but also the measure of their belonging to the Kingdom without borders promised by the Holy Scriptures."[15] Similarly, André Vauchez's article "A Campaign of Peacemaking in Lombardy around 1233" demonstrates "how certain Dominican and Franciscan friars, by placing themselves at the head of a popular devotional movement, were able to dominate briefly the governments of several Italian cities and enact a series of legislative measures embodying mendicant ideals."[16]

During the medieval period it was extremely difficult to pursue civic or military life and avoid either bearing arms or taking oaths. It was a necessary part of medieval government. Yet it was common to think that the Sermon on the Mount prohibited these actions. Consequently, it was understood by many that only those who chose a form of life separate from customary medieval society (namely, nuns and monks—or penitents trying to imitate them) would be able to keep these injunctions.[17] In

14. Melville, *World of Medieval Monasticism*, 16–17. We see another interesting combination of monastic withdrawal and political action by a powerful religious figure in the life of Bernard of Clairvaux (c. 1090–1153), the Cistercian abbot, spiritual writer, and medieval politician. See McGuire, "Bernard's Life and Works"; Pedersen, "Saving the World."

15. Todeschini, *Franciscan Wealth*, 131. This entire book documents many interesting examples of Franciscan political/economic creativity.

16. Bornstein, "Preface," ix.

17. For examples, see Andrews, *Early Humiliati*, 100–101; Thompson, *Cities of*

this sense medieval monastic expressions avoided specific political roles and activities. Yet consecrated Christians found many ways to express their convictions and use their influence to shape governmental processes. Thus Vauchez writes of a situation in tenth-century France when, "The weakness of royal power . . . as well as the renewed outbreak of violence caused by the installation of new feudal structures, soon led the monks, especially the Cluniacs, to abandon their isolation and actively intervene in profane society. Only a spiritual authority was capable of restoring the minimum of order necessary for the survival of the Church itself, as well as for that of the poor and humble."[18]

At times this led some to pursue less-approved tactics. Penitent and pilgrim St. Raimondo Palmerio (c. 1139–1200), was a shoemaker in Piacenza until God called him to travel, and then to work among the poor. Vauchez writes of Palmerio, "Not satisfied with fighting against prostitution and protecting the poor against unjust magistrates and magnates, he did not hesitate to organize a demonstration of beggars and poor people in Piacenza, who marched through the streets shouting 'Help me, help me, cruel harsh Christians, for I am dying of hunger while you live in abundance.'"[19] Another interesting example in the medieval period is that of Arnold of Brescia, Italy (1100–1155), head of a house of canons (a group who lived a combination of monastic and priestly vocations). Arnold's town (called a "commune") was torn by ecclesiastical schism and in the midst of this the population sought to reorganize their commune with a more democratic form of government. Arnold encouraged and organized a resistance movement that eventually controlled the commune, calling itself the Roman Republic.[20]

Space only permits a few examples from the modern period. First, Bartolomé de las Casas (1484–1566).[21] Las Casas was born in Seville, Spain. His father traveled with Christopher Columbus on his second voyage to the New World in 1493 and Las Casas was ordained as a priest and was serving as a catechist for the "Indians" when Dominicans such

God, 84–85; Howard, "What Does God Expect?," 15–16.

18. Vauchez, Laity in the Middle Ages, 13.

19. Vauchez, Laity in the Middle Ages, 61. See further for more examples.

20. On Arnold of Brescia see, for example, Little, Religious Poverty and the Profit Economy, 109–110; Davison, Forerunners of Saint Francis, 96–167.

21. On Bartolomé de Las Casas see especially Clayton, Bartolomé de las Casas; Sanderlin, ed., Witness. Zagano and McGonigle, Dominican Tradition, 60–65, provide a brief summary of La Casas's life and works.

as Fray Anton Montesino began to critique the colonists' abuse of the *encomienda*: an "agreement" that gave permission for Spaniards to collect tribute from the local population and use them as laborers in return for protection, provision, and instruction. In 1514, after an encounter with God and with the sufferings of the native population, Las Casas decided to free his own Indians and to join the Dominicans in their life of study, preaching, and action in order to promote a more just way of life in the New World. Las Casas the Dominican friar spent the rest of his life between Spain and the New World, writing drafts of laws (the *New Laws* were published in 1542), pleading with kings, castigating settlers, and mobilizing for a more beloved community. His writings are now considered early models of a "human rights" movement.

Next, Nano Nagle (1718–1784). Few outside Ireland know of Nagle but her influence has been significant, being voted in 2000 Irish Woman of the Millennium.[22] Nagle was a Catholic woman in eighteenth-century Ireland. She was a Catholic *woman*, at a time when models for women's active service (leaving the cloister) were rare. And she was an *Irish* Catholic woman, living during the era of the Penal Code, a system of laws enacted after England's Siege of Limerick. The result of these laws was an Irish populace reduced to near destitution. During this era it was illegal for Catholics to practice their religion, to hold public office, to purchase land, to bear arms, and much more. Most importantly for Nano, this system made it illegal to receive Catholic education, or to travel overseas for that purpose. Yet Nano Nagle was born into a wealthy family. Her family (secretly) provided her a Catholic education at home and then quietly sent her to Europe for formal Catholic education. She returned to Ireland and ultimately founded an underground school for poor children. More, she used her skills, her influence, and her wealth to found a *network* of schools and a *religious order* (eventually named The Sisters of the Presentation of the Blessed Virgin Mary) to support their work. She was the first woman in Ireland since St. Brigid (451–525) to found a new monastic expression, and she did so through the delicate tactics of illegal maneuvering.

Finally I must say something about Toyohiko Kagawa (1888–1960). Like Nagle, Kagawa is currently less well-known but was, in his time, highly influential: nominated twice for the Nobel Prize in Literature and

22. On Nano Nagle, see Flanagan, *Embracing Solitude*, 100–113; Flanagan et al. eds., *Nano Nagle and an Evolving Charism*; Clear, "Nano Nagle"; de Bhál, "Biographical Note"; Raftery et al., *Nano Nagle*.

at least three times for the Nobel Peace Prize.[23] Kagawa was a convert to (Protestant) Christianity in Meiji-era Japan, receiving seminary training at Princeton Theological Seminary (1914–1916). On Christmas Eve of 1909 Kagawa moved into one of the most notorious slums of Japan. There—aside from his time at Princeton—he devoted thirteen years to evangelism, pastoral ministry, writing, and social change. In 1920 he founded the Kobe Consumer Cooperative (which currently has over a million members). In 1923 he founded The Friends of Jesus Society, a semi-monastic fellowship that "synthesized Franciscan compassion for the deprived classes, Dominican evangelical ardor, Jesuit obedience and disciplines, . . . Paul's stress on the love and the cross, as well as the methodism and perfectionism of John Wesley."[24] This same year Kagawa was called to Tokyo to offer his services after the great earthquake and it was there he spent the rest of his life. Most importantly for our concerns here, Kagawa was a powerful political activist in a very complex environment. He preached solidarity with the poor long before "liberation theology." He organized labor strikes and spoke at rallies; he helped found political parties; he was rebuked by those who promoted violent tactics; he was arrested and spent time in jail for his political actions. He became a representative to the national government after World War II, pleading with the United States to help rebuild Japan. Today he is considered by many as a forgotten prophet, often compared with Gandhi, King, and Schweitzer.

Ancient, medieval, modern. Orthodox, Catholic, Protestant. Men and women. Cloistered monasteries, networks of friars, semi-monastic movements, all over the globe. And all of these nuns and monks investing themselves in some form of statecraft (or some form of resistance to the statecraft of their situation). Some served as influential political figures from their monastic setting. Others functioned as political renegades, serving God in secret. Still others joined or founded monastic communities in order to further their religious vocation of socio-political action. Formal strategies, illegal tactics, and everything in between. What we

23. On Kagawa's life, legacy, and thought see Kagawa, *Before the Dawn*; Kagawa, *Songs From the Slums*; Fukada, "Legacy"; Schildgen, *Toyohiko Kagawa*; Hastings, "Practicing the Redemptive Love"; Hastings, *Seeing All Things Whole*. Some of Kagawa's works and writings about him are available at archive.org. On Kagawa and socio-political engagement see Kagawa, *Brotherhood Economics*; Mullins, "Christianity as a Transnational Social Movement"; Byrd and Loucky, "Kagawa and Niebuhr."

24. Helen Topping, *Friends of Jesus* 4, no. 1, cited in Fukada, "Legacy," 20. By 1928 membership had grown to 1,300 (Hastings, "Practicing the Redemptive Love," 169).

discover is that monks and nuns—like the rest of us—try our best to follow God with our whole life. We follow God in rhythms of prayer and
community when that is needed. But when it is time to act, we act. It is
not a matter of some shallow *whether* Christians should act or not, but
rather a deeper *when* and *how* we act given the truth of the gospel, the
work of God in our lives, and the situation at hand. As I have been saying all along, devotion to Christ and socio-political engagement merge
within a life of discerning intimacy with God. We sink deep into God's
heart. We look wide in careful observation of the surrounding realities.
We attend to the Spirit's guidance in our midst. And when appropriate,
we act.

POLITICAL ACTION IN SCRIPTURE AND THEOLOGY

We have seen that at least on occasion sisters and friars and more have
seen fit to participate in the governmental processes of their contexts, employing the strategies of the dominant political structures or the tactics of
resistance. But perhaps this involvement should be considered a step too
far. Didn't the New Testament church avoid political involvement, choosing rather simply to submit to governments and to focus their attention
on community life and evangelism? In fact, wasn't that what Jesus came to
demonstrate: a *spiritual* rather than a *political* kingdom? As I mentioned
above, we must understand these matters by means of a careful examination of the governments of the first-century Mediterranean world and the
strategies and tactics available to people in that time and place.

Let's begin with Jesus. Was Jesus a revolutionary?[25] Unlike many
Sadducees, he did not curry favor with Roman elites. Unlike Josephus, he
did not lobby for policies. Those options simply were not available to the
Galilean carpenter's son. Unlike the Essenes, the Jesus movement was not
an isolated desert commune, but spread wherever Jesus traveled. Jesus,
like John the Baptist and unlike those in revolutionary uprisings, did not
advocate armed revolt.[26] Yet, as I mentioned in the previous chapter, both

25. This was the title of a well-known pamphlet published by New Testament
scholar Martin Hengel originally in 1970 (see Hengel, *Was Jesus a Revolutionist?*). I
return in this section to my conversation with "historical Jesus" literature (see footnote
2 of the previous chapter), only now rather than simply exploring the socio-political
significance of the way of life of the Jesus movement I am examining *actions* of Jesus in
light of his governmental context.

26. I touched on Essenes and revolutionary movements in the previous chapter.

those who admired him and those who crucified him perceived Jesus as some kind of resistance leader. What do we see when we examine Jesus's *actions* vis-à-vis the governments and options available to Jesus in his own context?

First, though for most of his ministry Jesus did not go out of his way to confront authorities, he felt free to exercise civil disobedience when necessary and was not shy when it came to offering critique of the dominant systems of government in his own setting. Jesus consciously violated the blue laws: harvesting grain (Mark 2:23–24) and providing medical services on the Sabbath (Luke 13:10–17). He consciously violated health regulations, affirming the bleeding woman who touched him (Luke 8:43–48), and reaching out his own hand to contact a leprous man (Matt 8:2–3; see also his contact with the bier of a dead son in Luke 7:14). Jesus ignored customs of both race and gender as he engaged with the Samaritan woman (John 4:1–10). Jesus replied to questions posed to him regarding paying taxes to Rome (a matter of deep concern among the various factions) by clever expressions of superficial compliance and thinly veiled condemnation of the Roman system (Matt 17:24–27; 22:15–22).[27]

Second, at times Jesus consciously chose symbolic ("direct") actions that he knew would be perceived as a threat to dominant political systems. This is particularly the case towards the end of his ministry, though even his choice of twelve disciples communicated a challenge to common understandings of the source of authority or renewal of the nation of Israel.[28] Jesus's "triumphal entry" (see Luke 19:29–40; John 12:12–16) was understood by his followers, his enemies, and probably by Jesus himself, as a religious-political "march," a declaration and demonstration of rightful kingship along the lines of Zechariah 9:9.[29] Likewise, his overturning

---

On John the Baptist and his relationship to Jesus, see especially Meier, *Marginal Jew: Mentor, Message, and Miracles*, 19–233.

27. On Matt 17:24–27 see Meier, *Marginal Jew: Mentor, Message, and Miracles*, 880–84. N. T. Wright's reading of Matthew 22:15–22 (Wright, *Jesus and the Victory*, 502–7) could be a bit stretched, but I still think the point is clear from the passages: Jesus cleverly responded with both compliance and critique. We must remember that open critique of the dominant system by a public figure was a dangerous affair, much as public figures in Cold War-era USA (such as Thomas Merton) suffered misrepresentation, out-of-hand rejection of their ideas, and sometimes worse, when they were labeled "communist" as a result of comments made in interviews.

28. On Jesus's selection of the twelve, see Meier, *Marginal Jew: Companions and Competitors*, 153, 162, 248–50.

29. See Wright, *Jesus and the Victory*, 490–91; Marshall, *Gospel of Luke*, 711.

of the tables at the Jerusalem temple (Mark 11:15–19) was at the least a confrontation of the current sacrificial system. Many scholars today read Jesus's action as a symbolic prophetic denunciation of the temple cult.[30]

Ultimately Jesus's life and ministry was a confrontation with the legitimacy of religious and political leadership. According to Matthew 2:1–18, Herod the Great perceived this threat even at Jesus's birth. Again and again, through his teachings, his miracles, his riddles,[31] and his symbolic actions, Jesus presented himself as the *true* authority—it was not just matter of following his ideas, but rather of following *him*—of Israel. Furthermore, he called others to join him in this movement. While Jesus did not engage in "politics" using the forms of modern statecraft, it would have been impossible in his own context not to see Jesus's movement and actions as an open critique of the existing system and therefore as a threat to political-religious authority. Ultimately he allowed himself to be judged guilty of blasphemy ("son of the Blessed One," Mark 14:61) and treason ("king of the Jews," Mark 15:2). This is what we affirm consistently in our theology of Jesus Christ: he is both divine Son and human king. Jesus simply demonstrated this politically dangerous fact and was executed accordingly. I return to the Assisi cross: Jesus hanging, eyes open looking at the crowds, his blood flowing deep and wide. The Jesus who encountered both individual sinners and corporate Sin held out his arms and offered mercy for all: oppressor and oppressed alike, his blood a fountain flowing deep and wide.

When we move from the Jesus Movement to the early post-Pentecost church we face slightly different, but similar, questions. In order to understand, for example, the early church's conservatism with regard to socio-political activity (see for example Rom 13:1–7; 1 Tim 2:1–2; 1 Pet 2:13–17), we must read the New Testament in light of the context and the options available. Christian leaders were planting churches and writing letters in a time that was volatile, to say the least. Ancient historian Josephus's description of the banditry, revolts, and messianic movements leading to the First Jewish-Roman War (66–70)[32] suggests

30. See Wright, *Jesus and the Victory*, 413–28; 490–93; Meier, *Marginal Jew: Mentor, Message, and Miracles*, 884–85. See also Douglass, *Resistance and Contemplation*, 82–83.

31. On Jesus's "royal riddles," see Wright, *Jesus and the Victory*, 493–510.

32. Josephus treats this period in the final book of his *Antiquities* (Josephus, *Jewish Antiquities*, XX, pp. 390–532) and in the second book of his *Jewish War* (Josephus, *Jewish War*, II, pp. 218–84; pp. 408–34). See also Horsley, *Bandits*, 67–69; 106–27. Not

to me the phrase "powder keg" to describe the political environment in the Middle East at that time. Christians were perceived by Romans as an insignificant minority within a problematic minority. Furthermore, the early Christian churches were planted in the midst of a wide range of geographic-political settings: Palestine, Greece, Syria, Mesopotamia, Rome, and more. The Roman Empire had distinct policies for handling religious minorities (and other concerns) within each region. There is simply no way that Paul, for example, could advise the Christian churches regarding how to influence governmental affairs. Not a realistic option.

There are also theological explanations for the New Testament's tendency toward less engaged relationships with governmental structures. I do think there is something to be said about the early church's expectations of an imminent "second coming" of Christ. As in my high school days, I suspect that many early Christians were less concerned with socio-political conditions and more interested in the universal message and the final appearance of the Lord Jesus Christ. I also think that the early Christian experience of Christ's powerful resurrection and exalting ascension ultimately served to relativize the importance of secular governments. Yes, governments served the purposes of God by maintaining a general peace and by punishing wrongdoing, but the victory of Christ and the outpouring of the Spirit inaugurated Christians into a more profound citizenship in heaven, with the result that the Christian's primary attention would be on standing firm to the way of Christ (Phil 3:20–4:1).[33]

Thus for various reasons the earliest Christians were not heavily engaged in governmental process, whether formal involvement or active resistance. Nonetheless, as we have already discovered in previous chapters, they lived the politics of Christ—reconciling Jew and Gentile, forgiving enemies, caring for the least, advocating for justice (see the exhortations in Luke 3:10–14; Jas 5:1–6)—among themselves and to those within their circles of influence. They followed Jesus's life and teachings and the Spirit's leading into a way of life that would equip them, when the context was appropriate, to care for abandoned children, to build hospitals, to challenge the political authorities regarding infanticide and gladiatorial games, and to offer their own voice within (or against) the political systems surrounding them.

to mention Nero's mistreatment of the Jews in Rome after the year 64 and other events.

33. Compare O'Donovan, *Desire of the Nations*, 120–157, with Yoder, *Politics of Jesus*, 163–214.

My March

I remember my first political "march." I dropped by Denver to visit my younger daughter Terese on my way back home from a speaking engagement. "So what's going on for you in the next couple days while I am here?" I asked. She answered, "Well, we're having a march on the 16th Street Mall tonight. Wanna join?" Of course I said yes (what's a father to do?). But then I asked her what it was all about. I learned the latest developments regarding the city of Denver planning to enact an urban camping ban, a law which would make it illegal for people without homes to cover themselves.[34] Terese and her circle wanted to draw attention to the fact that the Denver Business Partnership was a primary supporter of the ban. Terese saw a problem with powerful business forces pushing unneeded regulations through government process that would severely affect the survival of many for the sake of improving their profits. They felt like it would benefit the cause to make some public statement, some symbolic action that would send a message to the population that this "partnership" was wrong.

I asked Terese about the action. "Why not just go to the hearings and make your case there? Why do you need some kind of march? Don't these things get out of hand?" She reminded me of her stand on these matters, a stand stated so clearly to some well-meaning pastors on April 16, 1963 by Martin Luther King Jr. in his "Letter from Birmingham City Jail": "there is a type of constructive nonviolent tension that is necessary for growth."[35] Hearings and legal procedures are all well and good—and she tried her best to make sure that a crowd of people without homes were well represented in these proceedings—but often when standing against powerful forces it is necessary to exert pressure by drawing public attention to injustice. So we marched.

I carried a sign. I chanted slogans as we walked down 16th Street. We stopped in front of the Denver Business Partnership office and someone gave a talk, explaining the situation. And in the middle of it all a reporter came up to me with a microphone and asked me why I was there. I remember mentally freezing for a moment. "Uh, I'm spending a couple of days with my daughter and we're just hanging out?" No, that wouldn't work. And in that moment I was converted. I realized why I was there,

34. For more information, see for example, https://denverhomelessoutloud.org/homeless-survey/.

35. King, "Letter," 291.

more deeply. I *believed* in the cause. I took the microphone, introduced myself as Dr. Evan Howard, and went on to explain how the very lives of people without homes were threatened by a camping ban. I spoke of how it was wrong to cause this kind of suffering for the sake of a perceived improvement of business interests. Threatening a person's survival was wrong even if the intention of some was to "encourage" responsibility. I advocated for other more creative options. It was my first public lecture on the criminalization of homelessness. The reporter left, we returned home (those of us who slept in homes), and the city ultimately passed the camping ban. Was the march useless? With Terese and Martin Luther King Jr., I still think not. The ordering of society may require a variety of different strategies or tactics at different times. My place is to be available to express God's heart as best I can within the context I find myself.

Monastic Practice: Doing Politics the Monastic Way

I have a friend, Jose, who used to work with a new friars group befriending gang members and young men in the juvenile detention system. (He and his wife have since moved to Honduras and are working in a more severe environment yet.) This friend has a pretty tough background and is full of energy. I have known him as one who pours himself into anything he does. So I was interested to hear him share what happened when he spent a portion of his sabbatical in a contemplative monastery.

One of the stories Jose tells is about learning to "do dishes the monastic way." He was required, as part of his stay, to participate in some of the chores. Jose ended up doing dishes with one of the monks, and he went at it with his characteristic high energy and a desire to do a good job. You would have thought he was a young soldier with his commanding officer looking over his shoulder. After a few minutes the monk who was with him graciously thanked him for his hard work but told him that here at the monastery "we do things the monastic way." He instructed Jose to slow down a bit since they did not need to hurry in order to finish. Rather this was time to be present with God doing dishes, just as the previous hour was time spent with God in a common meal and the hour before that was time with God in prayer. He taught Jose how to notice the feel of each pan, each fork, transforming them from dirty to clean. In time the monk showed Jose how his approach to doing dishes had characterized his whole life: rushing from this to that thing, trying to get lots done so that he can accomplish good. A worthy and even inspirational approach to life, but not always sustainable or even profitable in the long run.

So now let's learn from this story. Let's think of a political campaign: running for election, promoting or opposing a piece of legislation, organizing support for a certain policy. How could we "do politics" in a monastic way in the context of a political campaign?

First, develop a rhythm of time involved and time away, even in the midst of the campaign. Jose was at this contemplative monastery as part of a required sabbatical. He knew he was leaving his gang kids to take this sabbatical. Not easy. There is a well-known story about Martin Luther King Jr. and Howard Thurman. In 1958 during a book signing, the twenty-nine-year-old King was stabbed and ended up in the hospital. Howard Thurman, who knew King, visited him at the hospital and advised him to take this tragic event as an opportunity to rest, reflect, and rebuild. Thurman encouraged King to extend his rest period by two weeks, for "the movement had become more than an organization; it had become an organism with a life of its own," which potentially could swallow up King.[36] Don't let it get to a hospital visit before you rest. Schedule appointments for times of rest and rebuilding. As any athlete will tell you, excellence comes from the proper rhythm of rest and work. My conviction is that an excellent campaign will need a wise rhythm.

Second, learn to make repetition your friend. Monasteries are good at repetition. Chants, prayer ropes, doing dishes. They have learned to make it an art. Very small actions are accomplished consciously (albeit a bit more slowly) before the presence of God, being aware of how the very small fits into the very large. Political campaigns are also filled with small, repetitive tasks: stuffing envelopes, making signs, composing emails. Why not perform these tasks the monastic way? Do them before the Lord, aware of how *this* small task—*this* one and *this* one—fits into the large task of spreading the glory of God. Learn to make repetition your friend.

Third, pay attention to the outer and the inner. I love the way the monk instructed Jose to get in touch with the feel of doing dishes, the sheer sensory experience of the work. There is something about a rally out in the cold, the physical feel of texting a network partner, the sound of music played as part of a political campaign. Wouldn't it be interesting to identify and appreciate some of the sights, sounds, and smells of a political campaign? Learn to pay attention. But at the same time there are inner things to notice as well. The monk helped Jose to recognize patterns in his

36. For this story, see https://theconversation.com/meet-the-theologian-who-helped-mlk-see-the-value-of-nonviolence-89938. Thanks to James Wilhoit for telling me of this story.

life that influenced the way he approached even this simple task of doing dishes. He learned to become aware of the "way" he was doing dishes, and what was underneath that. What is the "way" you do politics? How are you present to the tasks of folding leaflets, planning gatherings, writing speeches? What is going on inside? Where is God? Can you learn to pay attention? (First *after* the moment, then *during* the moment, then even *before*.)[37]

Finally, honor the process as much as the product. Jose did not realize that the process of doing the dishes had any real value at all. By the time he left the monastery he realized that every action in life has value. Can we learn to see the sacredness of the process? My daughter Terese says she still thinks direct actions are important, but now she talks as frequently about what they do for the participants. She rejoices, for example, when those who are most affected by laws criminalizing homeless people are empowered to speak. There are important things going on in the very act of our actions. Pay attention to these and respond accordingly. Furthermore, while we want change, it often takes time and how we invest in the long haul is an important part of the action itself. I talked about some of this in my discussion of "prefigurative politics." Can we learn to *be* in our political action what we want society to *become*?

I think it might help in a campaign to take a little time to journal (if you're that kind of person; or perhaps just talk with a friend) and reflect along the way on each of the elements of "doing politics the monastic way." What is your rhythm like? Have you identified a few repetitive tasks or played with contemplative political folding? What have you noticed as you paid attention? Can you summarize the feel of a committee meeting using your five senses? Can you summarize what goes on inside of you in that meeting—and why? Where is the Spirit of God in the process itself?

Authentic Action

We have been talking in this book about the value of living both deep and wide. It is time I clarify—or perhaps develop—my use of these terms a little further. You see, it is easy to get the impression that *wide* equals "outward" (things like speaking out, caring, political action) and that

37. Sometimes the term "mindfulness" is used to describe this kind of awareness. From a Christian perspective see Oden, *Right Here Right Now*.

deep equals "inward" (things like community, modeling, prayer). Perhaps this is helpful, but it is ultimately a false stereotype. We are becoming more aware today that our "inner" world (our personal life and modeling) is shaped by our socio-political location, our race, our national identity, and more. When I look within I see that which is without. Likewise, when we explore the stereotypically "wide" (caring or political actions) we find ourselves facing deep issues of self-interest, power dynamics, and more. Perhaps there is more to the song "Deep and Wide" than we might have thought in the beginning. The fountain of God's mercy flows both deep and wide at the same time to all aspects of life because they are necessarily caught up in each other. Deep *and* wide.

Let's take a look at this interpenetration of "deep" *and* "wide" a bit further as we develop a few things we have learned so far as they pertain to community or individual participation in governmental action.

First, Christian statecraft aims at the glory of God. Of course, many governments may not be open to hearing about "the glory of God." Some governments are downright hostile to this aim. But insofar as we are creatures placed on earth by God to order it, our goal as ambassadors of God is to foster a world—or a school district—that manifests God's concerns: care for creation, righteousness, justice, compassion, honoring the dignity of the human person. Thus, however we may debate issues about the environment, the point is that we advocate for those governmental measures that make the environment a primary concern. Likewise when we address issues of tariffs and international trade we do not try to squeeze the greatest possible profit for our own country, because our aim is a country that reflects God's heart. Statecraft is often a process involving representatives, procedures, populist movements, and more all mixed together. New monastic communities can contribute to this process at any of these elements: for example by having meetings with a representative in order to show how a well-considered idea (and a compassionate one) might best serve the objectives of the government. We model compassion through our life as a community. We then use our model as a demonstration plot of what could be accomplished on a larger scale (with appropriate modifications).

Most importantly, during our political action we constantly remind ourselves of why we are here. Is it just about unseating disliked representatives? Is it about the success of our plan, or the fear of what might happen if some particular agenda does not materialize? God is bigger than all our agendas. A tremendous amount of damage is inflicted upon society

through politics undertaken with poor motives. I urge us to remind ourselves frequently: "We are just trying to faithfully facilitate the greatest
glory of God we can in this place here and now with what we have at our
disposal." Take a look at our motives. Our look wide must also be deep.

Second, political action emerges from a deep awareness of our own
context and the options available. I have already shown this with regard
to biblical times and the history of monasticism. But we must face this
today right where we are. Times are changing. In some parts of the globe
Christians have greater potential for influence than ever, for example in
Europe after post-2008 "austerity measures." In other parts Christians
are experiencing diminished regard in governmental process—or worse.
Christians cannot control whether we are treated with minority status or
not. Our job is to influence when and how we can in each situation. At
times we will wish to confront situations (as the earliest Christians may
have wished to confront the practice of gladiatorial games) but cannot
because of our status or other complexities. In these situations we are
obliged, as Luke Bretherton suggests, to face these issues with *impatient
endurance* until God may grant us voice or change the circumstances.[38]

But sometimes we can act, and then the wisdom is in discerning the
most appropriate action. Part of this is seeing what we are best at. On the
one hand, Christian communities have often excelled at offering care and
experimenting with new ways of doing things. Yet, there have been times
(for example in the ministry of Arnold of Brescia or in the civil rights
movement in the USA) where monastic groups or churches were quite
effective in mobilizing people to support governmental change.[39] And
then there is the question of what is needed. At times organizing peaceful
negotiations is effective. At other times peaceful negotiations simply give
people in power freedom to delay action and keep the public unaware of
the need for change. Unfortunately, members of negotiation gatherings
are not always on a level playing field, and other tactics are more appropriate. We must look deep, to recognize the forces that are in play in any
governmental situation. Where is there unforgiveness? Do we perceive

38. Bretherton, *Christ and the Common Life*, 269. Bretherton distinguishes between
the *problems* we endure, which are systemic and often require societal change to
resolve, and *issues* we address, which are more specific and can be addressed through
policy and practice (see 270–72). What I am suggesting here is that at times Christians
may find themselves impatiently enduring unchangeable issues as well as intolerable
problems.

39. For a helpful assessment of the socio-political contributions of faith-based
organizations for example, see Wuthnow, *Saving America?*

corporate self-interest? Is there a relationship between ideology and fear in key individuals? Looking wide forces us to look deep. Do politics the monastic way. When we take the time to pay attention to what is there, we discover wisdom that shapes the direction of our action.

Third, as we have already seen, Christian political action will not only address ideas and plans but also personalities and power. An ordered society is about relationships and consequently government is not simply about what we decide, but also about how we decide and who gets to decide. Wayne Grudem, in his *Politics According to the Bible*, argues that "Genuine, long-term change in a nation will only happen (1) if people's *hearts* change so that they seek to do good, not evil; (2) if people's *minds* change so that their moral convictions align more closely with God's moral standards in the Bible; and (3) if a nation's *laws* change so that they more fully encourage good conduct and punish wrong conduct."[40] I agree for the most part with Grudem's comment here (and thus I am an advocate for evangelism and education as well as socio-political engagement), only I would add one additional component. I would say that long-term change also requires (4) an alteration in the *relationships* of groups of people. Government is not merely the rule of law, but the ruling of a configuration of people. And the health of that government is not only a reflection of the laws but of how people(s) relate to one another in the context of these laws.[41] We act within configurations of class, race, education, gender, and more that distribute different possibilities and limitations of influence to us all. Furthermore, we must recognize that power and relationship are not simply matters of who leads the system, but also of the character of the system itself, who the system "looks like." When we admit relationship we realize that the arts of confrontation and compromise are critical.[42] And in the middle of all this we honestly acknowledge our own power. We see our own configuration of possibilities and limits for what it is. We recognize the power of consumer choice. We celebrate the power of Christian non-retaliation. And we face our own mixed needs for power. Looking deep is a means of acting wide. When

40. Grudem, *Politics According to the Bible*, 54.

41. I find Augustine including this relational element (along with heart, mind, and law) in his understanding of the development of a true "commonwealth" (see Augustine, *City of God*, XIX.21–24, pp. 881–91). Bretherton explores the relational element in his discussion of "peopling" (Bretherton, *Christ and the Common Life*, 424–29.

42. See Kiefer, "50-50 Senate," Bretherton, *Christ and the Common Life*, 42–43.

we look deep into personalities and power we see strategies and tactics of effective ordering.

Finally, Christian political action acts. We can talk forever about *how* action should be done. But as any good activist knows, sooner or later we must get up from the planning table, roll up our sleeves, and do something. We send emails supporting a referendum. We go on a march. We make an appointment with a representative and lobby against a bill up for consideration. We vote, or even run for office. We act. Some of these actions are easier for communities than individuals (email lists, gathering people for a march). Others are only available to individuals (running for office).

We act, willing to experiment with strategies and tactics. The choice of action is a combination of both art and wisdom. Good political action grabs the attention of the intended audience, communicates clearly, and produces effects.[43] Thomas Merton, from his monastic distance, spoke periodically about choice of action. He warns Evora Arca de Sardinia in a letter, "You must be very careful of a false and noisy zeal that talks loudly about plans for action and conquest." He supports negotiation in another letter: "In terms of politics, I think that the issue is to get down to some real sincere and practical negotiation in regard to disarmament." Yet at the same time he supports those who march. He writes to his friend James Forest, "My Mass on February 1 will be for all of the strikers every-where in the world and all who yearn for a true peace, all who are willing to shoulder the great burden of patiently working, praying, and sacrific-ing themselves for peace."[44] There are times when we use our influence to give voice to those who have little voice (for example, the males who gave voice to the women mystics of the late medieval period). There is also a time to step aside and give others power so that they may emerge. Again, there are a variety of factors influencing any governmental situation we face: personal, situational, structural, and more. Wise discernment at one time may lead us to address the personal, pleading with the city to permit a tiny home village to be built in a vacant lot. Then again later we might address the structural, seeking to strike down a law that criminalizes sur-vival behaviors. Some individuals (like Merton) or communities (like the

43. This combination of art and wisdom is what stands out, to me, in the ministry of Shane Claiborne and the Simple Way. See also Lederach, *Moral Imagination*.

44. Merton, *Cold War Letters*, 64, 172, 58. See also 75, 91, 106, 122. On the importance of not villainizing our opponents see also Merton, *Turning Toward the World*, 125 and *Cold War Letters*, 95–97, 185–87.

Carthusians) might focus on prayer or writing. Others, like the Sisters of St. Joseph of Peace, may identify their vocation particularly in advocating for political change.[45]

We act, willing to face the consequences of our action. We have already discussed the consequences of Jesus's actions. Thomas Merton was also very conscious of the consequences of his action. Merton chose to critique both country and church and in turn he received his own share of criticism.[46] He complained about the silence of the church and was silenced by the church.[47] When we choose to act we face our potential and our limits. Can we see this through? What if we keep it up and this campaign just fizzles out? What if we keep it up and the movement turns into a monster that swallows us up? Should I try to work out a negotiation between opposing parties at a "shallower" level or can I invite them into a higher plane of dialogue? Different consequences can be imagined for each.[48] One consequence we face—and we can celebrate—is the knowledge we gain through action. Sometimes we step into political action with a stereotyped view of the issues and the parties. But through the action itself—if we are open—we gain an intuitive sense of things that "knows" the problem both wider and deeper than when we started. We see deep by acting wide.[49]

My conviction is that monastic expressions—communities of Christians holding common values, shared decision-making, a sense of alternative life, and so on—have great potential for supporting and sustaining political action, and even governmental action. When, like Toyohiko Kagawa and the Friends of Jesus, we live among those in need, pray together regularly, discern our actions and support one another through the actions, we have a strength that is not available to lone-ranger Christian activists. I think that monastic expressions can become powerful

45. For the Congregation of the Sisters of St. Joseph of Peace, see https://csjp.org.

46. For Merton's critique, see *Cold War Letters*, 38, 54, 141. For his own tensions with the church see 81,150, 177. For Merton's comments on others' criticism of his own position see 17, 125.

47. For Merton's comments on the church's silence see *Cold War Letters*, 25, 110, 147. For the church's censure of his work see 143.

48. On this, see Charles Taylor's discussion of two-dimensional space in Taylor, *Secular Age*, 706–7.

49. I am influenced here by Japanese philosopher Kitaro Nishida's understanding of action-intuition. See, for example, Masakatsu, "Nishida Kitarō's Philosophy."

networks of outrage and hope, influencing the private and public spheres for good.[50] It is a blend of God's mercy flowing deep and wide, integrating contemplation and action. And with the introduction of the term "contemplation" we turn to our chapter on prayer.

50. On networks of outrage and hope, see Castells, *Networks of Outrage and Hope.*

SEVEN

We Pray

Do you pray? What do you *do* when you pray? Does "politics" ever enter into your prayers? Why, and how? Is prayer a movement toward the "deep" or the "wide"?

In the earlier sections of this book it might have seemed like prayer equals *deep* and action equals *wide*. Yet as we have been developing this theme we see that our categories of "deep" and "wide" blend more and more together. We discover that prayer and action are perhaps best understood not as distinct tasks but rather as essential, interpenetrating components of a creative whole, a life of relationship with God and others. Consequently, in this chapter we will learn that prayer is a deep act of going wide: in solidarity, in motivation, in strategy, and more. These are more than the "sports event prayers" of "God help my team (my candidate, my party, my campaign . . .) to win." I closed the previous chapter by claiming that monastic (or semi-monastic) community can provide an excellent framework of support for socio-political action. In this chapter I want to make a further claim: monastic (or semi-monastic) prayer *is* socio-political action. You will see what I mean as we go further.

A few years ago, while filming a video lecture for a class I was teaching on "Monasticism(s) Old and New," I found myself spontaneously pleading to my students that "we need a new mysticism to accompany a new monasticism." I have mused on that statement ever since I made it. What would this "new mysticism" (or perhaps new mysticism(s)) look like? Where would I find it (them)? I suspect that I will find it among people living the life itself, just as the new mysticisms of the late-medieval period emerged from the creative experiments of the Beguines and other unique expressions of the times. Nonetheless, I think I see glimpses of it here and there and I will point them out as we go along.

I will divide up this chapter a bit differently than previous chapters. Whereas my reflections in previous chapters were often identified by a viewpoint from which the topic was explored (biblical/theological, historical, practical, and such), in this chapter I will organize my reflections according to different kinds of prayer: worship, repentance, contemplation, and intercession (with a "monastic practice" of praying the political Scriptures included).

WORSHIP AS SOCIO-POLITICAL PERSPECTIVE; SOCIO-POLITICAL ENGAGEMENT AS CHRISTIAN WORSHIP

Worship. I think "worship" is one of the most misused words in contemporary Christian conversation. "How was the worship last Sunday?" a friend might ask. We might answer, "Oh, the lead guitar was a bit loud, but on the whole I really felt God's presence through the songs." Churches hire "worship pastors," whose primary job is to supply the singing portion of a Sunday church service. Liturgical congregations might expand this a bit and see the whole event as a "worship service," a time where we offer prayers, sing songs, hear the Scripture, and receive communion. But even here I think we are falling short.[1]

The biblical words we translate as "worship" reveal a very big picture. Worship is an *act* we perform: we bow, we kneel, we prostrate ourselves. But it is an act performed with an attitude. Worship emerges from a sense of extravagant reverence or admiration. We say of a young woman smitten in love for a man, "She worships the ground he walks on." In religious worship this attribution of value toward the other takes on a cosmic proportion. We ascribe ultimate value to God. This posture of the worshipp*er* and the worshipp*ed* is an expression of a relationship of absolute unequals. Needless to say, this is a pretty political notion. We may complain that the idea promotes a monarchical view of God that facilitates awful abuses—I think Christian monotheism supports not authoritarianism, but rather reverence for a single God who requires a host of humans in collaboration to even approximate God's wisdom and

---

1. Regarding worship, see for example, Peterson, *Engaging with God;* Jones et al., eds., *Study of Liturgy;* Farhadian, ed., *Christian Worship Worldwide.* I have uploaded a series of video lectures on the spirituality of worship at https://www.youtube.com/watch?v=-KdhoYxDMxQ&list=PLiw_vQbcv1gOToTznf2fGUPBMFPlsdF1S.

power—but monotheism must remain or we lose authentically *Christian* worship. God is of ultimate value. Our relationship with God (Father, Son, Holy Spirit) begins here.

What does this mean for our socio-political engagement? It frees us from over-responsibility. I think of Moses and Aaron, following God's lead to confront the pharaoh (see Exod 4–5). They arrive and speak the word, just as God had instructed (note the strategy of diplomacy here). What happens? Everything gets worse. Pharaoh refuses to budge, the Israelites have more work, and Moses and Aaron are in the dog house with both the Egyptians and the Israelites. As readers, however, we know the rest of the story. God has a bigger plan. Moses and Aaron could have despaired—and they did confront God with the problem. They knew, however, that it did not depend on their work but on God's. Worship informs our sense of "who's really in charge here." We do our part and we trust God to do God's part.

Yet worship also refers to those *events* where God's people gather to praise, to hear the Word, to celebrate the Eucharist, to share our faith together. What is important to recognize about these events is that our times and places of worship gathering rehearse and reinforce our sense of the world within which we live.[2] As it is said in Latin: *lex orandi, lex credendi, lex agendi*: What we speak (the law of prayer), is what we believe (the law of our faith), and what we live (the law of life). When we lift up our hands to the ceiling and installed on that ceiling is a mosaic of the Pantocrator, the Almighty resurrected King Christ, we by that very act reinforce our sense of perspective. Our petty allegiances to this or that political system fall away as we remind ourselves of our citizenship in heaven. When we have a time of waiting upon the Spirit, perhaps quietly praying in tongues, sensing what God might have to say to the gathered community this day, we allow God to reorient our sense of time. Our addictions to busyness and effectiveness, the traps of outcomes and success, all fade as we do nothing, waiting for the Spirit. In waiting on the Spirit we remember that our sense of time is not necessarily God's sense of time. A profound lesson for our political life.

Similarly, when we "pray for one another," perhaps with some people coming to the front of the meeting place, we by this very act rehearse our conviction that God is actively present in the world, able and willing to restore what is broken and to use one another as vehicles of that restoring

2. For treatments of this theme from different traditions see Albrecht, *Rites in the Spirit*; Maximus the Confessor, "Church's Mystagogy"; Smith, *Imagining the Kingdom*.

grace. When we receive the sacramental elements—bread and wine—we welcome the fountain of Christ's sacrificial forgiveness flowing deep and wide. Some of us come to the sacrament, using Howard Thurman's language, as disinherited individuals: our backs against the wall, struggling with fear, with deception, with hate. The sacrament we receive reminds us "You are God's children." "From him nothing is hidden." "Neither do I condemn you."[3] Some of us come to the sacrament as those who benefit from the structures that put others' backs against the wall: and consequently who may carry not only appropriate guilt, but also a load of shame or confusion. The sacrament we receive communicates freedom from both personal sin and structural Sin. Our sacramental encounter with forgiveness, no matter who we are, is not an acknowledgment that "everything is OK." Rather it is the experienced perspective within which we can begin to do real work. Christian worship is the creation of sociopolitical perspective.

There is more. Worship not only speaks of particular acts of reverent trust or events of remembrance but also of an entire *life orientation*. When I say that I worship the God of Abraham and Isaac and not the gods of the Canaanites, I mean by this affirmation that I permit my way of living to be ordered in light of my sense of *this* God's reality. I am an advocate of God's concerns. The words for "serve" and "worship" are sometimes connected. Just as I may honor my wife by giving quality time with our children, so also we honor the God of Moses by treating our neighbors the way God likes, or by speaking out when they are not treated right (we learned about God's concerns in chapter 3). Worship is the way we order our entire lives in light of the reality of God's presence. It is prayer. It is action.

As you can see, this too is political. Our participation in a political campaign—or a food bank or in experimenting with an alternative life—is not just some effort to "make a difference." The way we serve God, the way we order our lives, is worship. John Howard Yoder speaks of this in terms of *doxology*, saying that, "Right action is a reflection of a victory already won as much as it is a contribution to a future achievement. It is more an act of praise rather than an act of servile obedience. We do not enter responsibly into the structures of social concern because we are sure of what we can get done there, but because we are proclaiming the lordship of Christ and predicting the day when every knee will bow

3. See Thurman, *Jesus and the Disinherited*, 50, 71, 106.

before him."[4] Our fundamental act of submissive worship before God reminds us of why we act. We are representatives of, witnesses to, the living God. I think of Martin Luther King Jr.'s decision, later in his career, to speak out against USA policies regarding Vietnam. Many of his own peers advised him to keep silent. He responded to their concerns in his 1967 address "A Time to Break the Silence": "I would yet have to live with the meaning of my commitment to the ministry of Jesus Christ. To me the relationship of this ministry to the making of peace is so obvious that I sometimes marvel at those who ask me why I am speaking against the war."[5] Our engagement is not merely an "action." Rather our engagement flows from our entire relationship with God. Socio-political engagement is Christian worship.

Some argue that "worship" (whatever it is) is a distraction from action. We get so caught up in meetings, songs, sermons, and personal experience, that the cause of justice is lost. I disagree. I would argue that worship is vital to socio-political engagement because it frames our worldview and orients us to the proper place of our action. Furthermore, with this worldview we can see our engagement—our service, our action—neither as an overly demanding "project" or a fruitless effort taking time away from community or devotion, but rather as one element of our wholehearted worship, which incorporates our songs and our community, along with our socio-political engagement.

Monastic Practice: Praying the (Political) Scriptures

If there is one thing you encounter in a monastery, it is a lot of Scripture. When you visit, you participate in Bible readings, Psalm recitations, and biblical meditations multiple times a day. Claude Peifer writes of the role of Scripture in monastic life, "Whatever factors may have been involved in the rise and development of the monastic movement, there is no doubt that the central factor, without which the monastic movement is simply unthinkable, is the Scriptures of the Old and New Testaments." He continues by making clear what this emphasis in Scripture is all about: "The

4. Yoder, "Biblical Mandate," 195. Thanks to Joe Gatlin of Hope Fellowship, a community of bilingual kindred spirits in Waco, Texas, who pointed out this article and shared his own encounter in El Salvador with mutual giving and receiving as an experience of doxological socio-political engagement.

5. King, "Time to Break Silence," 234.

monastic way of life was conceived as a response to the precepts of Scripture and was oriented toward the progressive assimilation of the truths of Scripture."[6] This is a worthy task. What might happen if committed communities and individuals today conceived of their life as a progressive assimilation of and response to the truths of Scripture? But how is this done?

One common monastic practice was known as *lectio divina*, or sacred reading. Sometimes we call it "praying the Scriptures": a way of reading Scripture and praying where the two blend into a single encounter.[7] When we pray the Scriptures we engage the text with our intellect, but also with imagination and feeling. We sit with the text, allowing the words to go deep, or perhaps allowing our own feelings about the text to emerge from the deep. Our interaction with Scripture becomes a time of prayer with God, or perhaps we are drawn to communicate with God through words found in Scripture. People have used a number of specific methods to stimulate this kind of prayer: reading slowly, imagining Bible stories, repeating phrases, putting Scripture words into our own words, singing the text, and so on.

We have been learning throughout this book that the Bible is more political than we had perhaps thought. The Bible begins with an ordering of the world that involves both God and humans. The story of the Israelites is a tale of God inviting a people to become light to the nations, demonstrating what it could look like to live in right relationship with God, self, others, and the created world. The story of Jesus and his followers—set within a complex drama of religious-political factions—recounts how the Son of God both modeled and mediated a path to this right relationship with God, self, others, and the created world. Laws proclaim the principles of righteousness. Psalmists cry out from the suffering of oppression. Prophetic visions dream of a new world. Thus, *lectio divina*, praying the Scriptures, can be—and perhaps *ought to be*—a very political practice.

For the sake of introducing the practice of praying the political Scriptures, I will use two examples: one from the book of Psalms and one from the Gospels. Psalm 72 is my favorite "Tuesday" psalm. It was a prayer for the success of the king and I often express my own prayers for government (on Tuesdays) using the words of this psalm as a guide. But since the psalms were written in a society where kings had absolute rule while I live in the midst of a different governmental structure, I find it helpful to make the words my own (trying my best to keep to the primary message of each

---

6. Peifer, "Role and Interpretation of Scripture," 467.

7. I, along with my friend James Wilhoit, have treated this practice more thoroughly in Howard, *Praying the Scriptures*; and in Wilhoit and Howard, *Discovering Lectio Divina*.

phrase). Thus, if I were living in the UK, I might express the following, slowly reflecting over each phrase as I offer my prayer to God:

verse 1 – Endow the Prime Minister with a sense of justice, oh God, a justice that ultimately comes from You. Give to the members of the Cabinet and the procedures of Parliament integrity and righteousness.

4 – May our county, district and parish authorities design laws that function to defend those who suffer most, and particularly the children of those who are most in need. May our laws give harsh penalties to those who take advantage of those who are weak.

6–7 – Throughout this cycle of leadership, may the interaction between political and economic sectors bring forth a time of authentic prosperity, a time of natural, healthy growth, where markets of blessing flourish like a garden.

11–12 – May other lands notice and appreciate our exemplary life together, following our model of compassionate attention to those who have no other help, consciously rescuing people from those who might harm them to their own profit.

19 – Praise be to Your name, Oh God, forever. We acknowledge that you are the Ultimate authority, and when we order well, we reflect your own Beauty. May this whole earth be filled with your Beauty (imagining *this* or *that* place, *this* or *that* situation). Amen and Amen.

Another way of praying the political Scriptures, especially popular among Jesuits, is to immerse yourselves in the drama of a passage. You do this by making use of your imagination, just picturing, experiencing, what it might have been like. The practice is especially fun when you pretend that you are a character in the story. A couple of years ago I imagined my way through the Gospel stories of Jesus's final week, from the triumphal entry through Easter. Every day or two I would read a different passage, moving one by one through the passion narratives. I ended up imagining that I was a follower of Jesus—but not one of the twelve. I was from Galilee, had been enthralled by the teachings and miracles of Jesus there, and just before this week I had finally decided to leave everything behind for a while to join the movement as it entered Jerusalem. Space does not permit me sharing the details—the smells, the sounds, all the moods—of my imaginative journey. But the point is to encourage you to take your own journey!

I was thrilled, as I joined with the crowd of fans at Jesus's triumphal entry, to think that perhaps through this man's leadership we would finally be free of the Roman rule of extraction, siphoning off nearly everything we produced for their own use elsewhere. I was not present when Jesus shared his Last Supper and time in the garden of Gethsemani with his closest disciples. News got to me that Jesus had been taken captive by soldiers and that he was going to appear before Pilate. I ran to the site, wondering, was *this* the moment when Jesus would do some powerful miracle? I found myself cheering Jesus on as he confronted Pilate in the first trial.

But after his meeting with Herod and as I attended his second appearance before Pilate, the tone of things changed and I was saddened. I watched my hopes for something new, something good, begin to die right before my eyes. Jesus was now the pawn being maneuvered by so many factions. Why didn't he *do* something? I saw my hero, my dreams, crushed: another victim of Roman supremacy, of Sadducean self-interest. As with his life, my experience at Jesus's cross exhibited both miracle and mystery. The sky grew dark. But Jesus did not rescue himself. I shared the questions of the onlookers: "Why don't you come down off the cross? You showed miracles before . . ." In the end, as Jesus spoke to John and Mary and then gave up his spirit, I found myself echoing the cry of Obi Wan Kenobi to Anakin Skywalker in *Star Wars* III: "You were the chosen one! You were supposed to bring balance to the Force!"

After his death and burial, I left for Galilee. Back home to start over again. I walked with a friend and on the way to Emmaus someone joined us. We talked, we ate, and in that meeting I realized that this man was *him*. Indeed, I realized that it was always and only really about *him*. Whether Rome stole our produce, whether Sadducees compromised the law, whether we lived or died, what mattered most was that I followed Jesus. I did not understand what it all meant but I knew that I would continue to follow Jesus. And in my devotional imagination in 2020, that decision to continue following was not just a matter of my imagined character; it was *me* making that decision in the midst of some pretty heavy personal and socio-political stuff.

I share my own journey to give you a taste of how the monastic practice of praying the Scriptures, employing our imagination and informed by a broader sense of the socio-political realities of Scripture and our lives can serve growth in full Christian maturity. This kind of practice can be done with a group as well as by an individual. One person reads the passage very slowly, waiting after each event, while the rest picture the development. Through the practice of praying the Scriptures, however we do it, we become more attuned to the socio-political context and message of the Bible, and we begin to allow the Scripture to penetrate our own socio-political lives ever deeper and wider.

Repentance as Socio-Political Solidarity

One common method of "doing prayer" is the ACTS method: Adoration, Confession, Thanksgiving, Supplication. It's easy to remember and it helps people learn that prayer is not just asking for things. I have, however, seen people struggle with the Confession part. On the one hand some people are experts at beating themselves up and find no end of things to confess, most of which they should have forgotten long ago. On the other hand others have a hard time noticing "sins" every day. And in the midst of all this, the Sin of our society gets lost. Sometimes I wonder if shifting the focus toward "repentance" rather than "confession" might help.

I mentioned in chapter 1 that from the beginning nuns and monks have seen their task as a "work of repentance" and that we needed to see this as part of our socio-political work. Indeed I suggested that one of the aims of this book was to help readers learn the integrated repentance of our personal life within and structural life without. I made mention of Merton's perspective in chapter 2, where he stated that "what we have known in the past as Christian penance is not a deep enough concept if it does not comprehend the special problems and dangers of the present age." Notice, Merton criticizes the practice of penance for not being *deep* enough. So, let us now look at this notion of repentance a little more deeply.

Monastic—and socio-political—life is a life of mourning and a life of turning. Mourning is reflected in the Greek word *penthos*.[8] Turning is reflected in the Greek word *metanoia*. Another Greek word that is often associated with these is "compunction" (*katanuxis*). Irénée Hausherr's struggle to define *penthos* describes our difficulties with this entire concept: "while definitions of *penthos* are not lacking, none of them is satisfactory."[9] One might, for example, speak of the presence of tears or sorrow in our prayers. Saint Ephrem (306–373) writes "Weep sinner, weep. You have no recourse but this." Gregory Nazianzen (329–390) writes that "baptism pardons freely, and requires nothing but faith. Repentance, after baptism, is not free, but requires exhausting effort, the afflictions of compunction, tears, prolonged weeping." Isaac of Nineveh (613–700) bewails his own life: "I have no heart in mourning to seek you with, I have neither repentance nor compunction, which bring the

---

8. Syrian monks were known as *penthikoi*, those who mourn.

9. Hausherr, *Penthos*, 17. See further, 17–25.

children back to their inheritance. Lord, I have no tears."[10] Early Christians regarded repentance as both a gift and command of God.[11] Peace activist and theologian James W. Douglass speaks of *metanoia* like this: "Metanoia is the demand for that wrench away from my household idols to confront the living God. If I dared to carry it through, it would result in my becoming a new man, someone whom I do not know and whom I fear to know."[12] From a slightly different angle, professor Soong-Chan Rah uses the word "lament": "But lament is not simply the presentation of a list of complaints, nor merely the expression of sadness over difficult circumstances. Lament in the Bible is a liturgical response to the reality of suffering and engages God in the context of pain and trouble."[13]

Mourning, repentance, compunction, lament: while difficult to define, these are important words in Scripture, monastic life, and—I will suggest—in our socio-political engagement. The key that holds all this together is the object of repentance, what we are repenting *for*. Confession tends to emphasize being sorry for personal sins.[14] Lament emphasizes grief in the midst of suffering. Repentance is open. I like the definition that Hausherr settles on in his description of *penthos*: "It is a mourning for salvation lost."[15] If we combine the moment of lament for salvation lost with a commitment that turns toward new salvation, we can begin to grasp a fuller idea of the repentance that I want to suggest is central to new monastic socio-political prayer.

The key is the object of our repentance: salvation lost and salvation sought. Which brings us to the next question: what is salvation? Jesus declares to the bleeding woman who touched his robe, "Take heart daughter; your faith has made you well" (Matt 9:22; see also Luke 18:42). This phrase "made you well" is the term we know as "saved." Jesus declares to Zacchaeus, a rich tax collector who decided to do good and

10. Cited in Hausherr, *Penthos*, 31, 131, 135. See also 24–25.

11. See Hausherr, *Penthos*, 54, 74, 138.

12. Douglass, *Resistance and Contemplation*, 59.

13. Rah, *Prophetic Lament*, 21. On lament more generally, see Billman and Migliore, *Rachel's Cry*.

14. *Penthos* in the early Christian East also tended to emphasize attention to personal sins (for example, Hausherr, *Penthos*, 139). It is important in this regard to recognize their value of nonjudgmentalism, particularly in the desert traditions. The point was to set aside judgment of others in order to work on one's own salvation. This may explain some of the intense personal focus in this literature.

15. Hausherr, *Penthos*, 25.

redistribute his wealth, "Today salvation has come to this house" (Luke 19:9). Paul declares in his Letter to the Romans regarding the obtaining of the righteousness that is from God, "For one believes with the heart and so is justified, and one confesses with the mouth and so is saved" (Rom 10:10). What is salvation? It is the restoring of any and every area of life into the wholeness of God.[16] Consequently, if salvation is the increase of restoration in any area of life (personal sins, lack of healing, economic unfairness, and more), our repentance is the mourning over the loss of wholeness and a turning toward wholeness in any area of life. This means that our prayerful repentance involves not only the personal, but the socio-political. Our "woe is me" not only comes from being *a person* of unclean lips, but also from one who lives among *a people* of unclean lips. This is a repentance of solidarity.

Thus Clement of Alexandria (150–215) acknowledges that "to weep and wear mourning for justice's sake is to bear witness to the most wonderful Law, that it is good."[17] Soong-Chan Rah urges the church to learn to lament on behalf of those who suffer from injustice, and to lament the broken system itself.[18] James Douglass speaks of "two wheels of bondage": the bondage of the individual self and the bondage of the extended or social self.[19] What does it mean to mourn over personal sins *and* social Sin? I think it is to declare and to *feel* the "Woe is me" with Isaiah, not only for our own personal sins, but to recognize deeply that we live among a people of unclean lips (here follows a sample list reflecting a variety of issues and viewpoints):

- where many of our lands and homes and places of business have been (and at times, still are) acquired at the cost of displacing others with little means from their lands or homes.

- where unborn children are put to death for social or economic reasons.

- where the color of our skin can affect whether we are treated fairly by police, represented fairly in the media, or respected fairly in the educational system.

---

16. I have treated this at greater length in Howard, *Brazos Introduction*, 186–89.

17. Cited in Hausherr, *Penthos*, 11.

18. This theme is replete in his *Prophetic Lament*.

19. Douglass, *Resistance and Contemplation*, 19, 69–70.

- where we escape our pains and pursue our pleasures through means that are harmful to ourselves and to society (such as drugs, pornography, or even suicide).

- where families and nations resort to contempt and violence far too quickly, neglecting to courageously and creatively pursue means of peace.

- where our lack of virtues, exhibited by a few, leads to the proliferation of laws restricting the many.

- where we maintain our standard of living at the cost of damage to air, water, soil, vegetation, and other kindred species.

- where we ignore, avoid, or reject the True King.

What would happen if we voiced these laments—these Isaiah 6, Daniel 9, Lamentations, Magnificat cries—to God as part of our "worship" services? Or our private devotions? We can create occasions of repentance (monasteries call this the "divine office"). We can develop structures and songs to hold our prayers of lament (monasteries call these "liturgies"), expressing our sincere grief over both the social and the personal. We can open ourselves to the Spirit through lament (monasteries call this "discernment"), attending to the voice of conviction, of wisdom, of response. The prayer of repentance will look different for the advantaged and the disinherited, but we all suffer from sins and Sin and we can all repent from the place of our own experience.

Some of our repentance will require a bit of study and education. It is helpful to have a clear sense of the connections between our life and the sufferings of others in order to repent sincerely. We grow to understand, for example, the impact of purchasing non-fair trade products. Our avarice is easy to see when we are consumed with financial worries. Our avarice is harder to see when we don't recognize how our need for what seems to be a normal standard of living requires purchases that harm others. Yes, we can get caught in the scrupulosity of nervously evaluating every purchase. Somewhere between unhealthy scruples and unhealthy negligence we learn to discern the appropriate posture for our own prayers of repentance.[20] Douglass writes that "my failure to correspond—

20. I have written a little piece on Quaker John Woolman and the practice of consumer ethics. See "Consumer Ethics, The Old Fashioned Way—Reflections on John Woolman's Interaction with Economics," https://spiritualityshoppe.org/wp-content/uploads/2022/02/WoolmanPresentation.pdf.

and my failure is no small one—to the living demands of love from my poorest brothers and sisters convicts me in conscience and act of the very same imperialism of which I indict my society. . . . But for resistance to survive long and fruitfully this deepening awareness of my own guilt, it will have to experience an infinitely forgiving Love and undergo the purifying fire of its own self-giving."[21] The repentance I seek for a new monasticism learns to live in this dialogue between the painful awareness of the breadth of sins/Sin and the grateful awareness of Christ's forgiving Love. This kind of repentance moves us beyond shallow confession into something much deeper and wider.

MONASTIC CONTEMPLATION AS A PLACE OF SOCIO-POLITICAL WISDOM AND STRENGTH

Another dimension of prayer that I suspect will be valuable for groups and individuals trying to pursue Christ in the twenty-first century—and which I believe has socio-political significance—is contemplation. I suggested in chapter 3 that through contemplative listening we can become aware of the various temptations of socio-political communication. But that is only the beginning. There are many benefits that contemplation has to offer our socio-political engagement.

"Contemplation" is even harder to define than repentance. Spiritual writers both past and present use the words "meditation" and "contemplation" variously, sometimes indicating by one word just what another person means by the other word. Both of these words have been associated with groups that some people don't like and consequently their use has made some people concerned. In my *Brazos Introduction to Christian Spirituality* I summarized contemplation by calling it a way of prayer (one which makes less use of words), an attitude of prayer (a posture of receptive listening), and an aim of prayer (a realization of the presence of God within a divine-human relationship).[22] Here I will focus on contem-

---

21. Douglass, *Resistance and Contemplation*, 188.

22. Howard, *Brazos Introduction*, 310, 315, 324–25. To explore the history and meaning of contemplation more thoroughly see, for example, McGinn, *Presence of God*; and Martin Laird's trilogy: *Into the Silent Land*; *A Sunlit Absence*; *Ocean of Light*. For the interplay between contemplation and socio-political see for example, Douglass, *Resistance and Contemplation*, Rohr, *Dancing Standing Still*; and the resources produced by the Center for Action and Contemplation. I have explored some of the features of contemplative prayer more closely in Howard, "Thoughtless Prayer."

plation as a practice, though we must understand that the practice cannot be truly separated from its other aspects.

The first thing to realize as we begin to integrate contemplation with socio-political engagement is that contemplation is a unique means of prayer whereby we may open ourselves to God and allow our depths (and those of our world) to be faced. In one sense this is simply a development of our discussion of repentance. Part of repentance is truly *seeing* what is broken, in us or in our world. Contemplation, even back to its origins, has been understood as an experience of *seeing*. Media tells us some things about ourselves and the world. Good hard-nosed research tells us other things. Contemplation tells us still other things. Jesuit Walter Burghardt has spoken of contemplation as a "long, loving look at the real."[23] Just think about this with regard to socio-political matters. First, we take time. We give our neighborhood, our own political frustrations, a *long* look. We do not want to miss the wide range of factors present in this situation. We do not want to neglect the deep things that lie slightly hidden. We choose the slow fix.[24] Second we give a *loving* look. The point in contemplation is to see, not to react. Seeing requires that we suspend judgment and simply observe. We let the real be before us with caring attention, aware that loving observation sometimes involves grief and pain. Finally, it is a look at the *real*. Yes, by this term we mean the *Real*, the God who is here. But we also mean the *real*, the real mess within which we dwell. The fact of the matter is, we dwell within both the real and the Real, and the long, loving look of contemplation helps us to recognize this.

Consider, for example, fear. Howard Thurman identifies fear as "one of the persistent hounds of hell that dog the footsteps of the poor, the dispossessed, the disinherited."[25] This fear has roots in the relations between those who control the environment and those who are controlled by it. It is the fear that emerges when I may be subject to violence or mistreatment and yet have no real power to make it different. Fear anticipates unavoidable suffering. How does it feel, knowing that just by walking through your neighborhood, you might be accosted, arrested, or worse? Thurman identifies a path through fear in knowing who and what we are, a child of God with dignity and ability. But how do we come to know who and what we are? How can we come to see the real in this situation? Often

23. Burghardt, "Contemplation."
24. See Honoré, *Slow Fix*.
25. Thurman, *Jesus and the Disinherited*, 36.

it is not enough just to proclaim "Si se puede" ("Yes we can"). We must come to a deeper existential knowledge that can overcome the roots of fear. Augustinian priest Martin Laird speaks directly of the relationship between contemplation and fear in his *Into the Silent Land: A Guide to the Christian Practice of Contemplation*. He writes that "learning to confront fear, indeed any afflictive emotion, is one of the great spiritual arts." He speaks of learning how to distinguish between an object of fear and the fear itself. Laird identifies this distinguishing skill with "watchfulness," a contemplative practice well-known among ancient monks.[26] He speaks of just being present before God, perhaps repeating a phrase, waiting and watching. When we allow ourselves to look long and care-fully at the real that confronts us—in this case, not just a situation, but our own inner posture toward that situation—we can open ourselves to the grace of recognizing both the child that God loves and the fear that we can leave behind. And when we leave that fear behind it is repentance, a transformation of one who lives among a people of unclean lips.

People are longing for a space within which they can simply be present with God. No need for prayer words that are often so hard to form or to say; no need to pretend we are pious Christians. We long for a space of human solidarity before God, a place where we can just present ourselves as those caught in the web of worldly, fleshly, and devilish entanglements without having to make sense of it all. People of every stripe are finding their way into prayer rooms and new monastic 24/7 prayer communities all over the world these days.[27] I think there is an important place that contemplation can serve in giving us a safe space to go deep.

Contemplation, thus, contributes to socio-political discernment. Contemplation is not only a place of leaving things behind, but also of imagining new options, and more. As I mentioned, I often teach that prayer involves speaking, listening, and the space in between, a space in between that involves the interpersonal dynamics which shape conversation. In the leisure of contemplation we permit our frustrations, our questions about trust, and more to come to the surface. Contemplation

26. Laird, *Into the Silent Land*, 98. He recounts a woman's story to illustrate his point. For the full story see 98–102.

27. See for example, https://www.24-7prayer.com/join_in_posts/how-to-run-a-prayer-room/ and Weber, *Even the Sparrow*. Thanks to Jill Weber with the Waverly Abbey in England, Andy Groen from the Greater Ontario House of Prayer in Canada, Aaron White from Vancouver, Canada, and others who have shared stories with me about the ministry of prayer rooms. We need more urban places of sanctuary!

opens the space in between God and us, and in doing so, allows the re-framing of the motives and of our image of our relationship with God from which our discernment of action emerges.

In chapter 3 we explored the practice of discernment and I mentioned the rhythm of listening, gathering, and prayer. The place of prayer is a place where things that we may not have considered come to mind. Things happen. Conversion. The term "repentance" is also connected to conversion, a commitment to live differently. Christian socio-political engagement involves what theologian Gustavo Gutiérrez calls a "conversion to our neighbor."[28] Once again, how does this "conversion to our neighbor" take place? Part of it certainly involves allowing ourselves permission to get to know our neighbor. But along with that there is the time we take to receive our neighbor's way of being, allowing it to soak into us. That, I think, is a task wonderfully suited for contemplation. Within this place of contemplative conversion healthy socio-political engagement is nurtured. When we are converted to our neighbor even the possibilities for action we might discern are transformed. Contemplation is not a time of planning. Indeed in contemplation we shut off our "planning mind" and allow our "default mode network" to permit unthought-of options to appear spontaneously.[29] Contemplation simply waits and sooner or later, ideas arise. Gandhi's idea of the Salt March in 1930 came, James Douglass states, "after weeks of silent searching and agonizing." He describes further: "To remain utterly still and concentrated, in a climate of violence, bitterness, and ringing demands for action, was Gandhi's way of revolution, and the source of his resulting action's enormous power when it was finally taken."[30] Sometimes the most powerful action we can take is to give space for contemplation.

Which brings me to a little note about withdrawal, solitude, and the role of monasticism in socio-political engagement. My aim in this book is not to argue that every monk, friar, nun or sister, whether traditional or semi-monastic, ought to be involved in statecraft. While none of us can

28. See Gutiérrez, *Theology of Liberation*, 116–20 and expanded in Gutiérrez, *We Drink from our Own Wells*. Donald Gelpi, developing the thought of Bernard Lonergan, has long spoken of the need for multiple conversions, speaking specifically of "socio-political" conversion (see Gelpi, "Converting Jesuit"), and I have developed these ideas further in Howard, *Brazos Introduction*, 254–59.

29. On "default mode network" see Pang, *Rest*, 33–50 and the references to the research described there.

30. Douglass, *Resistance and Contemplation*, 85, 95.

avoid involvement in politics at some level (this is the topic of chapter 2), I think some have more of a vocation to involvement in statecraft than others. I think, for example, that some people need to pursue a life of contemplation that requires a degree of distance from the political arena. Indeed, I think this is their strength, even for the sake of politics. It was certainly Thomas Merton's strength. Historian A. Gordon Mursell writes of Carthusian prior Guigo I (1083–1136), "For Guigo, the Carthusian vocation was not so much a flight *from* the world as a flight *for* it: the contemplative monk who addressed himself to secular concerns from his monastic solitude saw himself not as someone interfering in matters that did not concern him, but as someone who had the advantage of a clearer and surer perspective from which to view them."[31]

Finally, contemplation can equip us to become instruments of the divine radiating out from the spheres of our vocation. I have in mind here some combination of a broadly understood "organic intellectual," and the early Christian idea of a "holy man" or woman.[32] Take for example Abba Apollo (born around 305).[33] Apollo withdrew at age fifteen and spent forty years in the desert before the Lord encouraged him to move to more inhabited regions. He moved to a small cave adjoining a settled region where his primary work consisted in "offering prayers to God throughout the day, and in bending his knees a hundred times in the night and as many times again in the day." He performed miracles, attracted followers, and spread the gospel among locals, to the point where "there is no longer anybody in his district which may be termed a pagan." But for our purposes here we must look at other aspects of his ministry. "Not long afterwards, two villages came into armed conflict with each other in a dispute concerning the ownership of land. When Apollo was informed of this, he went down to them at once to restore peace among them." This history also records other stories of Apollo restoring peace between

31. Mursell, "Introduction," 14. Michel Foucault, for example in the essays collected in *Power and Knowledge,* argues that knowledge today is often at the service of institutional forces. For Foucault, there is no pure ivory tower. Yet, I wonder if contemplative environments might not provide just this kind of venue, detached (at least to some degree) from vested interests.

32. "Organic intellectual"—Antonio Gramsci's idea of one who is educated but targets the fruits of their education not for the academy but for local populations—and it spreads. "Holy person," one who mediates the presence of God for a local community—and it spreads. See https://www.oxfordreference.com/view/10.1093/oi/authority.20110803100253736.

33. Apollo's story is told in Russell, tr., *Lives of the Desert Fathers,* 70–79.

conflicting parties. David Brakke writes of Apollo, "Apollo's story, told in *The History of the Monks*, is a familiar one to students of late antiquity. A prestigious monk, after years of developing his identity as a man apart from other people through ascetic withdrawal, becomes the focal point of religious transition. He disrupts the practice of traditional religion and then provides the services that it had offered—mediation of conflict, healing of diseases, ensuring agricultural prosperity, and the like."[34] Notice the services offered: judicial, health care, economic assistance. This is all politics. God empowered Apollo through years of solitude to become a political force within the context of his own monastic life. God did this in the fourth century and I think God can do the same today.

There are a lot of dynamics to pay attention to when navigating the contemplative-active waters. Richard Rohr opens his book *Dancing Standing Still* with the sentence, "I believe that the combination of human action from a contemplative center is the greatest art form."[35] There are no easy formulae in art forms. You learn best by doing it. We discover our own limits and then celebrate them, using these very limits to create unique expressions. Such were the Beguines, limited by gender and formal education, yet able to articulate from their wild, prophetic voice an encounter with God and an influence in the world that was fresh and powerful not only for their own setting, but also for us today (I believe the rise of medieval women mystics to be a revival of the Holy Spirit). We will have to welcome our own darkness, lament, and ambiguity along the way. We will have to explore our own locations of wildness, learning to incorporate the mix of faith and doubt.[36] For some of us, perhaps addicted to the high energy culture of megachurch life or activist politics, the invitation to solitude and contemplation may be require some serious divine permission. Others of us, however, need to guard against the temptation of using solitude as an excuse for avoiding messy political involvement. Some of us are spiritually greedy, longing for the big experiences along the way. Others of us would do well to pursue a little experience. That is why we there is community, so others can help steer us in a good direction.

---

34. Brakke, *Demons and the Making*, 214.

35. Rohr, *Dancing Standing Still*, 8.

36. Wendell Berry speaks of the necessity of wildness in *Unsettling of America*, 130–31.

Praying for (Intercession) as Socio-Political Action

Worship, repentance, and contemplation. Yes, all of them good and appropriate. But sooner or later we get on our knees and pray *for* political situations. Such was the case with Nehemiah, exiled in Persia. When he heard word about the suffering of his fellow Israelites back in Judah, he was horrified. "When I heard these words I sat down and wept, and mourned for days, fasting and praying before the God of heaven" (Neh 1:4). Nehemiah repented in solidarity with his people for their failure to keep God's commandments. He reminded God of the promise to return the exiles to their land if they seek God. He asked God to give him success that very day. And then Nehemiah records this comment, "At the time, I was cupbearer to the king" (Neh 1:11). The reason he asked for success is that he had an idea—most likely one that emerged in his time of mourning and praying. As cupbearer, Nehemiah was a trusted associate to the king. What might happen if he asked the king for aid to rebuild Jerusalem? Kings can be capricious and Artaxerxes might think that Nehemiah was usurping his authority by suggesting foreign policy in this manner, especially a policy that sought to improve the status of a subject colony. But what if the king said "Yes"? So Nehemiah prayed, pleading with God for success. And, as we know from reading the rest of the book of Nehemiah, God granted his request. Nehemiah prayed for his political situation, recognizing that his own actions were only one piece of a much larger picture of the divine will. He prayed believing that the Almighty God was somehow sovereignly responsive to his own prayers. He dared to pray that God's own influence would be felt in this moment of ordering things. "And the king granted me what I asked, for the gracious hand of my God was upon me" (Neh 2:8).

Like Nehemiah, God's people often cry out, pleading that the gracious hand of our God would be upon our own political situations. I mentioned above that Psalm 72 is a favorite of mine, a prayer *for* God's influence upon government. "May he judge your people with righteousness, and your poor with justice" (Ps 72:2). Likewise we read in 1 Timothy 2:1–3, "First of all, then, I urge that supplications, prayers, intercessions, and thanksgivings be made for everyone, for kings and all who are in high positions, so that we may lead a quiet and peaceable life in all godliness and dignity. This is right and is acceptable in the sight of God our Savior." The point is that our prayers contribute to God's gracious hand involved in the ordering of leaders and nations. Intercession, prayer *for* things, even prayer for politics, is encouraged in the Bible. Nehemiah recognized that there was a cosmic King who stood even above his local king, and he pleaded with this King before he pleaded with his local king. So also we can recognize that our own politics are performed on a stage set by a much larger Politician. And we can ask this Politician to extend a gracious hand on behalf of righteousness, policies that reflect God's own concerns.

Monasteries have long sensed that this kind of prayer was part of their vocation. The author of the fourth-century *History of the Monks in Egypt* declared of these monasteries and monks that "through them the world is kept in being and that through them too human life is preserved and honoured by God. . . . And the people depend on the prayers of these monks as if on God himself."[37] We have already mentioned Columbanus and his relationship with kings and princes. Part of the structure of Columbanan monasteries was a pattern of prayer for the health of the surrounding political environment. Monastic historian Marilyn Dunn writes, "By establishing a pattern of intercession for named groups, Columbanus made a further move in the direction of the intercessory superstructure which had already begun and would come to surround the monastic office in subsequent centuries. Though specific groups are mentioned, the overall schema adds up to prayer for all of society—including 'our enemies.'"[38] Historian C. H. Lawrence recounts the founding of the highly influential monastery of Cluny in 909. Duke William III of Aquitane had taken abbot Berno on a trip to search for a proper location to build a monastery and Berno chose the richly wooded valley of Cluny. "William protested that the site was his favourite hunting ground, but Berno was inexorable: 'which will serve you better at the Judgment, O Duke, the prayers of monks or the baying of hounds?' So William yielded, and Berno became the first abbot of the new foundation."[39] Duke William charged the monks, in the charter through which he deeded the land to the foundation of the monastery, "that the venerable house of prayer there may be faithfully filled with prayers and supplications . . . and that prayers, requests, and entreaties may be assiduously addressed

---

37. Russell, *Lives of the Desert Fathers*, 50.

38. Dunn, *Emergence of Monasticism*, 172.

39. Lawrence, *Medieval Monasticism*, 80. For Cluny's ministry of intercession see also Constable, *Abbey of Cluny*, 65, 337.

both for me and for all those . . .",⁴⁰ Thus, from its inception the monastery of Cluny was committed to a ministry of intercession.

This was in keeping with the medieval sense of things that I mentioned earlier in this book: some fought and ruled, some labored, and still others prayed. It was this balance that held society together. The tenth-century *Regularis Concordia*, an agreement of the monks and nuns in England, states explicitly that those prayers made for the king and benefactors "shall not be chanted at excessive speed lest rashly we provoke God to anger, which God forbid, instead of wisely beseeching Him to forgive our sins."⁴¹ Historian David Knowles writes of the developments of monasticism in the eleventh century that, "By Lanfranc's day the emphasis had shifted, and although personal sanctification of the individual is not forgotten, the monk is now primarily one who devotes his life to the liturgical service of God and to intercession for the world."⁴² I could go on and on, but you get my point. Prayer, and specifically prayer *for* the political structures within which one dwells, is a pattern deeply engrained in monastic DNA. I think that this is part of the spirit of the later Moravian movement, which devoted itself to a project of 24/7 prayer not just for their local situation, but also for the spread of the gospel throughout the world.⁴³

And this brings me to the prayers of Thomas Merton. I mentioned in our first chapter that I would be referring to Merton's "Cold War Letters" throughout the book, stating that they offered a superb example of the interaction of monasticism and socio-political engagement. I also mentioned that there is a surprising end to Merton's "Cold War Letters" story. Now is the time to share that end.⁴⁴

Prior to Merton's first (October 25, 1961) Cold War Letter, he records in his journal (September 5, 1961) that he responded to a note

40. Halsall, "Charter of Cluny," 1.

41. Symons, *Regularis Concordia*, 5.

42. Knowles, tr., *Monastic Constitutions*, xiv–xv.

43. On the Moravians generally see Hutton, *History of the Moravian Church* and Langton, *History of the Moravian Church*. For a contemporary retrieval of the Moravian charism of prayer today see Greig, *Vision and Vow* and Greig and Roberts, *Red Moon Rising*.

44. My sources for this discussion include Douglass, "Foreword"; Merton, *Cold War Letters*; Merton, *Turning Toward the World*; White, "Robert Kennedy"; and Hayes, "Robert Kennedy." A comparison of the final two reveals the ongoing discussion regarding Robert Kennedy's role in the Cuban missile crisis. I do not think this matter needs to be resolved in order for me to make my suggestive point regarding prayer.

received from Ethel Kennedy with "an explicit objection to the resumption of nuclear testing." Two things must be understood here. First, Ethel Kennedy was the daughter of George and Ann Skakel, benefactors of Merton's own monastery of Gethsemani. Second, Ethel Kennedy was the wife of Robert Kennedy, then Attorney General and brother of President John F. Kennedy, the first Catholic President of the United States. By October, Merton had decided to work for the abolition of war, "primarily by prayer," expressing this commitment both in his first Cold War Letter and in his journal (October 30, 1961). Within the span of the five days between these two expressions American and Soviet tanks faced each other across "Checkpoint Charlie," engines running, poised to shoot and begin what easily could have been a nuclear war. Though the two superpowers pulled back from this offensive, the Cold War became hotter.

By December, the situation was grave. Merton wrote to Archbishop Thomas Roberts (Cold War Letter #9) lamenting that "the policy of the nation is more or less frankly oriented to a war of extermination." He states that "step by step we come closer to it because the country commits itself more and more to policies which, but for a miracle, will make it inevitable."[45] In this same month Merton wrote Cold War Letter #10, to Ethel Kennedy again. In this letter he explicitly states that

> The President can certainly do more than any one man to counteract this [pressure toward war] by word and example, by doing everything that can help salvage the life of reason, by maintaining respect for intelligence and humanist principles without which freedom is only a word. . . . I personally wish the Church in America and everywhere were more articulate and definite about nuclear war. Statements of Pius XII have left us some terribly clear principles about this. We cannot go on indefinitely relying on the kind of provisional framework of a balance of terror. If as Christians we were more certain of our duty, it might put us in a very tight spot politically but it would also merit for us special graces from God, and these we need badly.[46]

I wonder (and this is really just a wonder) what happened at the dinner table that night when Ethel received the letter from Thomas Merton, one of the most well-known and well-respected Catholic spiritual authorities of her time. What did she say to her husband, the Attorney General and brother to the President? "Hey, honey, look at this letter I received

45. Merton, *Cold War Letters*, 25.

46. Merton, *Cold War Letters*, 28–29.

from Thomas Merton! Do you know what he thinks about nuclear war? Perhaps you would like to read the letter. Perhaps you might like to talk to your brother about this." Yes, this is a conjecture, but you must realize that Ethel had sent and received mail from Merton already; that her family gave money to the monastery; that Robert, though Attorney General and technically involved in legal affairs, had, since the Bay of Pigs affair earlier, served as confidant and partner with his brother on various foreign policy issues. I think it only natural that Ethel would have shared Merton's concerns.

In January of 1962 Thomas Merton reaffirms his commitment to prayer, writing to his activist friend James Forest that "really we have to pray for a total and profound change in the mentality of the whole world."[47] James Douglass, in his "Foreword" to Merton's Cold War Letters inquires, "How did one even begin to act toward the goal of "a total and profound change in the mentality of the whole world"—especially when one was a cloistered monk whose greatest way to influence people on the critical subject of war and peace, by writing articles and a book, was about to be squelched by one's superiors?"[48]

Indeed, early in 1962 Merton's censors silenced him on the subject of war and peace. He writes in his journal (April 27, 1962), "The decision seems to be (it is not absolutely definite) that I am to stop all publication of anything on war. In other words I am to be in effect silenced on this subject for the main reason that it is not appropriate for a monk, and that it 'falsifies the message of monasticism.'"[49] James Douglass, after his account of Merton's silencing, repeats his question, "How was a monk, forbidden to publish his most prophetic thoughts, to seek the impossible goal of changing the mentality of millions of people?" Douglass answers, "Merton simply continued to write letters, one by one. Each of his letters is a prayer."[50] Between his April silencing and the end of October Merton wrote forty-two letters. Douglass summarizes Merton's spirit in these letters well: "Merton is trying to call forth the saving presence of God in each of his Cold War correspondents, and implicitly in everyone

47. Merton, *Cold War Letters*, 59.

48. Douglass, "Foreword," xiii.

49. Merton, *Turning Toward the World*, 216. See also his comments to James Forest in Cold War Letter #69. Also we must realize that this silencing stopped publication of a book that was nearly ready to be published. For this story see the introductory material to Merton, *Peace in the Post-Christian Era*.

50. Douglass, "Foreword," xiii.

on earth. Writing in what he perceived as total darkness, the monk is praying his way through these individual letters in pursuit of the global miracle needed to save us from our own violence."[51]

On October 16, 1962 the presence of Soviet missiles located in Cuba, ninety miles (140 km) from Florida was communicated to US officials. The President held a series of meetings with the Executive Committee of the National Security Council to discuss the situation (EXCOMM; composed of the regular members of the National Security Council and a few others, including President Kennedy's brother, Robert). The situation was extremely tense, particularly as military advisors for both the Soviet Union and the USA pushed for invasions, preemptive strikes, blockades, and other dangerous options. President John F. Kennedy himself was, during this time, also communicating privately with Communist Party Chair Nikita Khrushchev. At one point Robert Kennedy met secretly with Soviet Ambassador Anatoly Dobrinin to ask for help.[52] It appears that Khrushchev and Kennedy both agreed on the idea of Noah's ark as a symbol of their common predicament, believing that they and all of humanity needed to stay afloat amidst a sea of conflict.[53] The details of the public and private meetings are complicated and the roles of the persons involved are still under some dispute. Yet two points can be affirmed: (1) that in the end the two parties decided each to make compromises and war was averted, and (2) that Robert Kennedy played a significant part in these negotiations, though not perhaps as significant as sometimes claimed. Douglass writes, "Instead of annihilation, they chose, in Khrushchev's words, 'a common cause, to save the world from those pushing us toward war.'" And he continues, "Their willingness to turn at a critical point in history was the kind of miracle Merton was praying for."[54]

Again, I wonder. "Each letter a prayer." Ethel and Robert Kennedy. Robert Kennedy and the EXCOMM meetings, and the secret meetings. Miraculous peace at a moment when everything could easily have gone awry. Douglass continues further with a question: "How does prayer work? Thomas Merton gives no clear answer to that question in his letters or anywhere else, nor does any other spiritual writer. But Merton

---

51. Douglass, "Foreword," xiii–xiv.
52. See both Douglass, "Foreword," xiv, and White, "Robert Kennedy."
53. See Douglass, "Foreword," xv.
54. Douglass, "Foreword," xv.

knew that prayer takes many forms. He knew his Cold War Letters were a form of praying in darkness, a search for light with the companions he addressed, in a night of the spirit when everything seemed lost."[55] How does prayer work? Maybe we are not meant to know the answer; rather we are simply invited to pray.

As with the practice of contemplation, there are dynamics in socio-political intercession (prayer *for*) that we will learn to navigate. Some of us can easily express our heartfelt prayers in words. Others ponder, waiting for words. Some offer their intercessions through prayers without words or through the gift of tongues. Still others find that written prayers in a liturgical book seem to communicate better than any words we might invent. There are many "collects" or prayers for governments published in prayer books. No worry what we do. We can trust that the Spirit who births and breathes prayer inhabits it all (Rom 8:26–27). Often we pray and no answer comes. At times, this experience of unanswered prayer can threaten our faith. It is striking how key prayers of Jesus remain unanswered: "Thy kingdom come." "Make them one." Or perhaps they are gradually being answered? This is the confusion of prayer, and many find it necessary to face our prayer confusions head on in order to move forward in the practice of intercession.[56] Nevertheless, in spite of our questions we can persevere in prayers to Jesus, who modeled and mediated prayer and intercedes on our behalf. We may struggle with the whole idea of us "asking" Almighty God and God "answering." That's OK. We can just pray anyway, for the God who created and commanded prayer knows much more about all this than we do.

Worship, Repentance, Contemplation, Intercession. Is prayer a distraction from our socio-political engagement? No. If speaking, caring, modeling, and acting are *ways* of socio-political engagement (are streams of the river/fountain), perhaps prayer is not merely another way or stream, but rather the energy, the flow, that carries forward any and every way or stream of socio-political engagement.

55. Douglass, "Foreword," xvi.

56. On unanswered prayer see Greig, *God on Mute*. For an academic analysis of the relationship between intercessory prayer and our view of God see Tiessen, *Providence and Prayer*.

EIGHT

We Live

David Janzen from Reba Place Fellowship (profiled in chapter 1) tells of his socio-political engagement in earlier days.

> I remember standing in a picket line holding a sign in silent vigil with a bunch of Quakers in a civil rights (or was it peace movement?) witness about 1965. It was a boring, drizzly day, and I wondered, "If no one saw us and changed their mind, if no reporter put this event in the news, if no one around me was turning more radical because of our witness, did I still want to be here?" I came to the conclusion, "Yes, I still want to be here because this is an opportunity to pray and purify my own soul. If no one else was changed but I was changed, it was worth it. If this was a moment of communion with God and I was in the center of God's attention and going deeper in availability to God's purposes, then, indeed, it was worth it." Years later, in the late 1970s, I felt God calling me, personally, to go to one of the buried missile silos in the prairies of Kansas (near where we lived at the time) that aimed multiple warheads at population centers in Russia. God called me to announce I'd be there the first Sunday of the month vigiling and praying for an end to the suicidal arms race. Some Sundays there were two or three of us but one Good Friday we were two hundred, with reporters on the edges and helicopters overhead, and the speaker with the megaphone had us chanting, "It's Friday, but Sunday is coming." Had I not been faithful in little, the bigger witness would never have happened. Though the world still looks a lot the same, those missile silos are now deactivated and gone. In a semi-monastic way the witness I led at the missile silo was closely connected to

prayer, discernment, and guidance from our intentional Christian community, New Creation Fellowship, in Newton, KS, and from a wider network of communities in resistance. It was well understood that if any of us got arrested, the community would care for our families and visit us in prison, carry on by other means. It was a communal witness though some were more on the front lines and others in supporting roles.

I want to draw attention to a couple of things in David's story. First, notice David's engagement. Both in 1965 and in the 1970s his means of engagement was to pray, whether privately or with two hundred others. And yet his prayer was also a "direct action" and even mass communication at times, complete with reporters and helicopters. We have learned about a lot of ways to engage in the socio-political sphere in this book. David's story shows how the ways of engagement blend together in a life of trying to live the gospel faithfully. Second, I want us to pay attention to the significance of David's community, New Creation Fellowship. The community had his back. If something happened, they would cover. Some were "on the front lines" and others played "supporting roles." I wonder if some of those in the community who were parents would have even gone if it were not for the support of the whole.

In our first chapter, I talked about the challenges of socio-political engagement and the challenges of monasticism. After a chapter describing how we are political people, I have spent most of the time exploring the politics of "old" monasticisms, demonstrating how monasticism engaged in their socio-political spheres in a variety of ways (speaking, caring, modeling, acting, praying). Now, in this chapter, I will review what we have learned and take a step toward the future. As I mentioned at the beginning, I suspect this book will serve less to inspire an army of activists and more to provide a little wisdom for those associated with communities who desire to engage. At the same time I hope there are others reading who might not be associated with a Christian community but through this book see in consecrated Christian living potential for something new. If so, you have grasped something of my heart. As I mentioned, I believe that we are not left with either leaving the faith or leaving political engagement. Other ways are possible. In what follows I will review where we have been by talking about the possibilities of socio-political engagement and then offer something on the promise of new monasticism(s).

THE POSSIBILITIES OF SOCIO-POLITICAL ENGAGEMENT

Let's look back at some of the ground we have covered. Only now our interest will be less on what has happened in the past and more on what is available to us in the present and future. I will revisit some of the key statements introduced in chapter 2, returning in the process to the cross (and the empty tomb), seeing the life of Jesus flowing deep and wide.

We are political people

First, *we are political people*. I can't say this enough, and if all that some readers get out of this book is a sense that the Christian gospel is more "political" than they had previously understood, I will have accomplished something important. Human beings were put on earth to help facilitate godly order and we will be doing the same in the final new earth. In between Genesis and Revelation we read a story of God leading humanity through a process of learning (and failing to learn) to live in right relationship with the earth, with ourselves, with one another, and with God. We are placed on this planet not simply as isolated individuals but in the context of a "common humanity," of a life shared with others.[1] What does this mean for us today? A sense of our dignity and relationships can, for example, help us appreciate the significance of labor not merely as a material necessity in a fallen world but more so as a vehicle of our cooperation with God's loving ordering work, a viewpoint that can offer something to our political debates about labor.[2] Similarly we have learned to understand human failing in terms of both personal "sins" and corporate "Sin." We are persons of unclean lips who live among peoples of unclean lips. To my mind, our humble solidarity with the conflicts of race, class, and more—just as our awareness of our own personal sense of fear or avarice—are a distinctive element of *Christian* socio-political engagement. God's socio-political concerns (which I introduced in chapter 3—creation care, human dignity, righteousness, justice, compassion) are not simply extracurricular virtues for those who are interested in politics. No, they are fundamental to the Christian gospel itself.

1. Bretherton, *Christ and the Common Life*, 299–301, 320.

2. Bretherton, *Christ and the Common Life*, 170–71. An interesting comparison can be made by a review of Arendt, *Human Condition*; Berry, "What Are People For?"; and Volf, *Work in the Spirit*.

And with the word "Christian" we are brought to Jesus Christ. Jesus, as we have seen, lived a political life. He modeled ways of navigating economy, family, and power that were unique for his time, and he taught his disciples to follow his model. Indeed, this is what his disciples understood "following" Jesus to mean: not just a revision of doctrinal beliefs (though I do think it included this), but a transformation of one's way of life. Jesus also challenged the religious-political authorities of his day, employing the tactics available to his situation. Through his own life and teachings Jesus sought to demonstrate and to inaugurate a society (a "kingdom") that embodied the heart of God. Jesus lived a political life and ultimately he died a political death.

We turn once again to the Assisi cross: Jesus dying, looking over the people gesturing and "politicking" among themselves, his blood flowing deep and wide. Theologians discuss "the work of Christ" in part by speaking about various "theories of the atonement." What did Jesus's death (or life, death, resurrection) mean? How does it affect us today? I like to think of these views not so much as competing "theories" of the atonement, but rather as different "aspects" of Christ's work on our behalf.[3] I have already talked a bit about the moral aspect of Christ's work. By his life and his way of death Jesus modeled a way of life for us, a life of sacrificial nonviolent resistance in the journey toward an order of love.

A second aspect of Christ's work is the substitutionary aspect. Christ died on our behalf, forgiving our sins and paving the way for full acceptance with God. Private sins and corporate Sin, s/Sin both known and unknown, the wounds of the oppressed and those of the oppressor: all human dis-order was borne by Christ on the cross. The substitutionary aspect of Christ's atonement means, for example, that we who have been recently politically enlightened need not perform our socio-political engagement in a spirit of anxious self-atonement for horrible sins in which we have found ourselves complicit. Likewise, the engagement of we who have suffered from the hands of others, perhaps for generations, need not be performed simply as acts of rage. There is s/Sin enough to go around.

3. In Howard, *Brazos Introduction*, 180–89, I treated a set of these views in light of how they provide unique emphases for Christian spirituality. Here I want to see a few of them as mutually informing contributions toward a synthetic understanding of the mystery of Christ's life, death, and resurrection, an understanding that has political significance.

There is forgiveness enough to cover all, flowing deep and wide. Forgiveness, reconciliation, and life-giving order are all tied up together.[4]

Then there is the victory aspect of Christ's work. Some passages of Scripture speak of the cross as a "conquering" moment, a battle won over the enemies of God (Col 2:15; note also 1 Cor 2:8).[5] Furthermore, it appears that Christ's work not only conquered our enemies theoretically, but also that somehow through Christ and the Spirit we who follow Christ can share in his victory and have power to conquer our enemies practically in life today. We have been set free from s/Sin and have become slaves of righteousness (Rom 6:18). Violence may be a strong force, but through Christ love is stronger. Self-interest may appear fundamental to our economy, but through Christ we can take steps to toward an economy of considering other's interests (see Phil 2:3-4).

Finally, I want to mention the participation aspect of Christ's work. Christ's death—and especially his resurrection—was not just a model, not just a sacrifice, not just a victory, but the provision of a divine life in which we participate through the Spirit of Christ (2 Pet 1:3-4). On the one hand we become aware of our free potential to live anew as we know the act of God through Christ. On the other hand our faith in God ushers forth a life of joining with God's concerns. On the one hand, the resurrection of Christ reaffirms our continuity with creation and God's original plan for creation. But on the other hand, the resurrection institutes a new era and a new and discontinuous identity for the city of God. There is something here that draws us both deeper in identification with the world as common creatures and yet draws us out wider in distinction from the world in a unique, Christlike politics.[6] And this, of course, leads to a reconsideration of the relationship between eschatology and politics. Politics and hope have often been connected, whether through a revolution of the proletariat or the gradual improvement caused by some "invisible hand" of the economy.[7] Christian socio-political engagement is

---

4. Miroslav Volf's chapter on "Embrace" in his *Exclusion and Embrace* (99-165) is written from the angle of "those of us who see ourselves as "victims" (100) and provides helpful reflection on the implications of the life and work of Christ for those who suffer at the hands of others.

5. I find this theme present (from significantly different perspectives) in Pentecostal theology, the works of John Howard Yoder, and in the thought of Gil Baillie and his followers.

6. I find these tensions explored in the political theologies of Augustine, Oliver O'Donovan, and Wayne Grudem.

7. See for example, Douglass's comments in Douglass, *Resistance and*

radicalized by our participation in Christ's victory, which is summarized in the phrase "Christ has died. Christ is risen. Christ will come again."[8] My point in all this reflection on the cross and empty tomb is to draw attention to the profound, mysterious richness of Christ's work offered for us, a work that is done for the transformation of our spiritual and political life. And remember, this Trinitarian work has been and is currently being done: God is the primary agent on earth. Our engagement is a participation in God's prior engagement of bringing order to all things. We are political people and the good news of Christ is a political good news.

Politics is not merely statecraft

Second, *politics is not merely statecraft*. In chapter 2 I defined politics as an ordering activity of agents within given spheres of influence in the world. I defined politics this way not only because of my sense of the biblical story, but also because I see this in political life. Bringing life-giving order to a society or a place is often expressed as the aim of government, whether that order is understood as domination over surrounding territories, protection of individual rights, or providing for the common good.[9] However it is perceived, and whoever the order benefits, governments understand that their task is to facilitate order. Furthermore—and this is my point—government is not the only contributor to life-giving order. Indeed, governments themselves are aware of this. They expect families, voluntary associations, private enterprises, and art events to contribute to the common order.[10] Thus, institutions of care, networks of communication, and models of alternative living all give shape to the ordering process, the politics of any society.

Contemplation, 29.

8. Thanks to Phil Harrold for reminding me of this way of expressing the christological and eucharistic foundations of socio-political engagement.

9. Of course this definition of politics begs the question of "life-giving order for *whom?*" But that question is technically aside from the definition itself.

10. I think this is more or less assumed (though not always explicitly discussed) in many governmental frameworks. The mutual interpenetration of different spheres of society within the common ordering process is a central element of a "consociational" understanding of politics. On this, see Bretherton, *Christ and the Common Life*, 167–68, 184, 218, 359–99.

What this means, for our engagement as communities and individuals devoted to Christ, is that we have at our disposal a wide variety of means for influencing things. There is no "one right way" to be politically active, for the river of the struggle for freedom welcomes many streams. We have seen this variety in the history of monasticism and we can appreciate a similar variety when we look at intentional communities and new monastic groups today. Some expressions, such as Taizé or the hermits and contemplatives who contributed to *Solitude and Communion* give greater emphasis to providing space for people to pray.[11] Certainly the world needs our prayers. Others, like Church of the Sojourners in San Francisco and Reba Place Fellowship, emphasize living well together, welcoming the haves and have-nots and modeling Christlike community. Others, like Catholic Worker houses, place a greater priority on protesting violence or offering their influence to the governmental process.[12] And still others, like Christian Study Center Communities, place greater emphasis on the ministry of evangelism and discipleship, influencing the order of society through promoting an increase of righteous people.[13] While some seem to focus their attention more specifically on the cave, the refectory, or the road,[14] most groups I know organize around a blend of values. The global Order of the Mustard Seed organizes itself around values of creativity, prayer, justice, hospitality, learning, and mission.[15] The Iona Community, begun in Scotland in 1938 and currently with a few thousand members, associates, and friends worldwide, speak of a common Rule of daily prayer and reading the Bible, sharing and accounting for use of resources, spending time together in community, and action for justice, peace, and the integrity of creation.[16] The Community of the Beatitudes, a Catholic community birthed in France in 1973 and currently with members in twenty-eight countries, unites a vision for life in

11. We have been introduced to Taizé in chapter 5. See Allchin, *Solitude and Communion*. See also the expressions introduced in Flanagan, *Embracing Solitude*.

12. For the Catholic Worker movement see https://www.catholicworker.org/.

13. For the Consortium of Christian Study Centers see https://studycentersonline.org/. Some study centers have a residential expression where students live in community.

14. I mentioned this distinction in chapter 1 (cave—contemplative; refectory—community; road—mission). See Adams, "Cave, Refectory, Road."

15. See https://www.orderofthemustardseed.com/about/way-of-life/.

16. See Galloway, *Living by the Rule*.

the Spirit, the integration of priests, lay, and religious in a single residential expression, and apostolic works of mission.

In terms of socio-political engagement, some communities, like a few of the Candler Formation Communities, residential expressions integrating student life and intentional Christian community at Candler School of Theology (Atlanta, USA), are oriented around a single focus. Others, such as the members of Springwater community, a neighborhood-oriented ministry in Oregon, USA, are engaged in socio-political matters without any single focus that the members gather around.[17] We even find variety of socio-political engagement within stages of our own lives: in one season Henri Nouwen was deeply engaged in matters related to Central American politics; in another season his focus was on offering care for one disabled man. I find all this variety to be a blessing. There is room for us all to find a place, through discerning wisdom, to serve.[18]

Change within and change without go hand in hand

Finally, *change within and change without go hand in hand*. I have mentioned this a number of times. We begin with ourselves. The violence without can be seen in our own violence within. The Christian (political) life is a life of repentant solidarity. And so on. One way I speak of this—in terms of the options for communities or individuals today—is to employ the monastic notion of "renunciation." Renunciation from the world for the sake of the world. Consider the following descriptions of monastic life:

- "A monastic is someone who adopts a critical attitude toward the contemporary world and its structures, an attitude of protest toward society as it is, just as back in the 4th century the dwellers in the Egyptian desert did when they fled the Roman culture of the day."[19]

17. For the Candler formation communities, see https://candler.emory.edu/student-life/_documents/Formation-Communities-2021-22.pdf. For Springwater, see https://www.springwatercommunity.org/.

18. Augustine, *City of God*, speaks of the value of a variety of kinds of life: contemplative, active, and mixed. James Douglass records Julius Lester's grief over Bob Starobin's suicide in the winter of 1970–71, bemoaning that the radical political scene "is a politics which has no place in it for a quiet scholar like Bob Starobin. It is a politics which regards violent rhetoric and military action as the *sine qua non* of revolution." Douglass, *Resistance and Contemplation*, 138.

19. Laboa, *Historical Atlas*, 246.

- "The [early Syrian] monk led a life at the opposite extreme from the culture of the cities. Unwashed, unkempt, often homeless, usually poorly educated, making a positive virtue out of physical deprivation, he shocked and appalled a cultivated pagan like Libanius of Antioch; and even the Christian townsman had a prejudice to overcome before he could see in this uncouth figure the spiritual paragon of the age."[20]

- "A person's status within [Anglo-Saxon] society was permanently changed by their entry to the religious life, the transformation being marked with appropriate ceremony and ritual. . . . These ceremonies, together with the formalised rejection of personal property, conveyed the magnitude and meaning of the entrant's transition to the new life in a starkly physical manner, a process facilitated . . . through the structuring of the new self in relation to monastic time, ordered space, religious ceremony and a new material culture."[21]

Whether living in the city or the country, whether our focus is on the cave or the road, the nun or monk embodies a radically Christian life in full view of—and I would argue *for the sake of*—the surrounding world. Our personal and political lives are necessarily connected. Our distinctly Christ-centered lives are bound to be noticed, and at times will become politically significant. Historian Margaret Miles writes, "Monastic life, then, was a counter culture. In it, instincts of sex, power, and possession were consciously sacrificed in a rejection of secular culture. . . . In summary, the monastic Rules describe a new understanding of the failure of the secular world to orient human beings to 'life' and provide an alternative community."[22] This is prefigurative politics, where we live radically into the life we want to see emerge, and in so doing we face within the temptations that society faces without (just as Jesus did). Change within and change without.

One area that I consider to be especially important in this regard is the matter of power. As I have said throughout this book, it is time we take another look at power. It is time to drop our superficial stereotypes of political power and recognize the subtle and varied ways that we influence one another for good or for ill. It is so easy to cry out against the power struggles in wider political circles and ignore the dynamics within

20. Price, "Introduction," xxix.

21. Foot, *Monastic Life in Anglo-Saxon*, 152.

22. Miles, *Fullness of Life*, 143, 144.

our own micro-communities. An important step toward speaking to the powers is to face the powers in our midst. What types of power dynamics are at play at home?

Furthermore, I think it is important to see power as a gift as well as a problem. We all have ways we can offer influence to one another. This is mutual aid: a variety of influences given and received. Consider Charles Dickens's well-known description of employer Mr. Fezziwig in his timeless *Christmas Carol*. The miser Scrooge, upon being transported to his early adult workplace, praises Fezziwig and the Ghost of Christmas Past replies that it is a small thing to make these employees so full of gratitude.

> "Why! Is it not? He has spent but a few pounds of your mortal money: three or four perhaps. Is that so much that he deserves this praise?"
>
> "It isn't that," said Scrooge, heated by this remark, and speaking unconsciously like his former, not his latter self. "It isn't that, Spirit. He has the power to render us happy or unhappy; to make our service light or burdensome; a pleasure or a toil. Say that his power lies in words and looks; in things so slight and insignificant that it is impossible to add and count 'em up: what then? The happiness he gives is quite as great as if it cost a fortune."[23]

We are political people. Politics is more than statecraft. Change within and change without go hand in hand. All of this has significant implications for our socio-political engagement. When we understand that we are ordering our world in ordinary ways, in things "slight and insignificant," that politics is simply part of what we do all the time— touching us from different angles both deep and wide and available for our engagement as our situation grants—we can begin to see that the possibilities for socio-political engagement are endless. I see this as both a grave challenge and a blessed invitation.

The Promise of New Monasticism(s)

Now, we must turn our attention from community *engagement* to the *community* of engagement, for this is a book on "monasticism" and socio-political engagement. So far, we have mostly seen how monasticisms have engaged in the past. What might it look like for new monastic

---

23. Dickens, *Christmas Carol*, 56–57.

communities to live out an authentic Christian socio-political engagement today? I have a conviction regarding this question. My conviction is that it is good—enjoyable, creative, meaningful, effective—when we navigate our socio-political engagement in active relationship with a healthy community of kindred spirits.[24] Notice that I used the ominous word "healthy." Thus, in order for me to argue my point, I find it necessary to say something about the character of Christian community and "health," which leads to a corollary conviction: that Christian communities are generally stronger or healthier when they manifest the following features (of course assuming that each of these features, as part of *Christian* community, flows from and aims toward Christ):[25]

1. Common Aim toward Growth:

We make a journey together toward somewhere. It has been said that "If you aim at nothing you are sure to hit it." I have seen this repeatedly in Christian groups. Just "hanging out" seldom provides sufficient bonding to last. Groups need some kind of aim, purpose, vision—even a small one—to hold them together. It not only provides a common identity (we gather around *this* cause), but also a common process of growth (we are growing together in the skills and relationship work that facilitate our participation in this cause). The *somewhere* defines the *journey*. A common aim provides personal incentive for a member to join (I get to be a part of *this*) and it also provides reason for personal and group formation.

24. As I mentioned at the start if this book, I am not intending to diminish the role of devout solitaries. I have a phrase that I use about this: "Modern society has produced many collections but few real communities, many individuals, but few real solitaries." In this book I am giving focus to communities.

25. General definitions of healthy communities speak of "maintaining commitment," "vitality," "growth," or other terms. One can also think in terms of the continued fulfillment of group vision or effectiveness of purpose: perspectives that facilitate dialogue with discussion of socio-political engagement. Various features are identified in the literature on intentional communities. My list here is currently cobbled together from my glance at some of this literature, along with my own observations and musings. I must confess, however, that I have not yet examined the sociological literature nor conducted community surveys or other research as I would wish. My hope is to explore questions of the nature and health of community life (however socio-politically engaged) in future work. For a sample of literature on this topic from different angles see Wittberg, *Rise and Decline*; Kanter, *Commitment and Community*; Janzen, *Intentional Christian Community Handbook*; Killian, *Religious Vitality*.

2. Common Life and Resources:

Community is a shared life: it's as simple as that. Communities tend to be stronger when they share things. This is especially true regarding housing. When we live in geographic proximity we can easily share chores, front porch evenings, and the minor communication moments that go on when we are cleaning up personal and community food in a common kitchen. The "making room for another" needed for a thriving community life functions best when there is a sharing of heart, mind, and hand, and this often involves the sharing of the mundane as well as the profound. We transgress, especially today, when we expect to share our confessions when we have not shared a meal. True, the advent of the internet can create a level of proximity and sharing unavailable in previous times, but even here I think it is valuable to explore our ways of sharing as a feature of health in communities.

3. Common Values:

Healthy groups usually have some set of common values that structure how they conduct life together. While some groups (like universities) have detailed manuals specifying the procedures for participating in the community, others (like an ad hoc "circle group"[26]) operate with just a few mutual agreements. Whether few or many, however, it is important that members both understand and agree to the group's values. While a common aim expresses direction for the journey, common values identify how we are going to behave in the process of the journey, what is important along the way. Some might identify, for example, social justice, prayer, mutual conflict resolution, or creativity as key values for a given group. Commitment to these values is part of a member's commitment to the group generally and sharing these values in common enables both strength and health.

4. Common Decision-Making Process and Expectations:

We have already talked about discernment in the "Monastic Practice" for chapter 3. I think discernment is especially valuable for the health of a community, although discernment need not be conducted in the reflective manner I introduced in that practice. Group members should know how decisions are made and how members are expected to

26. See Pranis, *Little Book of Circle Processes.*

participate. Are we going to allow a new person into the group? How will we organize the work of the community? What about *this* problem over here? The community will collapse without a clearly understood means of making decisions on important matters that regard the group. Interesting to note, however—in my observations, it does not necessarily matter whether a single person makes all of the decisions, everybody votes on every decision, or the group decides by some loose consensus. What matters is that all members understand how decisions are made and willingly agree to that process. What is key to community health is a clear communication of expectations. Clear expectations consistently embodied leads to trust, and trust is at the core of healthy community life.

5. Common Practices:

Values do not mean much unless they are lived. Communities are groups of people who *do* things together. For example: We eat dinner together on Fridays and Sundays. We have community meetings twice a month. We submit half of our income into a common fund. We do not walk away from disagreements, but work them out, if necessary using the mediation skills of a third member of the community (or even an outside mediator). We all are engaged in some kind of socio-political action, though each individual decides their action and shares at the community meeting. Anyone can develop their own means of "employment."[27] Without clearly defined practices it is difficult to resolve questions regarding who is "in" or "out" and why. Related to the intersection of values and practices is the development of some kind of community Rule of Life, which we discussed in the chapter on modeling. Healthy communities do not require written Rules of Life. But members do need to know how and why things happen the way they do. Furthermore, as you can see by the language describing practices ("on Fridays and Sundays," "twice a month," and so on), healthy communities develop a sense of life rhythm, which acts as a stabilizing force when members understand how they can fit their own individual lives within the context of the whole.

27. I often distinguish between "common" practices (which we all do together), "shared" practices (which we all do, but not necessarily together or in the same way), and "personal" practices (which individuals have the freedom to choose as desired).

6. Common Prayer:

Perhaps you have heard the statement: "The family that prays to-gether stays together." It now appears there is some evidence to support this claim.[28] I would venture to say that the same goes for intentional Christian communities. The rituals of common prayer serve as a stabiliz-ing practice as well as a gathering that can creatively incorporate both sameness and diversity. All the communities I have visited practice some form of common prayer. I think that a regular return to core religious val-ues is important. Communities founded merely on socio-political issues can be short-lived, as viewpoints diverge or one issue fades and others rise. Common life comprehended in a spirit of relationship with God through Christ and enacted in prayerful ritual reminds us of the meaning of our lives conducted in ordinary worlds.

7. Common Support Framework:

One factor that contributes to the health of intentional Christian communities is the presence of some form of support and oversight. When things get messy, where do you go for help? We don't often talk about this one, but it is important. Often communities affiliate either with a larger organization or a mutually supporting network in order to partic-ipate in periodic visitation or urgent care. Common support frameworks can also provide much-needed assistance when a community is making major decisions and a "respected but outside" facilitator is desired.

8. Common or Shared Sentiments:

This category describes something slightly different than the previ-ous. As I have watched families or communities occasionally dissolve, sometimes people express that it is not about the change of structure (like common practices) but rather it is about the change in an interior sentiment or disposition. Thus, it seems like by meeting a set of basic emotional needs, we support continued, vital membership in commu-nity.[29] Are we able both to give and to receive *approval* or *affirmation* in

---

28. See the summaries of research in Dr. David Stoop's Marriage and Family Matters August 6, 2012 blog entry, "The Couple that Prays Together" (http://drstoop.com/the-couple-that-prays-together/); and in Ashley McGuire's Institute for Family Studies blog entry of April 20, 2016, "Does the Family That Prays Together Really Stay Together?" (https://ifstudies.org/blog/does-the-family-that-prays-together-really-stay-together).

29. My current notion has some loose ties to Maslow's hierarchy of needs and to

the group? Or perhaps there is something that prevents the flow of these? Do we have a sense of *acceptance* by the group, that we can be who we are without experiencing contempt? *Affection* is a feeling of tenderness or liking. Affection for a group grows with time and shared life. But it can diminish for various reasons. Such also is the case with *attachment*. Attachment can be strong in a group, especially if the group shares housing, many tasks, and deep personal matters. But if core values or basic affection shifts then attachment can be broken (sometimes painfully) as well. My current sense of this is that intentional communities live in the mix between individual and corporate life. What I see with regard to these sentiments is that when we focus our community on trying to meet the emotional needs of all the individual members we run into difficulties, but when we are clear about common values, shared practices, and so on, we are more likely to meet these basic emotional community needs. And yet, if we simply ignore the needs of individuals in the process of serving the whole (the community, the cause, etc.) we run the danger of losing the unity-in-diversity that is characteristic of authentic community.

9. Love:

And that brings us to love. The items listed above only provide a structure within which Christians can practice a life of love together. But it is love that holds the community together. Common resources, common values, and common prayer only ensure that the group has enough in common to make a real "go of it." But common values without the willingness to give another space when needed will not a community make. To reword a well-known passage of Scripture: "If we have thought through our values in detail and we pray together twice a day; if we share the same house, and even donate our money to a common purse, but have not love we are only a collection of bodies and a useless witness to the world." Love is patient and kind. Never jealous or envious or rude . . . (see 1 Cor 13).

Common aim, resources, values, decision-making process and expectations, practices, prayer, support, sentiments, and love. These are the virtues and practices that transform a group from an awkward collection into a living community. This is what I and other interpreters of

---

Leanne Payne's discussion of the blocks to spiritual growth in Payne, *Restoring the Christian Soul.*

community call "health" for communities of all types. Communities that are strong in these features are more likely to thrive. Thus—to repeat my conviction from a purely secular point of view—it is good when we navigate our socio-political engagement in active relationship with communities like this. But more directly for intentional *Christian* communities, there is much to be gained for the cause of Christ when we associate with Christian groups that exhibit these virtues in the context of a lived relationship with God through Christ. Needless to say, my point here is not to create a standard that the ordinary community cannot reach. I recognize that we are all more or less fragile depending on the forces of individuals, circumstances, and structures. We can be weak in one or more of these features and still live well enough. Yet I have also seen communities that have seriously neglected one or another of these factors to the demise of the group. The list simply gives an outline of factors to consider when establishing, joining, or navigating community. More importantly, my interest here is to draw attention to the promise of community when all of these are in place to some measure among those who love the Lord. Oh, the value of these elements all together! I am convinced that socio-political engagement can be well supported by relationship with such communities (and I will soon show you how). But where do we find such communities?

This leads us back to monasticism (perhaps you have already guessed where this is going). In our first chapter I defined monasticism as "an embodiment of concrete means of spiritual formation, chosen in conscious distinction from others who do not share a similar way of life, symbolized through a formal and serious commitment to a particular way of life, a way of life the general principles of which are usually clearly articulated and which exhibit a rhythmic blend of prayer, work, study, and/or ministry." "Concrete means of spiritual formation": this sounds like a *common aim toward growth*.[30] A life in "conscious distinction from others": this sounds like the communication of *common values*. A "way of life," "articulated": this speaks to me of *common decision-making and common expectations*. "Rhythmic blend of prayer, work . . .": this sounds

---

30. This statement assumes that Christian spiritual formation is not merely a matter of interior piety but rather a growth in the fullness of life in Christ and the gospel. I have treated this topic at length in Howard, *Guide*.

like a set of *common practices*, specifically mentioning *prayer*. Check. Check. Check.

Furthermore, we can examine the other features of healthy community not yet mentioned. What about *common life and resources*? Well, of course. This is what a traditional monastery *is*: a place where life and resources are completely shared. Even expressions of religious life that do not necessarily share common residence practice a high degree of shared life and resources. What about a *common support network*? Once again, traditional monastic expressions often have formal connections with a larger institution, or with parish bishops, or with the Roman papacy more directly, though we have already learned about some of the complications of oversight in monastic history. Protestant and other groups have addressed this question of support network variously, but usually it is part of monastic culture to make space for visitation and oversight. What about love? We have treated the place of love in monastic Rules in chapter 3.

One interesting matter of discussion is the question of *common sentiments*. How do monasteries navigate the role of approval, affection, attachment, and so on? There is a strong heritage in monastic culture regarding nonjudgmentalism. The common values in a monastery provide a framework where acceptance and approval can flourish. And certainly, in one sense, attachment grows with commitment over time. Yet the development of a sense of affection and friendship in religious life can be complicated.[31] On the one hand, monasteries have often discouraged the development of "particular friendships" within the community. Nurturing "favorites" within a community can lead to unhealthy attachments or even slight divisions. Rather than emphasizing the value of personal feelings for one another in community, love is more often understood as something that grows between members (sometimes with very different background or personalities) through the act of sharing life.

What we discover is that the very features that facilitate healthy community are also characteristic of monastic life, and in Christian monasteries explicitly the features are oriented around relationship with God through Christ. Together, they provide an environment of safety, freedom, support, availability of shared resources, trust, and more. Perhaps that is why the Benedictines have been around for fifteen hundred years, the Franciscans for a thousand, and so on, exercising an influence radically

---

31. See for example, the treatments in Leclercq, "Friendship and Friends"; and Driscoll, "Friendship."

disproportionate to their numbers. And so today. Pooled resources enable communities, like Reba Place and their housing ministries, to do more with less. Common values empower teams, like the Jesuits in El Salvador, to become prophetic voices to the church and the world. Common decision-making in a shared neighborhood gives communities, like the Communality community in Kentucky, USA, freedom to experiment with good ideas.[32] I have said elsewhere, "When lived out well, a religious community is a formational greenhouse. The orchestration of time, intensity, designated relationships, resources, and such is designed to facilitate the members' growth in gospel life."[33] Søren Kierkegaard wrote in an 1847 note: "Of this there is no doubt, our age and Protestantism in general may need the monastery again, or wish it were there. The 'monastery' is an essential dialectical element in Christianity. We therefore need it like a navigation buoy at sea in order to see where we are, even though I myself would not enter it. But if there really is true Christianity in every generation there must also be individuals who have this need."[34]

But what about support specifically for *socio-political engagement*? Once again I suggest that intentional Christian communities can offer a unique environment for the nurturing of appropriate engagement. A community of *common values* (regularly reaffirmed) provides an environment where ideas can be easily shared and developed. I think of Philadelphia or Minneapolis in the early 2000s—complete with their developing communities—as something akin to the Vienna Circle or the Inklings in the early twentieth century (Greenwich Village in the early sixties?), with the communities forming a center of the energy. People gather around the values and this, in turn, facilitates the engagement. Some fresh expressions of the new monasticism movement in the UK consciously aim toward helping communities identify common values that facilitate creative engagement in their neighborhoods or more widely.[35]

32. Though this community is no longer active, I remember hearing a number of delightful ideas developed through their decision-making process when I visited their community around 2010.

33. Howard, *Guide*, 169.

34. Kierkegaard, *Papers and Journals*, 7 VIII 1 A 403 (1847), p. 275. See also Dietrich Bonhoeffer's seminal reference to the need for a new monasticism in Bonhoeffer, *A Testament to Freedom*, 424. Author Tom Sine foreshadows the cry of Rod Dreher for an authentic Christian witness in the midst of a secularizing culture in a 1996 article exploring possibilities for the twenty-first century (see Sine, "Creating New Visions").

35. I sensed this as I attended a training in the formation of new monastic communities put on by Ian Mobsby and Mark Berry. See Mobsby and Berry, *A New*

I also see something positive about monastic-ish communities and the value of common wisdom for socio-political engagement. Think of the monastic practice exercises we have been doing in this book: political self-examination, discernment of political engagement, Rule of Life. When we do these kinds of exercises as a community we can, for example, see the contexts that surround us more clearly since more "eyes" are observing together. We also have more confidence, having gone through a discernment process together (*common decision-making*), that we are engaging not from a motive of guilt or prescription, but in partnership with a community open to the Spirit's call. The community Rule reminds us why we engage.[36]

Likewise I find Christian communities to be a valuable asset for the work of engagement itself. We are supported when we can share our ups and downs of engagement with kindred spirits, if not share in the work itself. Think of David Janzen's monthly prayer meetings, sometimes very small, sometimes much larger. When folks are behind you, both through encouragement and through covering if something happens, it just makes it more possible to engage. Think of the relationship between InnerCHANGE and the Church of the Sojourners, the good Samaritan and the innkeeper: each plays their own part. Even the hospitality required to care for someone in serious need may be possible for a community who can share the load while impossible for a single family to carry. Jubilee Partners (I mentioned them in chapter 4) welcomes refugees, often multiple families from a single region of the world. They provide temporary housing, counseling, opportunity for people to work with their hands, and more. All this simply could not be done without a community gathered for the cause. Doing politics the monastic way.

Certainly we can see the value of modeling good society by living together as a community. I have covered this in chapter 5, but let me say again how important visible, relevant, and possible models are for the sake of socio-political causes. People must see solutions before they can vote for them. I do not think that residential expressions of Christian

---

Monastic Handbook.

36. Ian Shelburne, from the Eden community—a group building a cohousing ecovillage, permaculture farm, and retreat/training center in Abilene, Texas—mentioned in a Nurturing Communities Roundtable meeting (March 19, 2022) that he thought that a Rule of Life gives emphasis to the "intentional" in intentional Christian communities.

community are the only way to witness to the gospel, but I certainly think that it is a worthy and underexplored means of prefigurative politics.

Finally, there is prayer. There is the common prayer at the missile site. There is the common cry of lament that rises from a community gathered to repent as those who live among a people of unclean lips. There is the prayer of a Thomas Merton, a solitary voice in the midst of a consecrated community. There is the liturgy of praying the political Scriptures, facing the pain of our unanswered political prayers together and encouraging each other to keep faith when hope seems so small. I think a community of prayer can support socio-political engagement in ways we have yet to learn. Let us hear again Vincent Harding's comments on the place of prayer in the Black struggle for freedom, only now let us hear it not as a record of what people did then, but of what Christian communities might do now:

> ... although it is hard to grasp in a secular age, large numbers of black people believed that their best contribution to the struggle was through unremitting prayer. Like some widespread, unorganized, unrecognized corps of spiritual resistants, these black men, women, and children were everywhere disciplining their wills, turning themselves to the work of praying for freedom.[37]

Could we believe that our best contribution to the political order was through unremitting prayer? Could we mobilize ourselves through some kind of new mystical, new monastic divine office as a corps of spiritual resistants, turning ourselves to the work of praying for freedom? What might the Spirit say? What might it mean to follow?

CONCLUSION

Let's return again to Jonathan Wilson-Hartgrove's comments mentioned at the start of the book. He stated in his *Reconstructing the Gospel*: "many of us resident aliens from new monastic communities and postliberal congregations realized that, in our absence, extremism flourished in statehouses across the nation."[38] What I heard in my conversation with Jonathan on the way to the airport, and what I hear in this statement, is concern that an emphasis on "monasticism" (prayer, formation, community life, modeling the faith) draws people away (absence) from

37. Harding, *There Is a River*, 162.
38. Wilson-Hartgrove, *Reconstructing the Gospel*, loc. 1697 out of 2983.

much-needed political engagement. The question we must ask now is "Is this concern legitimate?" It may be that Jonathan was voicing a worthy assessment of the new monastic scene. But as he passed the concern to me, the question shifted from being merely one about contemporary trends to something more historical and theological. What is the relationship between religious life and socio-political engagement in history and in the context of a Christian view of the gospel?

I began this book with some comments on a children's song. "Deep and wide, deep and wide, there's a fountain flowing deep and wide." I have been using this image since. In my first discussion I suggested that some may need the "deep" (associated with prayer and spiritual formation) and that others may need the "wide" (associated with socio-political engagement). Here is another way of asking Jonathan's question: Does the "deep" draw us away from the "wide"? And yet. I gave a hint of something more, even as I spoke of that song. I mentioned that "the "deep" and the "wide" are not as easily distinguished as we thought. "Inner" and "outer" blend together in a well-discerned life of following Christ.

In the course of this book two things have been demonstrated. First, monasticism(s) throughout history at numerous times have, rather than withdrawing from politics, chosen to engage. Second, the stereotypes of deep=inner and wide=outer are insufficient to grasp the nature of the Christian gospel. The deeper we immerse ourselves in prayer, formation, Scripture meditation, community life, and so on, the more we discover the socio-political forces that shape who we are inside and we find that our own "inner" development is caught up in the transformation of the world in which we live in solidarity. Similarly, when we engage ourselves in politics we find ourselves immersed in self-interest, fear, guilt, and all kinds of deep things that go back long in our own lives and have been around for generations in our societies.

My sense of things moving forward is that it will be important for us to break our stereotypes not only of deep/wide but of monasticism as well. Monasticism (or religious life, more strictly) should not be seen as simply a force of withdrawal from socio-political engagement. Rather, I think that consecrated Christian communities can serve as a most worthy environment to empower appropriate action: to help us face our own political life with the help of others, to co-discern our most appropriate political next step, and to support us in our best engagement as groups and as individuals. We need the monastery, not only for community stability, but also for empowered action. In a 1988 *Christianity Today* magazine editorial, Rodney Clapp speaks of evangelicals "remonking the church," suggesting that a new breed of monks might "point beyond themselves": teaching others how to live our world in line with that of the Bible and recovering a life of prayer.[39] A decade earlier Ralph Winter, missiologist and pioneer of Theological Education by Extension, wrote concerning the church's impact upon the world, "Is there a 'more excellent way'"? Winter was convinced that the Roman Catholic tradition, in its much longer experience with the phenomenon of the "order," embodies "a *superior structural approach to both renewal and mission*."[40] More recently, Jonathan Wilson (not Jonathan Wilson-Hartgrove) provided an outline of what a new monasticism could look like in his 2010 *Living Faithfully in a Fragmented World* (originally published in 1997): recovering the *telos* of the world through healing false divisions of secular and sacred, becoming a monasticism for the whole world, a disciplined people, rooted in theological reflection and commitment.[41]

One more thing. I write this book not merely because I have a historical interest in monasticism or politics (though I do). Nor am I writing simply because I think that monastic-like communities supporting sociopolitical engagement is a good idea (though I do). More than that, I think God is doing something and I want to draw our attention to it. I want to call some of us *into* it. I hinted at this when I spoke in the first chapter about the "continuum" of monasticism and described people who lived "in between" an ordinary family form of life and a strictly vowed religious form of life. I stated that "I celebrate families who live in the same urban neighborhood, who pray together daily, who commit to a life of simplicity, and who take concrete steps to follow ever closer in discipleship with Christ. I applaud individuals who meet weekly online to share how they have kept a common Rule of Life of prayerful rhythm, sexual fidelity, and humble service. Like the medieval beguines, these contemporary "semi-monastic" expressions may be exploring valuable options for Christianity today.[42] I will take one step further here. I believe the Spirit of God is moving among us, calling many into in-between forms of life: forms of life that do not shallowly separate devotion and action, but which seek to

---

39. Clapp, "Remonking the Church." Notice Clapp's references in this article to others who called for some kind of "remonking."

40. Winter, "Protestant Mission Societies," 141. See also Winter, "Two Structures." Italics original.

41. Wilson, *Living Faithfully*, 59–62.

42. See Howard, "Beguine Option."

integrate them, looking to live both deep and wide with all that this might mean. I see it everywhere.

Over the past few years as I have spoken about things monastic I have noticed how people respond. I would like to think that, like Francis of Assisi, I am offering an invitation to everybody as they are able to follow.[43] Most of those who hear me talk about things monastic (I call this group "the 80 percent") reflect how they might like to apply my message to their lives: perhaps setting aside time for regular Scripture reading and prayer in their favorite chair, decluttering their homes, or joining a small support group. I affirm their steps and I am glad for their response—*really glad*. There are also a very few people (I call this group "the 2 percent") who hear my message and want to know how to join a monastery. These few are ready to quit their jobs, sell all, and start over again. Usually I give these people a couple of referrals and let them take it from there. Hallelujah. And then there are "the 18 percent": families who want to scale down, join with others, and follow the gospel as best they can, couples nearing retirement who want to make the rest of their lives count for something, young singles who are dreaming into a different version of "success" than what has been fed to them by the mainstream. In all honesty, it is the 18 percent that touches my heart most. And it is a growing crowd, full of people from all kinds of viewpoints and traditions (just check out the Appendix). After teaching a course on "Early African Monasticism" in Egypt in 2015, I wrote a little note:

> Back in the USA. My conclusion, after teaching this lovely group of people, and after talking with teachers, pharmacists, engineers, students, monks and mothers: there is place for semi-monastic Christian expressions here and now in Egypt, just as in the West. We may not be able to build large monasteries where we all live, but we can rent apartments in the same neighborhood and one of us can have a room large enough where we can meet. We may not all be able to wake up daily at 4:00 AM to pray the Psalms together for two hours, but perhaps many of our group can meet three times a week to pray and read Scripture together for a half-hour. We may not all be able to meet regularly with a master Amma or Abba, but perhaps many of us can have monthly meetings with the wisest among us and we can talk about how we lead our lives to the glory of God. We may not be able to sell our possessions, take a vow of poverty, and own everything in common, but perhaps we can sell a few

43. See Vauchez, *Life and Afterlife*, 302–3.

things and share a car, or our power tools in common. We may not be able to live as strict a Rule as St. Shenoute might have liked, but we each can support one another as we try to embrace our "little rules" and learn to be the light of Jesus right where we are. I loved this journey: part of my heart will be in the Egyptian desert even as I return to the "high desert" of Montrose.

Needless to say, the politics in Egypt are nothing like the politics in Montrose. But I am convinced that God is raising up pockets of semi-monastic Christians who will help one another face our own socio-political lives, discern our appropriate socio-political next step, and persevere in authentic socio-political engagement. Who will join?

APPENDIX

Exploring or Inventing New Monasticism(s)

Exploring—Finding a "New Monastic" Community:

What follows below in this "exploring" section is an alphabetized list of intentional Christian communities, new monastic expressions, and networks of communities/expressions. I have provided names and website addresses, a brief summary of the life of the group, and contact information. My summary is greatly condensed and primarily drawn from website information. In many cases the groups request contact through an inquiry web page and I have noted this where appropriate.

Bruderhof Communities—https://www.bruderhof.com/

The Bruderhof is an intentional Christian community with Anabaptist roots of more than three thousand people living in twenty-nine settlements on five continents. The Bruderhof lives together in full community, committed to following Jesus and inspired by the example of the early church. They do their best to show by lived example that a just society is possible. Community members gladly renounce private property and share everything in common. They value such things as community of goods, family, education, caring for each other, working together, and living simply.

Contact information:

There are different global connection points depending on continent (see https://www.bruderhof.com/en/contact-us) or contact Toby Mommsen at tobymommsen@ccimail.com.

See also the website inquiry form.

Candler Formation Communities—https://candler.emory.edu/student-life/formation-communities.html

Focused on intentional living and spiritual formation, Candler School of Theology's formation communities provide students a distinctive opportunity to live and grow in faith alongside their peers. Each formation community creates a "Rule of Life" and lives in its own house with its own focus. Communities are organized around shared prayer, shared table, and shared celebration, and each is coordinated by a student rector who provides day-to-day leadership and a faculty chaplain who provides worship leadership and long-term guidance.

Contact information:

Candler School of Theology
Rita Anne Rollins Building
1531 Dickey Drive
Atlanta, Georgia 30322 USA
(404) 727-6322

Center for Christian Study—https://www.studycenter.net/

The Center for Christian Study is a nonprofit education and outreach ministry serving the University of Virginia and Charlottesville since 1976, facilitating lectures, small groups, hospitality, and a separate library. More particularly, their Elzinga Residential Scholars Program forms residential communities with the commonality of commitment to Christ. They have regular house meetings for sharing and prayer, gather on a weekly basis for Thursday dinners, and participate in a community retreat. The Center for Christian Study is a member of the Consortium of Christian Study Centers (see below).

Contact information:

The Center for Christian Study
128 Chancellor Street
Charlottesville, VA 22903
info@studycenter.net
(434) 817-1050

Church of the Sojourners—https://churchofthesojourners.org/

Church of the Sojourners is an intentional Christian community located in San Francisco since the 1980s. They share houses, cars, meals, and money, along with prayer, worship, and discernment. They gather together three times per week and welcome many guests. They see themselves as part of the Anabaptist movement and are a Mennonite church, though only a few were raised in that tradition. They desire to be deeply family to one another, seeing their family life as being partners in the gospel together.

Contact information:

Meeting Place
1129 Florida St.
San Francisco, CA 94110
(415) 226-9838

Community of Aidan and Hilda—https://www.aidanandhilda.org.uk/

The Community of Aidan and Hilda is a dispersed, ecumenical body drawing inspiration from the lives of the Celtic saints, with properties on Holy Island, UK, and members in several countries around the world. Members of the Community share the belief that God is once again calling us to the quality of life and commitment that was revealed in the lives of these Christians whose witness was so effective in the *new* Anglo-Saxon world of the time. The Community of Aidan and Hilda provide a program of retreats, events, and online courses around the UK and internationally.

Contact information:

Community of Aidan and Hilda
26 Woodlea Ave.
Acomb, YORK YO26 5JU
01904 793438 Mobile: 07963 617071

Community of the Beatitudes—https://beatitudes.org/en/

The Community of the Beatitudes was founded in France in 1973, was recognized in 2002 by the Holy See as an association of the faithful, and later transferred to the Congregation for Institutes of Consecrated Life and Societies of Apostolic Life in 2008. In 2010 the community numbers in the hundreds of both consecrated and lay members in thirty countries worldwide. The life of this community includes life in the Spirit, the communion of states of life, and apostolic works. They value mental prayer, liturgy, and the gifts of the Holy Spirit. They aspire to an authentic fraternal relationship between lay and consecrated members, ordained and non-ordained, all sharing life together. Through media, retreats, schools, family ministry, and more, the Community shares in the mission of the church.

Contact information:

Consult their website at https://beatitudes.org/en/contact-webmaster/
For the convent in Denver, CO, USA:
2924 W. 43rd Ave.
Denver, CO 80211
(720) 855-9412

The Community of St. Anselm—https://www.stanselm.org.uk/

The Community of St. Anselm is a one-year experience of monastic life for people aged twenty to thirty-five. The community is housed at Lambeth Palace, a center of Anglican life. Each year, young adults from different countries and Christian backgrounds commit to live, serve, study, and pray together for one year under a simple Rule of Life. They set aside one Saturday each month to explore our monastic spiritual inheritance from St. Benedict, St. Francis, and St. Ignatius. Participants meet regularly with a sharing group and spiritual companion, to help one another grow in trust, listening, and accountability.

Contact information:

The Community of St Anselm
Lambeth Palace, London SE1 7JU
0207 898 1210
stanselm@lambethpalace.org.uk

Consortium of Christian Study Centers—https://cscmovement.org/

The Consortium of Christian Study Centers grows out of the grassroots Christian Study Center movement in the 1970s and 1980s. In July 2007, a dozen directors gathered and resolved to formalize their collective endeavor, officially forming the Consortium of Christian Study Centers in 2008. By the end of the decade, the Consortium had twenty-nine member centers and thirty-two partner organizations. The aim of the Consortium is to serve various centers, multiply locations, and promote the movement.

Contact information:

Consortium of Christian Study Centers
485 Hillsdale Drive, Suite 112
Charlottesville, VA 22901
(434) 296-3333
info@cscmovement.org

Eden Community—https://www.edenfellows.com/the-eden-community

The Eden Community was established in 2013 and is gathering families to live on a piece of land near Abilene, Texas around values of intergenerational life, exploring permaculture, and ministry to college students and beyond.

Contact information:

Laura Callarman—Program Director
Eden Fellows
c/o Jesus Family Network
PO Box 819
Abilene, TX 79604
(479) 466-0215
laura@edenfellows.com

Englewood Christian Church—https://www.theenglewoodchurch.com/

Englewood Christian Church in Indianapolis, Indiana has since 1895 been a small neighborhood church, a booming influential megachurch, a magnet of urban mission, and an informally intentional community. They recognize God has called the church to be a real community: finding common work, bearing one another's burdens, playing together, and walking together through life's most challenging and important transitions. They seek to embody "the Jesus way" in many aspects of life in their community and in their neighborhood: education, health care, housing, nutrition, economics, public policy, and more.

Contact information:

Englewood Christian Church
57 N. Rural St.
Indianapolis, IN 46201
(317) 639-1541
office@theenglewoodchurch.com

Hope Fellowship—https://www.hopefellowshipwaco.org/

Hope Fellowship is a community of Christians, a family of neighbors, and a Mennonite church (though affirming their ecumenical unity with the worldwide body of Christ). They seek to live the way of Jesus in Waco, Texas and their neighborhood. They desire to love each other, serve their neighbors, and proclaim God's peace and forgiveness in Jesus Christ. They worship in English and Spanish and try to organize their lives so that they have daily contact with each other in a variety of ways, living close to or working with each other, sharing childcare or living space, and finding ways that their paths will cross whether for praying, socializing, or meetings.

Contact information:

Hope Fellowship
1721 Sanger Ave.
Waco, TX 76707
hopefellowshipwaco.info@gmail.com

InnerCHANGE—https://www.innerchange.org/

InnerCHANGE is a new friars, missional order with teams located in Europe, Asia, Africa, South and Central America, and the US. While the teams are involved in programs or activities within their communities, relationships with neighbors are the foundation and catalyst for everything they do. They value the contemplative, the prophetic, and the missional working together and are involved in things like walking alongside families who are suffering or in crisis, entering into relationships with youth involved in gangs, and equipping local churches to love those on the margins in their communities.

Contact information:

To receive their newsletter see the website.

Iona—https://iona.org.uk

The Iona Community is an international, ecumenical Christian movement working for justice and peace, the rebuilding of community and the renewal of worship. Founded in 1938 on the island of Iona in Scotland, they now have about 280 members and more than two thousand associate members, young adults, and friends across the world. People visit the Abbey for retreats and events, support one another through accountability, and are nourished through the resources of the Wild Goose ministry.

Contact information:

Iona Community
Suite 9 Fairfield
1048 Govan Road, Glasgow
G51 4XS
Scotland, UK
+4 (0)1414297281
admin@iona.org.uk

Jesus People USA—https://jesuspeoplechicago.org/

Jesus People USA is a church family of nearly two hundred people living together in intentional community, sharing a ten-story building in the Uptown neighborhood of Chicago. They host many visitors and groups each year from around the world who are interested in what communal living looks like and want to join in serving the poor. They have been living together communally since 1972. They sustain themselves through mission businesses, strengthen themselves by practicing forgiveness and unity, and extend themselves through serving the poor—within and outside their walls.

Contact information:

Jesus People USA
920 W. Wilson Ave.
Chicago, IL 60640
(773) 561-2450
coordinators@jesuspeoplechicago.org

Jubilee Partners—https://jubileepartners.org/

Jubilee Partners is a Christian service community in rural Georgia, founded in 1979. Their primary work is to offer hospitality to immigrants who have experienced violence or persecution. Jubilee offers refugees a place for recovery and healing as well as practical supports such as language classes, legal resources, and medical care. They also put a good deal of labor into tending 250 acres of land in a way that cares for its ecological health and lets it serve as a place of refuge and peace for those who come there.

Contact information:

Jubilee Partners
PO Box 68
Comer, GA 30629
(706) 783-5131
communications@jubileepartners.org

Koinonia Farm—https://www.koinoniafarm.org/

Koinonia Farm was founded in 1942 by Clarence and Florence Jordan and Martin and Mabel England as a "demonstration plot for the kingdom of God." Other families soon joined, and visitors to the farm were invited to serve a period of apprenticeship in developing community life on the teachings and principles of Jesus. Racial reconciliation has been a significant part of their story. Koinonia Farm values love through service to others, joy through generous hospitality, and peace through reconciliation called to share a life of prayer, work, study, service, and fellowship. While honoring people of all backgrounds and faiths, they strive to demonstrate the way of Jesus as an alternative to materialism, militarism, and racism.

Contact information:

Koinonia Farm
1324 GA Highway 49 South
Americus, GA 31719
(229) 924-0391
info@koinoniafarm.org

L'Abri Fellowship International—https://labri.org/

L'Abri sees itself as a "shelter for honest questions." The L'Abri communities are study centers where individuals have the opportunity to seek answers to honest questions about God and the significance of human life. There are seven residential branches in Europe, the US, and Asia. A typical day is divided into half a day of study and half a day of helping with the practical tasks of living together—cooking, cleaning, gardening, etc. Meals often involve discussions centered on a topic raised by a guest or worker.

Contact information:

See the Quick Reference guide to the locations at https://labri.org/contact-us/

L'Arche International—https://larche.org/en/web/guest/welcome

L'Arche is a collection of communities of people with and without intellectual disabilities, sharing life and belonging to an International Federation. Today there are more than 156 communities and twenty-eight projects in thirty-eight countries around the world from Belgium to Argentina, Uganda to Japan, and to the United States. Mutual relationships and trust in God are at the heart of their journey together. L'Arche communities hold in balance four elements: service, community, spirituality, and outreach, adapting to needs and culture of each situation.

Contact information:

L'Arche International
25 rue Rosenwald
75015 Paris France
+33 (0)1 53 68 08 00
international@larche.org

Missional Wisdom Foundation— https://www.missionalwisdom.com

In the recent past Missional Wisdom Foundation integrated Methodist vision and monastic practice in creative intentional Christian community experiments (see https://www.missionalwisdom.com/experiments). Some their experiments are summarized in Heath and Duggins, *Missional, Monastic, Mainline.*

Contact information:

Missional Wisdom Foundation
Main Office
185 S. White Chapel Road

Southlake, TX 76092

Contact Larry Duggins by phone: (817) 915-5181
General info and Dallas Hub: info@missionalwisdom.com
Contact the Asheville Hub: info@hawcreekcommons.com

New Monastic Roundtable—https://www.newmonasticroundtable.com/info

The New Monastic Roundtable is really an event more than a network of communities. Yet this annual event gathers people from all over Europe who wonder how a monastic lifestyle and rhythm could function in today's world; for those who are interested in community life and the founding of new monastic communities. The aim is that communities from all kinds of backgrounds will get to know each other by sharing from their experience, both good and bad. The initiator and sponsor of the gathering is Adventure 300, a learning journey for new monastic communities in Europe.

Contact Information:

Adventure 300
Sonnenweg 6
3612 Steffisburg
Switzerland
info@adventure300.com
See also the inquiry form on the website.

North American Network of Charismatic Covenant Communities—https://nanccc.org/

The North American Network of Charismatic Covenant Communities (NAN) was formed by the leaders of various Charismatic Communities to support the Catholic Charismatic Renewal. The leaders of Communities from the Catholic Fraternity desired to continue their fraternal association as well as expand their association with Catholic and ecumenical covenant communities worldwide with a focus on North America. There were eleven founding communities in North America in 2019–2020. They act as a network of mutual support. For a description of Catholic renewal communities worldwide (and a map of their locations) see https://www.charis.international/en/communities/.

Contact information:

Contact.the.NAN@gmail.com

Northumbria—https://www.northumbriacommunity.org/

Northumbria Community is a globally dispersed network of people from different backgrounds, streams, and edges of the Christian faith. As companions in community, they are united in a desire to embrace and express an ongoing exploration into a new way for living, through a new monasticism. They are also united by a Rule of Life which they sum up in two words: availability and vulnerability. Northumbria is particularly known through their *Celtic Daily Prayer* resources. They also have a place of retreat in Nether Springs, England.

Contact information:

Northumbria Community
Nether Springs, Croft Cottage
Acton Home Farm
Felton
Northumberland NE65 9NU
0 (+44) 1670 787645
office@northumbriacommunity.org

Nurturing Communities Network—https://www.nurturingcommunities.org/

The Nurturing Communities Network is an informal and growing network of Christ-centered intentional communities. Some of the communities in this "Explore" list are associated with NCN. Older established communities connect with newly established communities for the purpose of learning from each other, encouragement, and growing. Support is offered for communities in crisis or at a serious impasse in the community's life. Nurturing Communities Network hosts regular gatherings of Christian intentional communities—regionally and nationally. They also offer resources both practical and theoretical for groups in all stages of community life.

Contact info:

See the inquiry form on the website.

The Order of Mission—https://www.missionorder.org/

TOM is a global network of missional leaders bound by covenant in proclaiming the kingdom of God in the world, an apostolic missional order grounded in the global Anglican Communion. Members of TOM take vows to live their lives in purity, accountability, and simplicity, so that the mission of God is not hindered. Some members of TOM find themselves in full-time vocational ministry, but many are not paid to "do" the work of Jesus. They sense a call to serve and influence within whatever context and culture they live and work: cities and rural areas, developed and developing countries, business, education, arts, health and social care, public and private sector, family, and church.

Contact information:

The Order of Mission
c/o Kairos Network Church
2 Harlow Terrace
Harrogate
North Yorkshire
HG2 OPN
See website for email contact.

Order of the Common Life—https://www.orderofthecommonlife.org/

The Order of the Common Life responds to an invitation to a *common way of life*—rooted in ancient Christian practices, lived in spiritual friendship with others, and in service within the local church. They have close ties with the Vineyard movement. Some of their members gather at times in common cities while others are scattered across the globe and meet virtually. Their Rule of Life is based in a rhythm of bodily labor, prayer, study, and rest, and is expressed around shared commitments to values such as contemplation, spiritual direction, simplicity, healing, shared work, and others.

Contact information:

Order of the Common Life
401 W. Town St., 248C
Columbus, OH 43215

See the website inquiry form for more.

The Order of the Mustard Seed—https://www.orderofthemustardseed.com/

The Order of the Mustard Seed is an ecumenical, lay-led, dispersed community—formally acknowledged by the Anglican House of Bishops—of over three hundred members, inspired by the original Moravian Order of the Mustard Seed of the eighteenth century. They share the wider objectives of the 24/7 Prayer movement to revive the church and to rewire the culture through the mobilization of prayer, mission, and justice. The Order of the Mustard Seed is an international missional movement united and galvanized by a shared Rule of Life and a vow to be true to Christ (creativity, prayer), kind to people (justice, hospitality), and to take the gospel to the nations (mission, learning).

Contact information:

info@orderofthemustardseed.com.
Also see the website inquiry form.

Reba Place Fellowship—https://rebaplacefellowship.org/

Reba Place Fellowship is an intentional Christian community with locations in Evanston and Chicago, Illinois. They live together in a number of common houses. They hope to share life and resources with one another and with neighbors in order to demonstrate God's peace and justice in the world. This happens in many ways—through small groups, pastoral relationships and spiritual friendships, and also through a number of businesses they have established which draw people together and serve the community. Reba Place Fellowship is also involved in nurturing other communities of love and discipleship.

Contact information:

Reba Place Fellowship
737 B Reba Place
Evanston, IL 60202
(847) 328-6066
Fax: (847) 328-8431
RebaFellowship@gmail.com

Rutba House Community

Rutba House, a group of Christians who live in common houses and serve their neighborhood and more, has never had a website, but folks can reach out via www.schoolforconversion.org.

Sant'Egidio—https://www.santegidio.org/pageID/1/langID/en/HOME.html

Sant'Egidio is a Christian community born in 1968, after the Second Vatican Council. An initiative of Andrea Riccardi, it was born in a secondary school in the center of Rome. Over the years, it has become a network of communities in more than seventy countries of the world. The community pays attention to the periphery and peripheral people, gathering men and women of all ages and conditions, united by a fraternal tie through the listening of the gospel and the voluntary and free commitment for the poor and peace. Prayer, friendship with whoever is in a moment of need, and working for peace are their fundamental points of reference.

Contact information:

Sant'Egidio
Piazza Sant'Egidio 3a
00153 Roma
+39 06 4292929
Fax: +39 06 5800197
info@santegidio.org

Servant Partners—https://www.servantpartners.org/

Servant Partners is a movement centered on Jesus Christ, planted in urban poor communities, and empowered to pursue community transformation. They plant churches, organize communities, and partner with local leadership towards individual, communal, and systemic transformation. They equip both staff and local leaders for holistic ministry in their urban communities. Servant Partners currently have seventeen global sites and share core values of joy in God, incarnation, justice, servanthood, making disciples, and transformation.

Contact information:

PO Box 3144
Pomona, CA 91769

(626) 398-1010
See also the website inquiry form.

Servants (Servants to Asia's Urban Poor)—https://servantsasia.org/

Servants are "new friar" communities of Jesus-following, justice-loving people, living with the urban poor in Asian cities. They not only aim to preach the gospel, but to live it, sharing people's day-to-day lives and struggles as neighbors and friends. They value restoring broken relationships: relationship with God, with one's self, with others, and with creation, utilizing concrete projects to address each. They currently have teams in Cambodia, India, Indonesia, and the Philippines. In the past they have also been in the UK and Canada.

Contact information:

You can link with each of the teams on their website (see https://servantsasia.org/want-to-know-more/contact-us/) or email info@servantsasia.org.

Simple Way—https://thesimpleway.org/

Simple Way was once an intentional community but now is a small nonprofit organization supporting neighbors in building a neighborhood where all belong and thrive. They find ways to celebrate together. They garden and work to make the neighborhood beautiful. They collaborate locally in practical ways, like working for food security and connecting people with nearby resources. When they run into bigger systems that throw obstacles in their neighbors' way, they advocate for systemic change together. Ultimately, they envision all of their neighbors coming to a place of security that enables growth and flourishing.

Contact Information:

The Simple Way
PO Box 14751
Philadelphia, PA 19134
(215) 423-3598
info@thesimpleway.org

Solas Bhríde—https://solasbhride.ie/

Solas Bhríde is a Christian spirituality center that welcomes people of all faiths and of no faith. The vision of the center is to welcome all to know and be inspired by Saint Brigid, whose legacy is ever more relevant for our world today. The center is run by the Brigidine Sisters, who came to Kildare in 1992 with the intention of reconnecting with their Celtic Christian roots, and reclaiming St. Brigid of Kildare in a new way for a new millennium. They emphasize values of hospitality, ecological awareness, social justice, contemplation, compassion and peace, and tranquility.

Contact information:

Solas Bhride Centre & Hermitages
Tully Road
Kildare Town
Co. Kildare
Ireland
+353 (0)45 522890
info@solasbhride.ie

Springwater Community—https://www.springwatercommunity.org/

Springwater is a multigenerational community living within a short walk of each other in the Glenwood Park portion of Portland's eclectic Lents neighborhood. They give honor and allegiance to Jesus Christ in their life together, their work in the neighborhood, and in a sacred gathering every Sunday. They seek to fulfill the two great commandments of love God and neighbor through honoring such values as simple living and sustainability, generosity, hospitality, geographic proximity, mutual discernment, and more.

Contact information:

See their website inquiry page: https://www.springwatercommunity.org/contact.

Taizé—https://www.taize.fr/en

Taizé was founded in France by Brother Roger in 1949, taking their common vows of celibacy, a life of common ownership of goods, and a life under the authority of a prior. In keeping with their value of reconciliation, Protestants, Catholics, and Orthodox worship together at the site in Taizé, France, living a rhythm of prayer (three times a day), Bible studies, and manual labor. Their distinctive chants are well-known today. Some of the brothers live in troubled parts of the world and offer reconciliation there.

Contact information:

See especially the information page on the website: https://www.taize.fr/en_article332.html.

With regard to the community itself:

The Taizé Community
71250 Taizé, France.
+33 (0)3 85 50 30 30
Fax: +33 (0)3 85 50 30 15
communitytaize.fr (to contact one of the brothers)

Urban Neighbors of Hope—https://unoh.org/

Urban Neighbors of Hope is a new friar network that immerses themselves in the life of neighborhoods facing urban poverty, joining the risen Jesus to seek transformation from the bottom up. They live and serve as small, responsive neighborhood-based teams currently in Melbourne, Bangkok, Wellington, and Auckland. Urban Neighbours of Hope (UNOH) is a missional order affiliated with Churches of Christ (in Australia and Thailand) and the Baptist Union (in New Zealand).

Contact information:

UNOH Office
Boon Wurrung/Bunurong Country
PO Box 52
Somerville VIC 3912
0407 992 707
unoh@unoh.org

World Impact

World Impact exists to serve people who minister in communities of poverty—affirming their call and vocation. World Impact empowers urban leaders and partners with local churches to reach their cities with the gospel. They believe that the best way to change our world is the hope of the gospel in our cities. The best way to declare that hope is to partner with denominations, networks, and local church leaders. And the best way to partner with them is through relationships. They equip local leaders particularly through networking, resources, and training. Some of their members participate in a Religious Missionary Order and make commitments to submission, simplicity, and purity.

Contact information:

World Impact, Inc.
2001 S. Vermont Ave.
Los Angeles, CA 90007

Inventing: How to Start a "New Monastic" Community

If you are interested in starting a "new monastic" community of some sort, see:

- Janzen, *Intentional Christian Community Handbook*
- Mobsby and Berry, *A New Monastic Handbook*
- or, if you are really serious and want some help, write me. I have an idea about how to integrate a team of local and distance mentors, clear aims, individual and group formation, full-orbed learning, and self-paced development to foster successful planting of new monastic expressions. (spiritualityshoppe123@gmail.com)

Bibliography

Adams, Ian. "Cave, Refectory, Road: The Monastic Life Shaping Community and Mission." Kindle ed. In *New Monasticism as Fresh Expression*, edited by Graham Cray, et al., locs. 789–1009 of 2923. London: Canterbury, 2010.

Agamben, Giorgio. *The Highest Poverty: Monastic Rules and Form-of-Life*. Stanford, CA: Stanford University Press, 2013.

Albrecht, Daniel E. *Rites in the Spirit: A Ritual Approach to Pentecostal/Charismatic Spirituality*. Sheffield: Sheffield Academic, 1999.

Allchin, Donald. *Solitude and Communion: Papers on the Hermit Life*. Oxford: SLG, 1975.

Alexander, John F. *Being Church: Reflections on How to Live as the People of God*. Eugene, OR: Cascade, 2012.

Anderson, Gary A. *Charity: The Place of the Poor in the Biblical Tradition*. New Haven: Yale University Press, 2014.

Andrews, Frances. *The Early Humiliati*. Cambridge: Cambridge University Press, 1999.

Antoncich, Ricardo. "The Exercises and the Spiritual Discernment of Political Options." 1975. Unpublished paper written in Lima, Peru, and available at the Graduate Theological Union Library.

Antony of Egypt. *The Letters of Saint Antony the Great*. Translated by Derwas J. Chitty. Oxford: Will Print/Sisters of the Love of God, 1975.

Arendt, Hannah. *The Human Condition*. Chicago: The University of Chicago Press, 1958.

Arnold, Eberhard. "The Early Anabaptists Part I: Forerunners." Published online in 2014 by *Plough* and available at https://www.plough.com/en/topics/faith/anabaptists/early-anabaptists-1.

Athanasius. *The Life of Antony*. In *Athanasius: The Life of Antony and the Letter to Marcellinus*, translated by Robert C. Gregg, 29–99. Classics of Western Spirituality. New York: Paulist, 1980.

Augustine of Hippo. *Concerning the City of God against the Pagans*. Translated by Henry Bettenson. New York: Penguin, 1972.

———. "The Ordo Monasterii." In *Augustine of Hippo: The Monastic Rules*, translated by Agatha Mary, 106–9. The Works of Augustine—A Translation for the 21st Century. Hyde Park, NY: New City, 2004.

———. *Saint Augustine: On Christian Teaching*. Translated by R. P. H. Green. Oxford: Oxford University Press, 1997.

Bahnson, Fred. "Peacemaking in the Midst of Violence and Conflict Resolution Along the Lines of Matthew 18." In *School(s) for Conversion: 12 Marks of a New Monasticism*, edited by The Rutba House, 149–61. Eugene, OR: Cascade, 2005.

Barber, William J., II. "Poor People's Campaign: The Future of Our Democracy Depends on Us Completing the Work of a Third Reconstruction." *Think Progress*, May 15, 2017. https://archive.thinkprogress.org/rev-barber-why-america-needs-a-new-poor-peoples-campaign-dd406d515193/.

Barber, William J., II, and Jonathan Wilson-Hartgrove. *The Third Reconstruction: How a Moral Movement Is Overcoming the Politics of Division and Fear*. Boston: Beacon, 2016.

Barclay, John M. G. *Paul and the Gift*. Grand Rapids: Eerdmans, 2015.

———. "Poverty in Pauline Studies: A Response to Steven Friesen." *JSNT* 26.3 (2004) 363–66.

———. "Under Grace: The Christ-Gift and the Construction of a Christian Habitus." In *Apocalyptic Paul: Cosmos and Anthropos in Romans 5–8*, edited by Beverly Roberts Gaventa, 59–76. Waco, TX: Baylor University Press, 2013.

Barton, J. *Isaiah 1–39*. T&T Clark Study Guides. London: T&T Clark International, 2003. First published by Sheffield Press in 1995.

Basil of Caesarea [the Great]. *Letter 94: To Elias, Governor of the Province*. New Advent. https://www.newadvent.org/fathers/3202094.htm.

———. "The Long Rules." In *Saint Basil: Ascetical Works*, translated by M. Monica Wagner, 223–37. The Fathers of the Church 9. Washington, DC: The Catholic University of America Press, 1962.

———. *On Social Justice*. Translated by C. Paul Schroeder. Popular Patristics Series. Crestwood, NY: St. Vladimir's Seminary Press, 2009.

Beauvois, Xavier, dir. *Des Hommes et des Dieux* (English: *Of Gods and Men*). Los Angeles: Sony Pictures Classics, 2010.

Beilby, James K., and Paul Rhodes Eddy, eds. *The Historical Jesus: Five Views*. Kindle ed. Downers Grove, IL: InterVarsity, 2009.

Benedict of Nursia. *RB 1980: The Rule of St. Benedict In Latin and English with Notes*. Edited by Timothy Fry. Collegeville, MN: Liturgical, 1981.

Berman, Constance Hoffman. *The Cistercian Evolution: The Invention of a Religious Order in Twelfth-Century Europe*. Philadelphia: University of Pennsylvania Press, 2000.

Berry, Wendell. *The Unsettling of America: Culture and Agriculture*. 3rd ed. San Francisco: Sierra Club Books, 1996.

———. "What Are People For?" In *What Are People For?: Essays by Wendell Berry*, 123–25. New York: North Point, 1990.

Bessenecker, Scott. *The New Friars: The Emerging Movement Serving the World's Poor*. Downers Grove, IL: InterVarsity, 2006.

Billman, Kathleen D., and Daniel L. Migliore. *Rachel's Cry: Prayer of Lament and Rebirth of Hope*. Eugene, OR: Wipf & Stock, 1999.

Bock, Darrell L. "The Historical Jesus: An Evangelical View." In *The Historical Jesus: Five Views*, edited by James Beilby and Paul Rhodes Eddy, locs. 3655–4159 of 6531. Kindle ed. Downers Grove, IL: InterVarsity, 2009.

Boda, Mark J., and Shannon E. Baines. "Wisdom's Cry: Embracing the Vision of Justice in Old Testament Wisdom Literature." In *The Bible and Social Justice: Old*

Testament and New Testament Foundations for the Church's Urgent Call, edited by Cynthia Long Westfall and Bryan R. Dyer, 35–63. Eugene, OR: Pickwick, 2015.

Boggs, Carl. "Marxism, prefigurative communism, and the problem of worker's control." Libcom.org, submitted online September 23, 2010. https://libcom.org/library/marxism-prefigurative-communism-problem-workers-control-carl-boggs.

———. "Revolutionary Process, Political Strategy, and the Dilemma of Power." *Theory and Society* 4.3 (1977) 359–93.

Böhringer, Letha, Jennifer Kolpacoff Deane, and Hildo van Engen, eds. *Labels and Libels: Naming Beguines in Northern Medieval Europe*. Turnhout, Belgium: Brepols, 2014.

Bonhoeffer, Dietrich. *A Testament to Freedom: The Essential Writings of Dietrich Bonhoeffer*. Rev. ed. Edited by Geffrey B. Kelly and F. Burton Nelson. New York: Harper One, 1990.

Bornstein, Daniel. "Preface." In *The Laity in the Middle Ages: Religious Beliefs and Devotional Practices*, by André Vauchez, translated by Margery J. Schneider, ix–xiii. Notre Dame: University of Notre Dame Press, 1993.

Bourdieu, Pierre. *Outline of a Theory of Practice*. Translated by Richard Nice. Cambridge Studies in Social Anthropology. Cambridge: Cambridge University Press, 1977.

Brakke, David. "Care for the Poor, Fear of Poverty, and Love of Money: Evagrius Ponticus on the Monk's Vulnerability." In *Wealth and Poverty in Early Church and Society*, edited by Susan R. Holman, 76–87. Holy Cross Studies in Patristic Theology and History. Grand Rapids: Baker Academic, 2008.

———. *Demons and the Making of the Monk: Spiritual Combat in Early Christianity*. Cambridge: Harvard University Press, 2006.

Breines, Wini. *Community and Organization in the New Left, 1962–1968: The Great Refusal*. New Brunswick, NJ: Rutgers University Press, 1989.

Bretherton, Luke. *Christ and the Common Life: Political Theology and the Case for Democracy*. Grand Rapids: Eerdmans, 2019.

———. "Power to the People: Orthodoxy, Consociational Democracy, and the Move beyond Phyletism." In *Christianity, Democracy, and the Shadow of Constantine*, edited by George E. Demacopoulos and Aristotle Papanikolaou, 61–77. New York: Fordham University Press, 2016.

Brooks, Arthur. *Love Your Enemies: How Decent People Can Save America from the Culture of Contempt*. New York: Broadside, 2019.

Brother Roger. *Parable of Community: The Rule and Other Basic Texts of Taizé*. New York: Seabury, 1981.

brown, adrienne maree. *Emergent Strategy: Shaping Change, Changing Worlds*. Chico, CA: AK, 2017.

Brueggemann, Walter. *Money and Possessions*. Interpretation: Resources for the Use of Scripture in the Church. Louisville: Westminster John Knox, 2016.

———. *Theology of the Old Testament: Testimony, Dispute, Advocacy*. Minneapolis: Fortress, 1997.

Buell, Denise Kimber. "Be Not One Who Stretches Out Hands to Receive But Shuts Them When It Comes to Giving: Envisioning Christian Charity When Both Donors and Recipients Are Poor." In *Wealth and Poverty in Early Church and Society*, edited by Susan R. Holman, 37–47. Holy Cross Studies in Patristic Theology and History. Grand Rapids: Baker Academic, 2008.

Burghardt, Walter J. "Contemplation: A Long Loving Look at the Real." *Church* 5 (Winter 1989) 14–18.

Burton-Christie, Douglas. *The Word in the Desert: Scripture and the Quest for Holiness in Early Christian Monasticism*. New York: Oxford University Press, 1993.

Buschart, W. David, and Kent D. Eilers. *Theology as Retrieval: Receiving the Past, Renewing the Church*. Downers Grove, IL: InterVarsity, 2015.

Butterfield, Rosaria. *The Gospel Comes with a Housekey*. Wheaton, IL: Crossway, 2018.

Byrd, Brian G., and John Paul Loucky. "Toyohiko Kagawa and Reinhold Niebuhr: The Church and Cooperatives." *Journal of Interdisciplinary Studies* 28, nos. 1–2 (2016) 63–88.

Cahill, Thomas. *How the Irish Saved Civilization: The Untold Story of Ireland's Heroic Role from the Fall of Rome to the Rise of Medieval Europe*. New York: Doubleday, 1995.

Calhoun, Adele Ahlberg. *Spiritual Disciplines Handbook: Practices That Transform Us*. Downers Grove, IL: InterVarsity, 2005.

Caner, Daniel. "Wealth, Stewardship, and Charitable 'Blessings' in Early Byzantine Monasticism." In *Wealth and Poverty in Early Church and Society*, edited by Susan R. Holman, 221–42. Holy Cross Studies in Patristic Theology and History. Grand Rapids: Baker Academic, 2008.

Castells, Manuel. *Communication Power*. Oxford: Oxford University Press, 2013.

———. *Networks of Outrage and Hope: Social Movements in the Internet Age*. 2nd ed. Cambridge: Polity 2015.

Catherine of Siena. *The Dialogue*. Translated by Suzanne Noffke. Classics of Western Spirituality. New York: Paulist, 1980.

Chittister, Joan D. *Wisdom Distilled from the Daily: Living the Rule of St. Benedict Today*. San Francisco: HarperSanFrancisco, 1990.

Clapp, Rodney. *Families at the Crossroads: Beyond Traditional and Modern Options*. Downers Grove, IL: InterVarsity, 1993.

———. "Remonking the Church: Would a Protestant form of monasticism help liberate evangelicalism from its cultural captivity?" *Christianity Today* (August 12, 1988) 20–21.

Clarke, Thomas E. "Public Policy and Christian Discernment." In *Personal Values in Public Policy: Essays and Conversations in Government Decision-Making*, edited by John C. Haughey, 212–31. New York: Paulist, 1979.

Clarke, W. K. Lowther. *St. Basil the Great: A Study in Monasticism*. Cambridge: Cambridge University Press, 1913.

Clayton, Lawrence A. *Bartolomé de las Casas: A Biography*. Cambridge: Cambridge University Press, 2012.

Clear, Caitriona. "Nano Nagle (1718–1784): Educator." *Studies: An Irish Quarterly Review* 98.390 (Summer 2009) 135–43.

Cleary, Miriam. "A Societal Context for Supervision." *Presence: The Journal of Spiritual Directors International* 4.2 (May 1988) 26–31.

Cleaver, Eldridge. "Speech to San Francisco Barristers' Club." San Francisco, CA, September 1968.

Colson, Charles. *God and Government: An Insider's View on the Boundaries between Faith and Politics*. Grand Rapids: Zondervan, 2007.

Cone, James H. *A Black Theology of Liberation*. Fiftieth anniversary ed. Maryknoll, NY: Orbis, 2020.

Constable, Giles. *The Abbey of Cluny: A Collection of Essays to Mark the Eleven-Hundredth Anniversary of its Foundation*. Berlin: LIT Verlag, 2010.

Corbett, Steven, and Brian Finkkert. *When Helping Hurts: How to Alleviate Poverty without Hurting the Poor . . . and Yourself.* Chicago: Moody, 2012.

Cox, Doug. "Sidney Cox Sings 'Deep and Wide' accompanied by John and Jean Cox." http://dougcoxfamilyhistory.com/sample-page/sec-music-library/audio-recordings/sidney-cox-sings-deep-and-wide-accompanied-by-john-and-jean-cox/.

Cray, Graham, et al., eds. *New Monasticism as Fresh Expression of Church.* Kindle ed. Norwich: Canterbury, 2010.

Crislip, Andrew. *From Monastery to Hospital: Christian Monasticism and the Transformation of Health Care in Late Antiquity.* Ann Arbor: University of Michigan Press, 2005.

Crossan, John Dominic. "Jesus and the Challenge of Collaborative Eschatology." In *The Historical Jesus: Five Views,* edited by James K. Beilby and Paul Rhodes Eddy, locs. 1427–1895 of 6531. Kindle ed. Downers Grove, IL: InterVarsity, 2009.

Croasmun, Matthew. *The Emergence of Sin: The Cosmic Tyrant in Romans.* Oxford: Oxford University Press, 2017.

Daly, Lowrie J. *Benedictine Monasticism: Its Formation and Development Through the 12th Century.* New York: Sheed and Ward, 1965.

Davison, Ellen Scott. *Forerunners of Saint Francis And Other Stories.* Boston: Houghton Mifflin, 1927.

de Bhál, Dolores. "A Biographical Note: Nano Nagle: 1718–1784." *Studies: An Irish Quarterly Review* 89.355 (Autumn 2000) 274–79.

de Certeau, Michel. *The Practice of Everyday Life.* Translated by Steven Rendall. Berkeley: University of California Press, 1984.

de Ridder-Symoens, Hilde. *Universities in the Middle Ages. A History of the University in Europe 1.* Cambridge: Cambridge University Press, 1991.

deVries, Jennifer. "The Proper Beguine's Interaction With the Outside World: Some Beguine Rules from the Late Medieval Low Countries." In *Shaping Stability: The Normation and Formation of Religious Life in the Late Middle Ages,* edited by Krijn Pansters and Abraham Plunkett-Latimer, 137–50. Disciplina Monastica 11. Turnhout, Belgium: Brepols, 2016.

Delany, Sheila, ed. *Counter-Tradition: A Reader in the Literature of Dissent and Alternatives.* New York: Basic, 1971.

Dickens, Charles. *A Christmas Carol.* New York: Weathervane, 1977.

Dieter, Melvin E., et al. *Five Views on Sanctification.* Rev. ed. Grand Rapids: Zondervan Academic, 2011.

Dixon, Ejeris, and Leah Lakshimi Piepzna-Samarisinha, eds. *Beyond Survival: Strategies and Stories from the Transformative Justice Movement.* Chico, CA: AK, 2020.

Donatus of Besançon. *The Rule of Donatus of Besançon.* In *The Ordeal of Community: The Rule of Donatus of Besançon,* by Jo Ann McNamara, 5–77. Toronto: Peregrina, 1990.

Douglass, James W. "Foreword." In *Cold War Letters,* by Thomas Merton, edited by Christine M. Bochen and William H. Shannon, x–xviii. Maryknoll, NY: Orbis, 2006.

———. *Resistance and Contemplation: The Way of Liberation.* Garden City, NY: Doubleday, 1972.

Dreher, Rod. *The Benedict Option: A Strategy for Christians in a Post-Christian Nation.* New York: Sentinel, 2017.

Driscoll, Jeremy, ed. *Evagrius Ponticus: Ad Monachus: Translation and Commentary.* Ancient Christian Writers 59. New York: Newman, 2003.

Driscoll, Michael. "Friendship." In *The New Dictionary of Catholic Spirituality*, edited by Michael Downey, 423–29. Collegeville, MN: Michael Glazier/Liturgical, 1993.

Dryer, Elizabeth. "Humility." In *The New Westminster Dictionary of Christian Spirituality*, edited by Philip Sheldrake, 348–49. Louisville: Westminster John Knox, 2005.

Dunn, Marilyn. *The Emergence of Monasticism: From the Desert Fathers to the Early Middle Ages.* Malden, MA: Blackwell, 2000.

Edwards, Jonathan. *Religious Affections.* The Works of Jonathan Edwards 4. New Haven: Yale University Press, 1959.

Ellacuría, Ignatio. *Essays on History, Liberation, and Salvation.* Edited by Michael E. Lee. Maryknoll, NY: Orbis, 2013.

Eller, Vernard. *Christian Anarchy: Jesus' Primacy over the Powers.* Eugene, OR: Wipf and Stock, 1999.

Ellul, Jacques. *Anarchy and Christianity.* Translated by Geoffrey W. Bromiley. Grand Rapids: Eerdmans, 1991.

———. *Propaganda: The Formation of Men's Attitudes.* Translated by Konrad Kellen and Jean Lerner. New York: Vintage, 1965.

Elm, Kaspar. "*Vita regularis sine regula*: The Meaning, Legal Status and Self-Understanding of Late-Medieval and Early-Modern Semi-Religious Life." In *Religious Life Between Jerusalem, the Desert, and the World: Selected Essays by Kaspar Elm*, translated by James D. Mixon, 277–316. Studies in the History of Christian Traditions 180. Leiden: Brill, 2016.

Esquivel, Julia. "Confession." In *Threatened with Resurrection: Prayers and Poems from an Exiled Guatamalan*, 37–43. 2nd ed. Elgin, IL: Brethren, 1994.

Evans, Craig A. "Social Justice or Personal Righteousness? What Jesus Has to Say in Matthew and Mark." In *The Bible and Social Justice: Old Testament and New Testament Foundations for the Church's Urgent Call*, edited by Cynthia Long Westfall and Bryan R. Dyer, 84–101. Eugene, OR: Pickwick, 2015.

Evans, Paul S. "Imagining Justice for the Marginalized: A Suspicious Reading of the Covenant Code (Exodus 21:1–23:33) in Its Ancient Near Eastern Context." In *The Bible and Social Justice: Old Testament and New Testament Foundations for the Church's Urgent Call*, edited by Cynthia Long Westfall and Bryan R. Dyer, 1–34. Eugene, OR: Pickwick, 2015.

Farhadian, Charles, ed. *Christian Worship Worldwide: Expanding Horizons, Deepening Practices.* Grand Rapids: Eerdmans, 2007.

Flanagan, Bernadette. *Embracing Solitude: Women and New Monasticism.* Eugene, OR: Cascade, 2014.

Flanagan, Bernadette, et al., eds. *Nano Nagle and an Evolving Charism: a Guide for Educators, Leaders and Care-Providers.* Dublin: Veritas, 2017.

Flood, David. *The Daily Labor of the Early Franciscans.* St. Bonaventure, NY: The Franciscan Institute, 2010.

———. "Franciscans at Work." *Franciscan Studies* 59 (2001) 21–62.

Foot, Sarah. *Monastic Life in Anglo-Saxon England c. 600–900.* Cambridge: Cambridge University Press, 2006.

Foucault, Michel. *Power/Knowledge: Selected Interviews and Other Writings 1972–1977.* Edited by Colin Gordon. New York: Pantheon, 1980.

Fox, George. *Abridgment of the Journal of George Fox.* In *Quaker Spirituality: Selected Writings,* edited by Douglas V. Steere, 127–36. Classics of Western Spirituality. New York: Paulist, 1984.

Fox, Yaniv. *Power and Religion in Merovingian Gaul: Columbanian Monasticism and the Frankish Elites.* Cambridge Studies in Medieval Life and Thought Fourth Series. Cambridge: Cambridge University Press, 2014.

Francis and Clare of Assisi: Early Documents. Published by the Commission on the Franciscan Intellectual Tradition (CFIT) 2022. https://www.franciscantradition.org/early-sources.

Freeman, James M. *The New Manners and Customs of the Bible.* Newberry, FL: Bridge-Logos, 1998.

French, Dorothea R. "Rhetoric and the Rebellion of 387 in Antioch." *Historia: Zeitschrift für Alte Geschichte* 47.4 (4th Qtr, 1998) 468–84.

Friesen, Steven J. "Injustice or God's Will: Early Christian Explanations of Poverty." In *Wealth and Poverty in Early Church and Society,* edited by Susan R. Holman, 17–36. Holy Cross Studies in Patristic Theology and History. Grand Rapids: Baker Academic, 2008.

———. "Poverty in Pauline Studies: Beyond the So-called New Consensus." *JSNT* 26.3 (2004) 323–61.

Fukada, Robert M. "The Legacy of Toyohiko Kagawa." *International Bulletin of Missionary Research* 12.1 (January 1988) 18–22.

Galloway, Kathy. *Living by the Rule: The Rule of the Iona Community.* Glasgow: Wild Goose, 2010.

Gates, Henry Louis, Jr. *Stony the Road: Reconstruction, White Supremacy, and the Rise of Jim Crow.* New York: Penguin, 2019.

Gatlin, Joe, et al. *Compañeros: Two Communities in a Transnational Communion.* Eugene, OR: Wipf and Stock, 2017.

Gaudet, Stephen J. *A Christian Utopia: Paul's Community of Equality and Justice.* Eugene, OR: Wipf and Stock, 2017.

Gelpi, Donald. "The Converting Jesuit." *Studies in the Spirituality of Jesuits* 18.1 (January 1986) 1–38.

Gilliard, Dominique. *Rethinking Incarceration: Advocating for Justice that Restores.* Downers Grove, IL: InterVarsity, 2018.

Goossen, Rachel Waltner. "'Defanging the Beast': Mennonite Responses to John Howard Yoder's Sexual Abuse." *The Mennonite Quarterly Review,* 89.1 (January 2015) 7–80.

Gordon, Uri. "Prefigurative politics between ethical practice and absent promise." *Political Studies* 66.2 (2018) 521–37. https://doi.org/10.1177/0032321717722363.

Gregory Nazianzen. *Oration 43: Funeral Oration on the Great S. Basil, Bishop of Caesarea in Cappadocia.* New Advent. https://www.newadvent.org/fathers/310243.htm.

Grenz, Stanley J. *The Social God and the Relational Self: A Trinitarian Theology of the Imago Dei.* Louisville: Westminster John Knox, 2001.

Greig, Pete. *God on Mute: Engaging the Silence of Unanswered Prayer.* Grand Rapids: Baker, 2007.

———. *The Vision and the Vow: Rediscovering Life and Grace.* Lake Mary, FL: Relevant, 2004.

Greig, Pete, and Dave Roberts. *Red Moon Rising: Rediscover the Power of Prayer.* Colorado Springs: David C. Cook, 2015.

Grudem, Wayne. *Politics According to the Bible: A Comprehensive Resource for Understanding Modern Political Issues in Light of Scripture.* Grand Rapids: Zondervan, 2010.

Grundmann, Herbert. *Religious Movements in the Middle Ages.* Translated by Steven Rowan. Notre Dame: University of Notre Dame Press, 1995. First published in 1935 and expanded in 1955/1961.

Gutiérrez, Gustavo. *A Theology of Liberation.* Fifteenth anniversary ed. Maryknoll, NY: Orbis, 1988.

———. *We Drink from our Own Wells: The Spiritual Journey of a People.* Translated by Matthew J. O'Connell. Maryknoll, NY: Orbis, 1995.

Halsall, Paul. "Medieval Sourcebook: Foundation Charter of Cluny, 910." In Internet Medieval Sourcebook. https://web.mit.edu/aorlando/www/SaintJohnCHI/Church HistoryReadings/Charter of Cluny.pdf. Posted 1996.

Hambrick-Stowe, Charles E. *The Practice of Piety: Puritan Devotional Disciplines in Seventeenth-Century New England.* Chapel Hill: The University of North Carolina Press, 1982.

Harding, Vincent. *There Is a River: The Black Struggle for Freedom in America.* New York: Vintage, 1981.

Harmless, William. *Desert Christians: An Introduction to the Literature of Early Monasticism.* Oxford: Oxford University Press, 2004.

Harris, Marguerite Tjader. *Birgitta of Sweden: Life and Selected Revelations.* Classics of Western Spirituality. New York: Paulist, 1990.

Hasselhoff, Görge K. "James 2:2–7 in Early Christian Thought." In *Wealth and Poverty in Early Church and Society,* edited by Susan R. Holman, 48–54. Holy Cross Studies in Patristic Theology and History. Grand Rapids: Baker Academic, 2008.

Hastings, Thomas John. "Practicing the Redemptive Love of Jesus: The Enduring Witness of Kagawa Toyohiko (1888–1960)." *Theology Today* 70.2 (July 2013) 160–80.

———. *Seeing All Things Whole: The Scientific Mysticism and Art of Kagawa Toyohiko.* Eugene, OR: Pickwick, 2015.

Hatlie, Peter. *The Monks and Monasteries of Constantinople, ca. 350–850.* Cambridge: Cambridge University Press, 2007.

Hauerwas, Stanley. *A Better Hope: Resources for a Church Confronting Capitalism, Democracy, and Postmodernity.* Grand Rapids: Brazos, 2000.

———. *A Community of Character: Toward a Constructive Christian Social Ethic.* Notre Dame: University of Notre Dame Press, 1981.

———. *The Hauerwas Reader.* Edited by John Berkman and Michael Cartwright. Durham: Duke University Press, 2001.

———. *Vision and Virtue: Essays in Christian Ethical Reflection.* Notre Dame: University of Notre Dame Press, 1974.

Hauerwas, Stanley, and William H. Willimon. *Resident Aliens: Life in the Christian Colony.* Nashville: Abingdon, 1989.

Hausherr, Irénée. *Penthos: The Doctrine of Compunction in the Christian East.* Kalamazoo, MI: Cistercian, 1982.

Hayes, John. *Sub-Merge: Living Deep in a Shallow World.* Ventura, CA: Regal, 2006.

Hayes, Matthew. "Robert Kennedy and the Cuban Missile Crisis: A Reassertion of Robert Kennedy's Role as the President's 'Indispensable Partner' in the Successful Resolution of the Crisis." *History: The Journal of the Historical Association* 104.361

(July, 2019) 473–503; also available at Wiley Online Library, https://onlinelibrary.wiley.com/doi/abs/10.1111/1468-229X.12815.

Heath, Elaine A., and Larry Duggins. *Missional. Monastic. Mainline.: A Guide to Starting Missional Micro-Communities in Historically Mainline Denominations.* Eugene, OR: Cascade, 2014.

Hengel, Martin. *Was Jesus a Revolutionist?* Translated by William Klassen. Philadelphia: Fortress, 1971.

Henriot, Peter J. "The Public Dimension of the Spiritual Life of the Christian: The Problem of 'Simultaneity.'" *Soundings: Center of Concern* (1976) 13–14.

Heyne, Thomas. "Reconstructing the world's first hospital: the Basiliad." *Hektoen Institute of Medicine* (Spring 2015). https://hekint.org/2017/02/24/reconstructing-the-worlds-first-hospital-the-basiliad/.

Hiers, Richard H. *Justice and Compassion in Biblical Law.* Kindle ed. Edinburgh: T & T Clark, 2009.

Hill, Jonathan. *What Has Christianity Ever Done for Us? How it Shaped the Modern World.* Downers Grove, IL: InterVarsity, 2005.

Hodson, Derek. "Becoming Part of the Solution: Learning about Activism, Learning through Activism, Learning from Activism." In *Activist Science and Technology Education*, edited by Larry Bencze and Steve Alsop, 67–98. Dordrecht: Springer Science + Business Media, 2014.

Holland, Joe, and Peter Henriot. *Social Analysis: Linking Faith and Justice.* Rev. ed. Maryknoll, NY: Orbis, 1983.

Holman, Susan R., ed. *Wealth and Poverty in Early Church and Society.* Holy Cross Studies in Patristic Theology and History. Grand Rapids: Baker Academic, 2008.

Holmén, Tom, and Stanley Porter, eds. *Handbook for the Study of the Historical Jesus.* 4 vols. E-Book (pdf). Leiden: Brill, 2019.

Holmes, Augustine. *A Life Pleasing to God: The Spirituality of the Rules of St. Basil.* Kalamazoo, MI: Cistercian, 2000.

Honoré, Carl. *The Slow Fix: Solve Problems, Work Smarter, and Live Better in a World Addicted to Speed.* New York: HarperOne, 2013.

Horsley, Richard A. *Bandits, Prophets and Messiahs: Popular Movements in the Time of Jesus.* Harrisburg, PA: Trinity International, 1999.

———. "Jesus-in-Context: A Relational Approach." In *Handbook for the Study of the Historical Jesus*, edited by Tom Holmén and Stanley Porter, 1:207–39. Leiden: Brill, 2019.

Howard, Evan B. *Affirming the Touch of God: A Psychological and Philosophical Exploration of Christian Discernment.* Lanham, MD: University Press of America, 2000.

———. "The Beguine Option: A Persistent Past and a Promising Future of Christian Monasticism." *Religions* (2019), 10(9) 491, published August 21, 2019 and available at https://www.mdpi.com/2077-1444/10/9/491.

———. "Beneath the Plan, Beyond the Call: The Practice of Discernment and the Mission of God." *Catalyst: Contemporary Evangelical Perspectives for United Methodist Seminarians*, March 5, 2014. https://www.catalystresources.org/beneath-the-plan-beyond-the-call-the-practice-of-discernment-and-the-mission-of-god-2/.

———. *The Brazos Introduction to Christian Spirituality.* Grand Rapids: Brazos, 2008.

————. "Getting Away to It All: The Place of Withdrawal in Fourth Century Monasticism and Postmodern Christianity." Spirituality Shoppe. https://spiritualityshoppe.org/getting-away-to-it-all-the-place-of-withdrawal-in-fourth-century-monasticism-and-postmodern-christianity/.

————. A Guide to Christian Spiritual Formation: How Scripture, Spirit, Community, and Mission Shape Our Souls. Grand Rapids: Baker, 2018.

————. Love Wisdom: A Global and Practical Introduction to Philosophy. Self-published volume with chapters available at Spirituality Shoppe. https://spiritualityshoppe.org/love-wisdom-a-global-and-practical-introduction-to-philosophy/.

————. "The Metaphysics of Power: Reflections on the Basic Framework of Psychology, Community, Politics, and Spiritual Formation." Spirituality Shoppe. https://spiritualityshoppe.org/the-metaphysics-of-power/.

————. Praying the Scriptures: A Field Guide for Your Spiritual Journey. Downers Grove, IL: InterVarsity, 1999.

————. "Is Thoughtless Prayer Really Christian? A Biblical/Evangelical Response to Evagrius of Pontus." Journal of Spiritual Formation and Soul Care. 7.1 (2014) 118–39.

————. "What Does God Expect? From Whom? And Why? Commands, Counsels, Community, and the Theology of Religious Life." Spirituality Shoppe. https://spiritualityshoppe.org/what-does-god-expect-from-whom-and-why-commands-counsels-community-and-the-theology-of-religious-life/.

————. "Who Should be Poor, How Poor, and Why? Reflections on a Franciscan Theme." Spirituality Shoppe. https://spiritualityshoppe.org/who-should-be-poor/.

Howard-Brooke, Wes. "Come Out, My People!": God's Call Out of Empire in the Bible and Beyond. Maryknoll, NY: Orbis, 2010.

Howe, Jon. "The Nobility's Reform of the Medieval Church." The American Historical Review 93.2 (April 1988) 317–39.

Hughes, Patrick, dir. Guess Who's Coming to Breakfast? Privately produced film. See https://vimeo.com/7320809.

Hutton, J. E. A History of the Moravian Church. New Century Kindle Format. nd.

Ignatius of Loyola. The Spiritual Exercises. In Ignatius of Loyola: The Spiritual Exercises and Selected Works, edited by George E. Ganss, 113–214. Classics of Western Spirituality. New York: Paulist Press, 1991. Note: I refer to this work by section number within square brackets [#xx].

Janzen, David. The Intentional Christian Community Handbook: For Idealists, Hypocrites, and Wannabe Disciples of Jesus. Brewster, MA: Paraclete, 2013.

Jennings, Willie James. Acts. Belief: A Theological Commentary on the Bible. Louisville: Westminster John Knox, 2017.

Johnson, Mark. Introduction to St. Thomas Aquinas and the Mendicant Controversies: Three Translations, by Thomas Aquinas, translated by John Proctor, vii–xxxiv. Leesburg, VA: Alethes, 2007.

Johnson, Mary, et al., eds. New Generations of Catholic Sisters: The Challenge of Diversity. Oxford: Oxford University Press, 2014.

Jonas of Bobbio. "The Life of St. Columban by the Monk Jonas," #31. In the Fordham University Medieval Sourcebook, https://sourcebooks.fordham.edu/basis/columban.asp, part of the Internet History Sourcebooks Project, with the latest revision January 2021.

Jones, Cheslyn, et al., eds. The Study of Liturgy. Rev. ed. London: SPCK, 1992.

Josephus. *Jewish Antiquities: Books XVIII–XX*. Translated by L. H. Feldman. Loeb Classical Library. London: William Heinemann, 1965.

———. *The Jewish War: Books I–III*. Translated by H. St. J. Thackeray. Loeb Classical Library. London: William Heinemann, 1961.

Kagawa, Toyohiko. *Before the Dawn*. Translated by I. Fukumoto and T. Satchell. New York: George H. Doran Company, 1924.

———. *Brotherhood Economics*. Kindle ed. New York: Harper and Brothers, 1936.

———. *Songs From the Slums*. London: Student Christian Movement, 1935.

Kahneman, Daniel. *Thinking Fast and Slow*. New York: Farrar, Straus and Giroux, 2011.

Kahneman, Daniel,et al. *Judgment Under Uncertainty: Heuristics and Biases*. Cambridge: Cambridge University Press, 1982.

Kanter, Rosabeth Moss. *Commitment and Community: Communities and Utopias in Sociological Perspective*. Cambridge: Harvard University Press, 1972.

Kardong, Terrance G. *Benedict's Rule: A Translation and Commentary*. Kindle ed. Collegeville, MN: Liturgical, 1996.

Kärkkäinen, Veli-Matti. *Hope and Community*. A Constructive Christian Theology for the Pluralistic World 5. Grand Rapids: Eerdmans, 2017.

———. *Spirit and Salvation*. A Constructive Christian Theology for the Pluralistic World 4. Grand Rapids: Eerdmans, 2016.

———. *Trinity and Revelation*. A Constructive Christian Theology for the Pluralistic World 2. Grand Rapids: Eerdmans, 2014.

Kauffman, Ivan J. *"Follow Me": A History of Christian Intentionality*. Eugene, OR: Cascade, 2009.

Kelly, R. A. "Righteousness." In *The International Standard Bible Encyclopedia*, edited by Geoffrey W. Bromiley, 4:192–95. Grand Rapids: Eerdmans, 1988.

Kendi, Ibram X. *How to Be an Antiracist*. New York: One World, 2019.

Kiefer, Francine. "How Does a 50-50 Senate Work? Two leaders who tried it explain." *The Christian Science Monitor Weekly* (February 15, 2021) 6–7.

Kierkegaard, Søren. *Papers and Journals: A Selection*. Kindle ed. Translated by Alastair Hannay. New York: Penguin Classics, 2015.

Killian, Mark. *Religious Vitality in Christian Intentional Communities: A Comparative Ethnographic Study*. Lanham, MD: Lexington, 2017.

King, Martin Luther, Jr. "A Christmas Sermon on Peace." In *A Testament of Hope: The Essential Writings and Speeches of Martin Luther King, Jr.*, edited by James M. Washington, 289–302. San Francisco: HarperSanFrancisco, 1986.

———. "Letter from Birmingham City Jail." In *A Testament of Hope: The Essential Writings and Speeches of Martin Luther King, Jr.*, edited by James M. Washington, 253–58. San Francisco: HarperSanFrancisco, 1986.

———. "A Time to Break Silence." In *A Testament of Hope: The Essential Writings and Speeches of Martin Luther King, Jr.*, edited by James M. Washington, 231–44. San Francisco: HarperSanFrancisco, 1986.

Knowles, David, trans. *The Monastic Constitutions of Lanfranc*. London: Thomas Nelson and Sons, 1951.

Kreider, Alan. *The Change of Conversion and the Origin of Christendom*. Christian Mission and Modern Culture. Harrisburg, PA: Trinity International, 1999.

———. *The Patient Ferment of the Early Christian Church: The Improbable Rise of Christianity in the Roman Empire*. Grand Rapids: Baker Academic, 2016.

Laboa, Juan María. *The Historical Atlas of Eastern and Western Christian Monasticism*. Collegeville, MN: Liturgical, 2001.

Laird, Martin. *Into the Silent Land: A Guide to the Christian Practice of Contemplation*. Oxford: Oxford University Press, 2006.

———. *An Ocean of Light: Contemplation, Transformation, and Liberation*. Oxford: Oxford University Press, 2019.

———. *A Sunlit Absence: Silence, Awareness, and Contemplation*. Oxford University Press, 2011.

Langton, Edward. *A History of the Moravian Church: The Story of the First International Protestant Church*. London: George Allen and Unwin, 1956.

Lau Branson, Mark, and Juan F. Martinez. *Churches, Cultures, and Leadership: A Practical Theology of Congregations and Ethnicities*. Downers Grove, IL: InterVarsity, 2011.

Lawrence, C. H. *Medieval Monasticism: Forms of Religious Life in Western Europe in the Middle Ages*. 3rd ed. Essex: Pearson Education, 2001.

Leclercq, Jean. "Friendship and Friends in the Monastic Life." *Cistercian Studies* 24.4 (1989) 293–300.

———. *The Love of Learning and the Desire for God: A Study in Monastic Culture*. Translated by Catherine Misrahi. New York: Fordham University Press, 1962.

Lederach, John Paul. *The Moral Imagination: The Art and Soul of Building Peace*. Oxford: Oxford University Press, 2010.

Lee, Michael E. "Ignatio Ellacuría: Historical Reality, Liberation, and the Role of the University." In *A Critical Pedagogy of Resistance: 34 Pedagogues We Need to Know*, edited by James D. Kirylo, 41–44. Rotterdam: Sense, 2013.

Leithart, Peter J. *Defending Constantine: The Twilight of an Empire and the Dawn of Christendom*. Downers Grove, IL: InterVarsity, 2010.

Liebert, Elizabeth. "Linking Faith and Justice: Working with Systems and Structures as a Spiritual Discipline." *Christian Spirituality Bulletin* (Spring 1997) 19–22.

———. *The Soul of Discernment: A Spiritual Practice for Communities and Institutions*. Louisville: Westminster John Knox, 2015.

———. *The Way of Discernment: Spiritual Practices for Decision Making*. Louisville: Westminster John Knox, 2008.

Lindberg, Carter. *Beyond Charity: Reformation Initiatives for the Poor*. Kindle ed. Minneapolis: Fortress, 1993.

Little, Lester K. *Religious Poverty and the Profit Economy in Medieval Europe*. Ithaca, NY: Cornell University Press, 1978.

Lohfink, Gerhard. *Does God Need the Church?: Toward a Theology of the People of God*. Translated by Linda M. Maloney. Collegeville, MN: Liturgical, 1999.

———. *Jesus and Community: The Social Dimension of Christian Faith*. Translated by John P. Gavin. Philadelphia: Fortress, 1984.

Longenecker, Bruce W. *Remember the Poor: Paul, Poverty, and the Greco-Roman World*. Grand Rapids: William B. Eerdmans, 2010.

Lupton, Robert D. *Toxic Charity: How Churches and Charities Hurt Those They Help*. New York: HarperOne, 2011.

MacIntyre, Alasdair. *After Virtue: A Study in Moral Theory*. Notre Dame: University of Notre Dame Press, 1981.

Malatesta, Edward, ed. *Discernment of Spirits*. Translation of the article "Discernment des Esprits" in the *Dictionnaire de Spiritualité* by Sr. Innocentia Richards. Collegeville, MN: Liturgical, 1970.

Markus, Robert. *The End of Ancient Christianity.* Cambridge: Cambridge University Press, 1990.

Marshall, I. Howard. *The Gospel of Luke: A Commentary on the Greek Text.* New International Greek Testament Commentary. Grand Rapids: Eerdmans, 1978.

Martin, Stephen L. *Healing and Creativity in Economic Ethics: The Contribution of Bernard Longergan's Economic Thought to Catholic Teaching.* Lanham, MD: University Press of America, 2008.

Masakatsu, Fujita. "The Development of Nishida Kitarō's Philosophy: Pure Experience, Place, Action-Intuition." In *The Oxford Handbook of Japanese Philosophy*, edited by Bret W. Davis. Oxford: Oxford University Press, Online Publication 2017. https://www.oxfordhandbooks.com/view/10.1093/oxfordhb/9780199945726.001.0001/oxfordhb-9780199945726.

Maximus the Confessor. "The Church's Mystagogy." In *Maximus Confessor: Selected Writings*, translated by George C. Berthold, 181–226. Mahwah, NJ: Paulist, 1985.

McClain, George D. "Spiritual Discernment and Social Justice." *Christian Social Action* (May 1995) 8–10.

McDonnell, Ernest W. *The Beguines and Beghards in Medieval Culture with Special Emphasis on the Belgian Scene.* New York: Octago, 1969.

McGinn, Bernard. *The Flowering of Mysticism : Men and Women in the New Mysticism.* The Presence of God: A History of Western Christian Mysticism 3. New York: Crossroad, 1998.

———. *The Presence of God: A History of Western Christian Mysticism.* Nine volumes to date. New York: Crossroad, 1994–.

McGuire, Brian Patrick. "Bernard's Life and Works: A Review." In *A Companion to Bernard of Clairvaux*, edited by Brian Patrick McGuire, 18–61. Leiden: Brill, 2011.

McNamara, Jo Ann Kay. *Sisters in Arms: Catholic Nuns through Two Millennia.* Cambridge: Harvard University Press, 1996.

Meier, John P. *A Marginal Jew: Rethinking the Historical Jesus, Volume Three: Companions and Competitors.* New York: Anchor/Doubleday, 2001.

———. *A Marginal Jew: Rethinking the Historical Jesus, Volume Two: Mentor, Message, and Miracles.* New York: Anchor/Doubleday, 1994.

Melville, Gert. *The World of Medieval Monasticism: Its History and Forms of Life.* Translated by James D. Mixson. Collegeville, MN: Liturgical, 2016.

Merton, Thomas. *Cold War Letters.* Edited by Christine M. Bochen and William H. Shannon. Maryknoll, NY: Orbis, 2006.

———. *Conjectures of a Guilty Bystander.* New York: Doubleday, 1966.

———. *Emblems of a Season of Fury.* Norfolk, CT: New Directions, 1963.

———. *The Monastic Journey.* Edited by Patrick Hart. Kalamazoo, MI: Cistercian Publications, 1992. Originally published in 1977 by Sheed Andrews and McMeel.

———. *Original Child Bomb: Points for Meditation to be Scratched on a Cave.* N.p.: New Directions/Abbey of Gethsemani, 1962.

———. *Passion for Peace: The Social Essays.* Edited by William H. Shannon. New York: Crossroad, 1997.

———. *Peace in the Post-Christian Era.* Edited by Patricia A. Burton. Maryknoll, NY: Orbis, 2004.

———. *Turning Toward the World: The Journals of Thomas Merton Volume Four 1960– 1963.* Edited by Victor A. Kramer. New York: HarperSanFrancisco, 1996.

Merton, Thomas, ed. *Breakthrough to Peace: Twelve Views on the Threat of Thermonuclear Extermination.* Norfolk, CT: New Directions, 1962.

Merton, Thomas, tr. *The Wisdom of the Desert: Sayings from the Desert Fathers of the Fourth Century.* New York: New Directions, 1960.

Miles, Margaret. *Fullness of Life: Historical Foundations of a New Asceticism.* Eugene, OR: Wipf and Stock, 2000.

Miller, Tanya Stabler. *The Beguines of Medieval Paris.* Philadelphia: University of Pennsylvania Press, 2014.

Mobsby, Ian, and Mark Berry. *A New Monastic Handbook: From Vision to Practice.* Norwich: Canterbury, 2014.

Moe-Lobeda, Cynthia D. *Resisting Structural Evil: Love as Ecological-Economic Vocation.* Minneapolis: Fortress, 2013.

Mollat, Michel. *The Poor in the Middle Ages: An Essay in Social History.* Translated by Arthur Goldhammer. New Haven: Yale University Press, 1986.

Moo, Douglas J., and Jonathan A. Moo. *Creation Care: A Biblical Theology of the Natural World.* Grand Rapids: Zondervan, 2018.

Mott, Michael. *The Seven Mountains of Thomas Merton.* Orlando, FL: Harcourt Brace, 1993.

Mullins, Mark. "Christianity as a Transnational Social Movement: Kagawa Toyohiko and the Friends of Jesus." *Japanese Religions* 32.1–2 (2007) 69–87.

Mursell, A. Gordon. "Introduction." In *The Meditations of Guigo I, Prior of the Charterhouse,* translated by A. Gordon Mursell, 7–60. Kalamazoo, MI: Cistercian, 1995.

Musaddiquue, Shafi. "MP's killing highlights value and risk of in-person democracy." *The Christian Science Monitor Weekly* (November 15, 2021) 10–11.

Nikodemos of the Holy Mountain and St. Makarios of Corinth, compilers. *The Philokalia: The Complete Text.* Vol. 1. Translated by G. E. H. Palmer, Philip Sherrard, and Kallistos Ware. London: Faber and Faber, 1979.

Oden, Amy G. *Right Here Right Now: The Practice of Christian Mindfulness.* Nashville: Abingdon, 2017.

Oden, Amy G., ed. *And You Welcomed Me: A Sourcebook on Hospitality in Early Christianity.* Nashville: Abingdon, 2001.

O'Donovan, Oliver. *The Desire of the Nations: Rediscovering the Roots of Political Theology.* Cambridge: Cambridge University Press, 1996.

———. *Finding and Seeking: Ethics and Theology 2.* Grand Rapids: Eerdmans, 2014.

———. *The Problem of Self-Love in St. Augustine.* Reprint ed. Eugene, OR: Wipf and Stock, 2006.

———. *Resurrection and Moral Order: An Outline for Evangelical Ethics.* 2nd ed. Grand Rapids: Eerdmans, 1994.

———. *The Ways of Judgment.* Grand Rapids: Eerdmans, 2005.

O'Donovan, Oliver, and Joan Lockwood O'Donovan, eds. *From Irenaeus to Grotius: A Sourcebook in Christian Political Thought.* Grand Rapids: Eerdmans, 1999.

Olasky, Marvin. *The Tragedy of American Compassion.* Wheaton, IL: Crossway, 1992.

O'Sullivan, Michael. "A Mysticism of Open Eyes: Ignatio Ellacuría, SJ (1930–1989)." Presentation given at the American Academy of Religion November of 2019, and later published in *Jesuit Lives: At Home in the World,* edited by Patrick Carberry, 134–43. Dublin: Messenger, 2019.

Palladius, *The Lausiac History.* Ancient Christian Writers 34. New York: Paulist, 1964.

Pang, Soojung-Kim. *Rest: Why You Get More Done When You Work Less*. New York: Basic, 2016.

Patitsas, Timothy. "St. Basil's Philanthropic Program and Modern Microlending Strategies for Economic Self-Actualization." In *Wealth and Poverty in Early Church and Society*, edited by Susan R. Holman, 267–86. Holy Cross Studies in Patristic Theology and History. Grand Rapids: Baker Academic, 2008.

Patterson, Kerry, et al. *Crucial Conversations: Tools for Talking When the Stakes are High*. 2nd ed. New York: McGraw Hill, 2012.

Payne, Leanne. *Restoring the Christian Soul: Overcoming Barriers to Completion in Christ through Healing Prayer*. Grand Rapids: Baker, 1991.

Pedersen, Else Marie Wiberg. "Saving the World: Shaping Europe: The Relation between Church and Politics in the Theology of Bernard of Clairvaux." In *Religion and Normativity*, edited by Anders-Christian Jacobsen, Kirsten Nielsen, and Peter Lodberg, 138–50. Acta Jutlandica. Theological Series volume III. Aarhus, Denmark: Aarhus University Press, 2009.

Peifer, Claude "The Role and Interpretation of Scripture in the Rule of Benedict." In *RB 1980: The Rule of St. Benedict In Latin and English with Notes*, edited by Timothy Fry, 467–77. Collegeville, MN: Liturgical, 1981.

Peirce, Charles S. *Peirce on Signs: Writings on Semiotic by Charles Sanders Peirce*. Chapel Hill: University of North Carolina Press, 1991.

Peters, Greg. *The Story of Monasticism: Retrieving an Ancient Tradition for Contemporary Spirituality*. Grand Rapids: Baker Academic, 2015.

Peterson, David. *Engaging with God: A Biblical Theology of Worship*. Downers Grove, IL: InterVarsity, 1992.

Phillips, Susan S., and Patricia Benner, eds. *The Crisis of Care: Affirming and Restoring Caring Practices in the Helping Professions*. Washington, DC: Georgetown University Press, 1994.

Pohl, Christine D. *Making Room: Recovering Hospitality as a Christian Tradition*. Grand Rapids: Eerdmans, 1999.

Porter, Stanley. "Reframing Social Justice in the Pauline Letters." In *The Bible and Social Justice: Old Testament and New Testament Foundations for the Church's Urgent Call*, edited by Cynthia Long Westfall and Bryan R. Dyer, 125–51. Eugene, OR: Pickwick, 2015.

Pranis, Kay. *The Little Book of Circle Processes: A New/Old Approach to Peacemaking*. The Little Books of Justice and Peacebuilding. New York: Good Books, 2014.

Pratt, Lonnie Collins. *Radical Hospitality: Benedict's Way of Love*. New and expanded ed. Brewster, MA: Paraclete, 2011.

Price, R. M. "Introduction." In *A History of the Monks of Syria*, by Theodoret of Cyrrhus, ix–xxxvi. Kalamazoo, MI: Cistercian, 1985.

Pritchard, James B., ed. *Ancient Near Eastern Texts Relating to the Old Testament*. Princeton: Princeton University Press, 1969.

Raekstad, Paul, and Sofa Saio Gradin. *Prefigurative Politics: Building Tomorrow Today*. Cambridge: Polity, 2020.

Raftery, Deirdre, et al. *Nano Nagle: The Life and the Legacy*. Newbridge, Ireland: Irish Academic, 2019.

Rah, Soong-Chan. *Prophetic Lament: A Call for Justice in Troubled Times*. Downers Grove, IL: InterVarsity, 2015.

Rauschenbusch, Walter. *Christianizing the Social Order*. New York: MacMillan, 1912.

————. *A Theology for the Social Gospel*. Nashville: Abingdon, 1945.

Rawls, John. *Justice as Fairness: A Restatement*. Edited by Erin Kelly. Cambridge: Harvard University Press, 2001.

Reyes, Patrick B. *Nobody Cries When We Die: God, Community, and Surviving to Adulthood*. St. Louis: Chalice, 2018.

Rohr, Richard. *Dancing Standing Still: Healing the World from a Place of Prayer*. New York: Paulist, 2014. First published in 2011 as *A Lever and a Place to Stand: The Contemplative Stance, the Active Prayer*.

Rosenberg, Marshall B. *Nonviolent Communication: A Language of Life*. 3rd ed. Encinitas, CA: Puddledancer, 2015.

Roth, John D., ed. *Constantine Revisited: Leithart, Yoder, and the Constantinian Debate*. Eugene, OR: Pickwick, 2013.

Rousseau, Philip. *Basil of Caesarea*. Transformation of the Classical Heritage. Berkeley: University of California Press, 1995.

Russell, Norman, tr. *The Lives of the Desert Fathers: The* Historia Monachorum in Aegypto. London: Mowbray, 1980.

Rutba House, eds. *School(s) for Conversion: 12 Marks of a New Monasticism*. Eugene, OR: Cascade, 2005.

Ryle, J. C. *Holiness: Its Nature, Hindrances, Difficulties, and Roots*. Peabody, MA: Hendrickson, 2007.

Sande, Ken. *The Peacemaker: A Biblical Guide to Resolving Personal Conflict*. 3rd ed. Grand Rapids: Baker, 2004.

Sanderlin, George, ed. *Witness: Writings of Bartolomé de Las Casas*. Maryknoll, NY: Orbis, 1971.

Santos, Jason Brian. *A Community Called Taizé: A Story of Prayer, Worship and Reconciliation*. Downers Grove, IL: InterVarsity, 2008.

Sassen, Saskia. *Expulsions: Brutality and Complexity in the Global Economy*. Cambridge: The Belknap Press of Harvard University Press, 2014.

Schattenmann, J. "Koinonia." In *The New International Dictionary of New Testament Theology*, edited by Colin Brown, 1:639–44. Grand Rapids: Zondervan, 1975.

Schmidt, Alvin J. *How Christianity Changed the World*. Grand Rapids: Zondervan, 2004.

Schildgen, Robert. *Toyohiko Kagawa: Apostle of Love and Social Justice*. Berkeley: Centenary, 1988.

Schmitt, John J. "Prophecy (Postexilic Hebrew)." In *The Anchor Bible Dictionary*, edited by David Noel Freedman, 5:482–89. New York: Doubleday, 1992.

Schneider, Andrew, and David McCumber. *An Air That Kills: How the Asbestos Poisoning of Libby, Montana, Uncovered a National Scandal*. New York: G. P. Putnam's Sons, 2004.

Schroeder, C. Paul. "Introduction." In *On Social Justice*, by Basil of Caesarea, 15–39. Popular Patristics Series. Crestwood, NY: St. Vladimir's Seminary Press, 2009.

Shea, Elinor. "Spiritual Direction and Social Consciousness." *The Way Supplement* 54 (Autumn 1985) 30–42.

Silvas, Anna M. *The Ascetikon of St. Basil the Great*. Oxford: Oxford University Press, 2005.

Simons, Walter. *Cities of Ladies: Beguine Communities in the Medieval Low Countries 1200–1565*. Philadelphia: University of Pennsylvania Press, 2001.

Sine, Tom. "Creating New Visions for a New Millennium." *Green Cross* 2 (Summer 1996) 22–23.

Sittser, Gerald L. *Resilient Faith: How the Early Christian "Third Way" Changed the World*. Grand Rapids: Brazos, 2019.

Smith, James K. A. *Imagining the Kingdom*. Cultural Liturgies 2. Grand Rapids: Baker Academic, 2013.

Sobrino, Jon, Ignatio Ellacuría, and others. *Companions of Jesus: The Jesuit Martyrs of El Salvador*. Maryknoll, NY: Orbis, 1990.

Sojourners magazine editors. "A Change of Heart." *Sojourners* (August, 1979). https://sojo.net/magazine/august-1979/change-heart.

Stark, Rodney. *For the Glory of God: How Monotheism Led to Reformations, Science, Witch-Hunts, and the End of Slavery*. Princeton: Princeton University Press, 2003.

Stassen, Glen H., et al. *Authentic Transformation: A New Vision of Christ and Culture*. Nashville: Abingdon, 1996.

Steenwyk, Mark Van. *The Unkingdom of God: Embracing the Subversive Power of Resistance*. Downers Grove, IL: InterVarsity, 2013.

Steere, Douglas V. *On Listening to Another*. New York: Harper and Brothers, 1955.

Stock, Jon. "Stability." In *Inhabiting the Church: Biblical Wisdom for a New Monasticism*, by Jon Stock et al., 87–118. Eugene, OR: Cascade, 2007.

Swan, Laura. *The Wisdom of the Beguines: The Forgotten Story of a Medieval Women's Movement*. Katonah, NY: BlueBridge, 2014.

Swidler, Ann. "Culture in Action: Symbols and Strategies." *American Sociological Review* 51 (April, 1986) 273–86.

———. *Talk of Love: How Culture Matters*. Chicago: University of Chicago Press, 2001.

Symons, Dom Thomas, tr. *Regularis Concordia; The Monastic Agreement of the Monks and Nuns of the English Nation*. New York: Oxford University Press, 1953.

Taylor, Charles. *Modern Social Imaginaries*. Durham: Duke University Press, 2004.

———. *A Secular Age*. Cambridge: The Belknap Press of Harvard University Press, 2007.

———. *Sources of the Self: The Making of the Modern Identity*. Cambridge: Harvard University Press, 1989.

Tiessen, Terrance. *Providence and Prayer: How Does God Work in the World?* Downers Grove, IL: InterVarsity, 2000.

Thompson, Augustine. *Cities of God: The Religion of the Italian Communes 1125–1325*. University Park, PA: The Pennsylvania State University Press, 2005.

Thurman, Howard. *Jesus and the Disinherited*. Boston: Beacon, 1976.

Todeschini, Giacomo. *Franciscan Wealth: From Voluntary Poverty to Market Society*. Translated by Donatella Melucci. Saint Bonaventure, NY: The Franciscan Institute, 2009.

Todorov, Tzvetan. *The Conquest of America: The Question of the Other*. Translated by Richard Howard. New York: HarperPerennial, 1984.

van Alten, Eric. "'. . . they had all things in common': Calvin's exposition of the community of goods in some key texts in Acts." *Studia Historicae Ecclesiasticae* 39.2 (December 2013) 181–96.

van de Pavard, Frans. *St. John Chrysostom, The Homilies on the Statues: An Introduction*. Rome: Pontificum Institutum Studiorum Orientalium, 1991.

Vauchez, André. *The Laity in the Middle Ages: Religious Beliefs and Devotional Practices.* Edited by Daniel E. Bornstein and translated by Margery J. Schneider. Notre Dame: University of Notre Dame Press, 1993.

———. *The Life and Afterlife of a Medieval Saint.* Translated by Michael F. Cusato. New Haven: Yale University Press, 2012.

Villegas, Diana L. "Catherine of Siena's spirituality of political engagement" *HTS Teologiese Studies/Theological Studies* 77.2 (2021) 1–9. Also available at Research Gate, https://www.researchgate.net/publication/349072168_Catherine_of_Siena %27s_spirituality_of_political_engagement.

Volf, Miroslav. *Exclusion and Embrace: A Theological Exploration of Identity, Otherness, and Reconciliation.* Nashville: Abingdon, 1996.

———. *Work in the Spirit: Toward a Theology of Work.* Eugene, OR: Wipf and Stock, 2001.

Wallis, Jim. *God's Politics: Why the Right Gets It Wrong and the Left Doesn't Get It.* San Francisco: HarperSanFrancisco, 2005.

Ward, Benedicta, tr. *The Sayings of the Desert Fathers: The Alphabetical Collection.* Kalamazoo, MI: Cistercian, 1975.

Watson, Sethina. *On Hospitals: Welfare, Law, and Christianity in Western Europe 400–1320.* Oxford Studies in Medieval European History. Oxford: Oxford University Press, 2020.

Weber, Jill. *Even the Sparrow: A Pilgrim's Guide to Prayer, Trust, and Following the Leader.* Edinburgh: Muddy Pearl, 2019.

Weiss, John T. "Origins of the French Welfare State: Poor Relief in the Third Republic, 1871–1914" *French Historical Studies* 33.1 (Spring 1983) 47–78.

Westfall, Cynthia Long. "Continue to Remember the Poor: Social Justice within the Poor and Powerless Jewish Christian Communities." In *The Bible and Social Justice: Old Testament and New Testament Foundations for the Church's Urgent Call,* edited by Cynthia Long Westfall and Bryan R. Dyer, 152–75. Eugene, OR: Pickwick, 2015.

Westfall, Cynthia Long, and Bryan R. Dyer, eds. *The Bible and Social Justice: Old Testament and New Testament Foundations for the Church's Urgent Call.* Eugene, OR: Pickwick, 2015.

White, Mark. "Robert Kennedy and the Cuban Missile Crisis—A Reinterpretation." *American Diplomacy* (September 2007). *American Diplomacy.* https://american diplomacy.web.unc.edu/2016/09/reflection-on-robert-kennedy-and-the-cuban-missile-crisis-a-reinterpretation/.

Wilhoit, James C., and Evan B. Howard. *Discovering Lectio Divina: Bringing Scripture into Ordinary Life.* Downers Grove, IL: InterVarsity, 2012.

Whitfield, Teresa. *Paying the Price: Ignatio Ellacuría and the Murdered Jesuits of El Salvador.* Philadelphia: Temple University Press, 1995.

Willard, Dallas. *The Disappearance of Moral Knowledge.* Edited and completed by Steven L. Porter, Aaron Preston, and Greg A. Ten Elshof. London: Routledge, 2018.

Williams, Bernard. *Ethics and the Limits of Philosophy.* Cambridge: Harvard University Press, 1985.

———. *Truth and Truthfulness.* Princeton: Princeton University Press, 2002.

Wilson, Jonathan. *Living Faithfully in a Fragmented World: From* After Virtue *to a New Monasticism.* 2nd ed. Eugene, OR: Cascade, 2010.

Wilson-Hartgrove, Jonathan. *Reconstructing the Gospel: Finding Freedom from Slave-Holder Religion*. Kindle ed. Downers Grove, IL: InterVarsity, 2018.

Wink, Walter. "The Powers Behind the Throne." *Sojourners* 13 (September, 1984) 22–25.

Winter, Ralph. "Protestant Mission Societies: The American Experience." *Missiology* 7.2 (April, 1979) 139–78.

———. "Two Structures of God's Redemptive Mission." *Missiology* 2.1 (January 1974) 121–39.

Wirzba, Norman. *From Nature to Creation: A Christian Vision for Understanding and Loving Our World*. Grand Rapids: Baker Academic, 2015.

Wittberg, Patricia. *The Rise and Decline of Catholic Religious Orders: A Social Movement Perspective*. Albany, NY: The State University of New York Press, 1994.

Woolman, John. *The Journal of John Woolman and A Plea for the Poor*. John Greenleaf Whittier Edition Text. New York: Corinth, 1961.

Wright, Christopher J. H. *The Mission of God: Unlocking the Bible's Grand Narrative*. Downer's Grove, IL: InterVarsity, 2006.

Wright, N. T. *Jesus and the Victory of God*. Minneapolis: Fortress, 1997.

Wuthnow, Robert. *Communities of Discourse: Ideology and Social Structure in the Reformation, the Enlightenment, and European Socialism*. Cambridge: Harvard University Press, 1989.

———. *Saving America? Faith-Based Services and the Future of Civil Society*. Princeton: Princeton University Press, 2004.

Yoder, John Howard. "The Biblical Mandate for Evangelical Social Action." In John Howard Yoder, *For the Nations: Essays Public and Evangelical*, 180–98. Grand Rapids: Eerdmans, 1997.

———. *Body Politics: Five Practices of the Christian Community Before the Watching World*. Nashville: Discipleship Resources, 1992.

———. *The Christian Witness to the State*. Scottsdale, PA: Herald, 1964.

———. *Discipleship as Political Responsibility*. Scottsdale, PA: Herald, 2003.

———. *For the Nations: Essays Public and Evangelical*. Grand Rapids: Eerdmans, 1997.

———. "How H. Richard Niebuhr Reasoned: A Critique of *Christ and Culture*." In *Authentic Transformation: A New Vision of Christ and Culture*, by Glen H. Stassen et al., 31–90. Nashville: Abingdon, 1996.

———. *The Politics of Jesus: Vicit Agnus Noster*. Grand Rapids: Eerdmans, 1972.

———. *The Priestly Kingdom: Social Ethics as Gospel*. Notre Dame: University of Notre Dame Press, 1984.

Zagano, Phyllis, and Thomas C. McGonigle. *The Dominican Tradition*. Spirituality in History Series. Collegeville, MN: Liturgical, 2006.

Zehr, Howard. *The Little Book of Restorative Justice*. The Little Books of Justice and Peacebuilding. New York: Good Books, 2014.

Zerbolt of Zutphen. *The Spiritual Ascents*. In *Devotio Moderna: Basic Writings*, edited by John van Engen, 243–315. New York: Paulist, 1988.

Zinzendorf, Nicolas Ludwig [Count von]. "Brotherly Union and Agreement at Herrnhut." In *Pietists: Selected Writings*, edited by Peter C. Erb, 325–30. New York: Paulist, 1983.

Zumkeller, Adolar. *Augustine's Ideal of the Religious Life*. New York: Fordham University Press, 1986.

Name/Subject Index

I have here indexed all the names mentioned in the text itself or regarding whom I have engaged in substantive discussion in the footnotes, identifying the appropriate locations.. For a complete list of authors and sources, see the bibliography or the footnotes.

Scripture Index